D1441970

D-DAY TO VICTORY

OSPREY
PUBLISHING

D-DAY TO VICTORY

with the men and machines that won the war

Stephen Bull

First published in Great Britain in 2011 by Osprey Publishing,
Midland House, West Way, Botley, Oxford, OX2 0PH, UK
44-02 23rd Street, Suite 219, Long Island City, NY 11101, USA
E-mail: info@ospreypublishing.com

OSPREY PUBLISHING IS PART OF THE OSPREY GROUP

© 2011 Stephen Bull

All rights reserved. Apart from any fair dealing for the purpose
of private study, research, criticism or review, as permitted
under the Copyright, Designs and Patents Act, 1988, no part
of this publication may be reproduced, stored in a retrieval
system, or transmitted in any form or by any means, electronic,
electrical, chemical, mechanical, optical, photocopying,
recording or otherwise, without the prior written permission
of the copyright owner. Enquiries should be addressed to the
Publishers.

Every attempt has been made by the Publisher to secure the
appropriate permissions for material reproduced in this book.
If there has been any oversight we will be happy to rectify the
situation and written submission should be made to the
Publishers.

A CIP catalogue record for this book is available from the
British Library.

Print ISBN 978 1 78096 179 8 for UK and Rest of World
edition
Print ISBN 978 1 84908 838 1 for North America edition

Page layout by: Ken Vail Graphic Design, Cambridge, UK
Index by Alison Worthington
Originated by PDQ Digital Media Solutions
Printed in Spain through Orymu

11 12 13 14 15   10 9 8 7 6 5 4 3 2 1

Osprey Publishing is supporting the Woodland Trust, the UK's leading
woodland conservation charity, by funding the dedication of trees.

www.ospreypublishing.com

Front Cover: Jeremy Llewellyn-Jones
Back Cover: IWM B7683
Title Page: Jeremy Llewellyn-Jones
All part openers and photographs taken during the making of the documentary
series are courtesy of Jeremy Llewellyn-Jones

CONVERSION TABLE

1 millimetre (mm)	0.0394 in.
1 centimetre (cm)	0.3937 in.
1 metre (m)	1.0936 yards
1 kilometre (km)	0.6214 miles
1 kilogram (kg)	2.2046 lb
1 inch	2.54cm
1 foot	0.3048m
1 yard	0.9144m
1 mile	1.609km

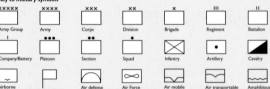

Key to military symbols

Army Group	Army	Corps	Division	Brigade	Regiment	Battalion
Company/Battery	Platoon	Section	Squad	Infantry	Artillery	Cavalry
Airborne	Unit HQ	Air defense	Air Force	Air mobile	Air transportable	Amphibious
Antitank	Armor	Air aviation	Bridging	Engineer	Headquarters	Maintenance
Medical	Missile	Mountain	Navy	Nuclear, biological, chemical	Ordnance	Parachute

Key to unit identification

Unit identifier — Parent unit
Commander
(+) with added elements
(−) less elements

CONTENTS

ACKNOWLEDGEMENTS

This book could not have been written without the making of the six-hour television series *World War II: The Last War Heroes* (UK title) *From D-Day to Victory* (North American title) for which it forms the permanent written record. Much has also been included here that could not be fitted into the programmes. Huge thanks are due accordingly to series producer Jeremy Llewellyn-Jones (who also acted as official photographer) and his colleagues Henrietta Mitchell, Justin Rickett and Kim Lask at Impossible Pictures, as also to the commissioning teams at Channel 4 and History Television. Special thanks in particular should go to Paul Wooding, originator for the series and Executive Producer, Jonathan Drake, Associate Producer, David Glover, Commissioning Editor at Channel 4 and Michael Kot, Executive Producer for Entertainment One Television. The interviewers and transcribers are especially thanked for their sterling work with the many thousands of words in English and Russian – and a wide variety of accents – over a long period, and at various points around the globe. Likewise my appreciation goes to Kate Moore, Editor at Osprey, who first saw possibilities for this collaboration, and to Emily Holmes, Project Editor. Naturally extensive use has been made of memoirs, diaries, histories and archive sources for the construction of the background narrative, and investigation of technical detail, and these appear in the bibliography. Photographs and other illustrations have been provided by the production team, archives, publisher and author, and are these are credited on an individual basis as they occur. Personal thanks also go to David Rogan, David Wollweber, Bill Hulbert and Alun Edwards who have variously made possible, or accompanied me on, visits to many of the battlefields, towns and museums mentioned in these pages.

What makes this venture genuinely unique however are the contributions of the living veterans who so readily agreed to relive the often painful experience of their youth for camera and subsequent transcription – two-thirds of a century after the cataclysmic events they describe. Many of these particular personal stories have not been told in public before. It is sincerely hoped that their words are here done justice, and convey at least some inkling to new generations of what it was to be a serviceman, witness, and often victim, of the events in North-West and Central Europe in the last year of World War II. Not only does the humanity of these people shine through the decades, but so does their contribution to humanity, in ridding the world of a tyranny and so reshaping for the better all our histories. In this very real sense it is both their story and ours.

INTRODUCTION: THE GREAT CRUSADE

> **We were so proud of being in it: on the other hand we were scared as hell...**
>
> Donald McCarthy, US 116th Infantry

By the summer of 1944 Western Europe had been under Nazi occupation for four very long years. Yet much had changed since the Panzer divisions spearheaded a victorious *Blitzkrieg* over France and the Low Countries. The United Kingdom had narrowly survived a similar fate – but only by dint of the escape of much of her army, if very little of its equipment, from Dunkirk; the fortitude of her Royal Navy; and the remarkable performance of her Royal Air Force (RAF), in what was quite literally a battle for, as well as of, Britain in 1940. Significant as this might be it was only one short chapter in an ever spreading war, as Germany had already occupied Austria and invaded Czechoslovakia, Poland, Norway and Denmark. In early 1941 Hitler struck south and east into Yugoslavia, Greece and North Africa in support of his ally Mussolini. In June the even more ambitious Operation *Barbarossa* had unleashed war on the Soviet Union. That year ended in apparent triumph for the Axis as Japan not only struck at Pearl Harbor, but attacked, and soon occupied, British, Dutch, French and American territories in the Far East. But not all was as it seemed.

Like the last link in some Mephistophelian chain reaction, December 1941 had linked the world in war. The day after Japan struck at the United States, Hitler ordered his forces in Russia onto the defensive: on

11 December, in what has been described as the 'greatest error' of World War II, he also declared war on America. The Third Reich was now in conflict with the 'Big Three' – the United States, United Kingdom and USSR, plus 23 other nations, while the most important of her own Axis partners were Japan and Italy. Those with a careful eye on the diplomatic scene, and an awareness of world balance of power, breathed a huge sigh of relief, and not least of them Winston Churchill. For although millions were yet to die, many of them in vicious and ideologically inflamed combat on the Eastern Front – and millions more in the gas chambers of the Holocaust – the tide had begun to turn, albeit almost imperceptibly at first. Britain marked her own 'end of the beginning' with Field Marshal Bernard Montgomery's victory at El Alamein in

October 1942, but there were further key turning points in other theatres: Guadalcanal, Moscow, Kursk, Midway, Stalingrad and Leningrad to name only some of the most obvious. Now there would be a different pressure: a demand from Stalin to open a 'Second Front' against the Nazis in the West. In point of fact the Soviet leader was technically inaccurate for the Western Allies and Commonwealth were already in action in many places – notably by sea and air – against Germany as well as Japan. Canada and Britain launched the ill-fated raid on Dieppe in August 1942, and Anglo-American forces had already landed in Italy in mid 1943 following the success of their North African campaign.

Yet Stalin's basic argument was compelling for many reasons. For ending the war in Europe entailed breaking the Third Reich, and to do this effectively meant a massive direct strike to the heart of the beast – in a manner that the Mediterranean, long since proven to be no 'soft underbelly', could not answer. It was also the case that at the 'Arcadia' Washington Conference, as long ago as the winter of 1941–42, Roosevelt and Churchill had agreed a policy of 'Germany First'. Only after this could all available resources be turned against Japan. Moreover, not answering the call to fight in North-West Europe might have many unspoken and undesirable effects. Europe would remain occupied for much longer, and perchance almost all the continent might simply swap a Fascist dictator for a Communist. Inadequate pressure on Hitler in the West might allow him to rebalance his forces, draw further strength from his ill-gotten gains, and beat the Russians to a standstill even if he could not defeat them. Quite what new wonder weapons the Nazis could produce, given time, was also unpredictable. American Chief of Staff George C. Marshall was therefore not exaggerating very much when he later offered the opinion that 'victory in this global war' depended on the cross-Channel effort.

INVASION PLANS

As early as 1942 an invasion plan code-named 'Bolero' was hatched for the landing of 48 divisions in northern France in 1943. Yet not everyone was convinced that the time was ripe, and Dieppe, planned during this period as a demonstration of intent, was taken as an omen of the difficulty of the undertaking. Moreover, there were not enough landing

PREVIOUS SPREAD
A landing caft, such as the ones used on D-Day, shown here being hit by an 88mm shell, during a recreation sequence in the making of the accompanying documentary series. (Jeremy Llewellyn-Jones)

OPPOSITE
This M4A2 Sherman at Arromanches, Normandy stands as memorial to Free French forces. The Sherman may not have been the fastest, best armoured or most powerful of tanks: indeed it was sometimes referred to as the 'Tommy Cooker' or 'Ronson' because it 'lit at first strike' and had a habit of incinerating its crew. Nevertheless, the Sherman was significant in the history of warfare, and a milestone of industry, being available in vast numbers just when it was needed. (Author's Collection)

Russian gunners at work. The ideologically fuelled slaughter on the Eastern Front proved relentless, from the summer of 1941 and the start of Operation *Barbarossa* to the end of the war in Europe. The D-Day landings of 1944 were the response to a strategic opportunity to hit at the Third Reich from a new direction, opening up the quickest route to the heart of the Reich. (Alamy)

craft for multiple amphibious efforts. So it was that, with the fight in Italy well underway, Western Europe was left to wait for another year. Nevertheless the first draft of the new Operation *Overlord* plan was completed in July 1943 with the invasion forces intended for Normandy, France. This was not to be just an isolated invasion but a series of phases that, taken together, would ensure the return of Allied forces to France. In the first period came operations *Pointblank* and *Fortitude*. *Pointblank* aimed to gain superiority of the skies, destroying the *Luftwaffe* and breaking German ability to field new air fleets. In *Fortitude* the enemy would be misled as to the locations and composition of the landings. These achieved, the naval phase, Operation *Neptune*, could be launched. The objectives of *Neptune* were defined as:

> to carry out an operation from the United Kingdom to secure a lodgement on the continent from which further operations can be developed. This lodgement area must contain sufficient port facilities to maintain a force of 25 to 30 divisions and enable this force to be augmented by follow up formations at the rate of from three to five divisions per month.

The 'Supreme Commander Allied Expeditionary Force' (SCAEF), selected that December, was 53-year-old General Dwight D. Eisenhower. His task,

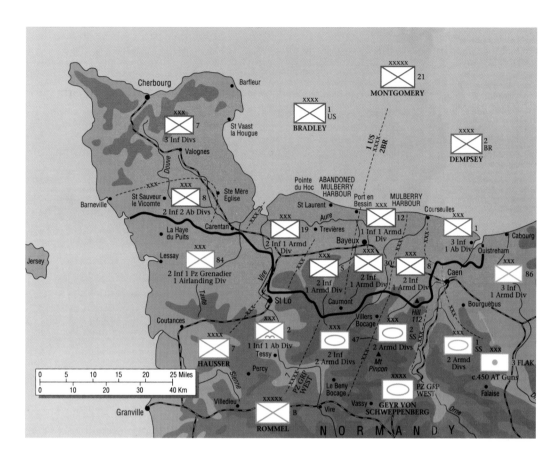

as formally stated a few months later, was to 'enter the Continent of Europe, and in conjunction with other Allied nations, undertake operations aimed at the heart of Germany and the destruction of her armed forces'. Eisenhower was an interesting choice, for while an experienced staff officer of long service, encouraged and supported by Chief of Staff Marshall, his familiarity with combat command was negligible. But what he brought to the proceedings was equally valuable: the tact and diplomacy to facilitate a truly Allied effort, what he himself defined as 'confidence, enthusiasm and optimism', an ability to inspire, and, perhaps unusually at this time, a media friendly disposition.[1] Under Eisenhower, and his British deputy Air Chief Marshal Sir Arthur Tedder, came a layer of arm of service commanders also drawn from the United Kingdom: Admiral Sir Bertram Ramsay for the navy; Field Marshal Sir Bernard Montgomery for the army; and the air commander Air Chief Marshal Sir Trafford Leigh-Mallory. Initially at least General Omar Bradley and the US First Army came under the purview of Montgomery. Controversially this would be changed in

A map detailing the Allied designated landing beaches, Utah, Omaha, Gold, Juno and Sword. The main landings were preceded by the landing of a small detachment of US Rangers as well as airborne troops of the 101st and 82nd. The German defenders are also indicated. (© Osprey Publishing Ltd.)

September 1944 when Eisenhower himself took over as land forces commander, a decision that the prickly Montgomery regarded as a demotion, though Eisenhower stated that this had been his intention all along – the original arrangement being only temporary while American forces in Europe were being built up.

While early planning under the previous Chief of Staff to Supreme Allied Commander (COSSAC) organization had already laid much of the groundwork many had doubts as to whether the projected landings were powerful, numerous and on a broad enough frontage to guarantee success. From early 1944 Montgomery became the mouthpiece for articulating the need for more men and more craft in the first wave. As he later explained:

> In deciding the degree to which the assault could be strengthened, the main factor was availability of craft and shipping but, in order to cover the front and facilitate organising the operation on a frontage of two armies, I recommended invading on a five division frontage, with two divisions in the immediate follow up, and using two, and if possible three, airborne divisions to be dropped prior to the actual sea borne assault.[2]

So it was that under the revised plan as finally implemented there were five large beach areas identified in Normandy, being, west to east, Utah, Omaha, Gold, Juno and Sword. Utah and Omaha, astride the Carentan estuary, fell to the Americans; Gold and Sword to the British; and Juno to the Canadians.

The major forces under Montgomery's 21st Army group for the invasion were the US First Army under Bradley, Canadian First Army under General Harry Crerar and the British Second Army under General Miles Dempsey, but there were also small contingents of French, Belgian, Dutch and Polish troops. Of this impressive array only a modest portion could be deployed in the first wave, even with expansion of the landing areas. On the attackers' right at Utah came the US 4th Infantry Division, aided by the preliminary dropping inland of the 82nd and 101st Airborne Divisions. Two American infantry divisions, the 29th and 1st, were allotted to Omaha, supported by a Ranger attack to eliminate the dangerous enemy battery at Pointe du Hoc. Five American tank battalions were also deployed. The British 50th Infantry Division was for Gold; the Canadian 3rd for Juno; and the British 3rd for Sword. British and Canadian efforts on the attackers'

Technical Recreation

The documentary series that accompanies this book recreated many different environments and munitions bringing to life the daily perils of the Allied soldier. Most of the work was on location in Canada where there were ranges with enough space to allow firing of weapons and the building of sets to represent parts of France, the Netherlands and Germany. Scenes varied from beaches to towns, and the munitions from individual bullets to explosives rigged to replicate full size bombs.

A pillbox is subjected to the attentions of a flame-thrower. As the American manual *Attack on a Fortified Position* explained, 'The flame thrower is an effective weapon for the last minute close in protection of a man or men placing the breaching charges or mopping up the bunker after it has been breached … the flame and smoke spread when they hit, fill the embrasures, and pour into ports or other openings, while the operator can stand at an angle from which he cannot be seen from the embrasure.' (Impossible Pictures)

A direct hit on a pillbox by a heavy naval shell, a difficult feat, but something that was achieved more than once on D-Day creating modest, but critical, chinks in the enemy defence. To be effective against reinforced concrete, guns and bombs had to be of considerable size. A 155mm howitzer could penetrate about 5ft of concrete given the right type of shell, a performance not much inferior to that of a 500lb bomb dropped from above. (Impossible Pictures)

left were bolstered by two Commando brigades – deployed individually to take out batteries and link the attacking forces – three assault tanks, and one armoured brigade, and on the extreme eastern flank the 6th Airborne Division, whose task was to shield an otherwise open flank, and seize the River Orne and Caen Canal bridges.

Supplies and equipment

Despite experience gained in the Mediterranean and elsewhere Allied planners remained intensely worried about both the consequences of failure, and the intervention of imponderables such as last minute changes to enemy dispositions and weather conditions. They were also acutely aware that a contested landing against a long prepared enemy offered challenges that ordinary formations and basic battlefield tactics were ill suited to overcome. So it was that a range of specialist equipment was deployed in the assault. To support troops over beaches and obstacles was seen as the niche of armour: but simply loading masses of ordinary tanks onto landing ships was no ideal solution as this would

lead to concentrated, easy targets for enemy guns, and existing tank designs were not built to cater specifically for sea walls, fortifications and mine fields. The remedy was a range of designs, some new, some long in gestation, each with its own defined task and often collectively referred to as the 'Funnies'. The amphibious DD or 'Duplex Drive' tanks, under development for some time, would be released from their parent craft some way off the beaches making their way independently to shore, arriving to drop their flotation screens and move up in direct close support of infantry. 'Flail' tanks were fitted with rotating chains to detonate mines, 'Bobbins' had large reels unwinding to create track ways, while bridging tanks laid ramps to span sea walls. The AVRE – 'Armoured Vehicle Royal Engineers' – was a conversion of the heavily armoured Churchill fitted with a 'Petard', or short-range bomb thrower, projecting a hefty 40lb high explosive charge. The British saw such developments as crucial, lumping together many specialist vehicles under Major-General Percy Hobart's 79th Armoured Division, the 1st Assault Brigade of which was deployed on D-Day. While the Americans were much less convinced by this new technology they still operated Sherman DD tanks on Utah and Omaha.

To answer supply problems after 6 June also required bold and ambitious solutions if the umbilical cord from the United Kingdom to the French coast was not to prove too delicate or slender to support the massive forces required on the continent. Perhaps the most obvious issue was fuel: the enemy were already short, and air attacks had deliberately interfered with production of synthetic oils, refineries and similar facilities in Occupied Europe. Thousands of vehicles would require millions of gallons, and tankers, even if enough were available, were a poor proposition taking up vital port facilities that would be difficult to capture. The radical answer was PLUTO – the definition of which appeared in official documents as either 'Pipe Line Under the Ocean' or 'Pipe Line Underwater Transport of Oil'. In fact there would not be one pipeline but several, the two main ones being 'Bambi' from the Isle of Wight to Cherbourg, and 'Dumbo' from Kent to Boulogne. Approximately 710 miles of flexible metal tubing were laid from a huge steel bobbin known as 'Conundrum', so called because it was a 'cone ended drum'. The potential lack of a port in the immediate aftermath of the landings was tackled by the 'Mulberry Harbour'. Two of these, made of huge prefabricated units, were towed across the Channel in the wake

OPPOSITE
Staff of the American Springfield Armoury check and stack MI rifles and unfinished stocks. Designed by Canadian-born arsenal employee John Cantius Garand, the MI semi-automatic was the first such weapon to be generally adopted by a major power. A robust and versatile weapon the .30 MI was loaded with an eight-round clip and was both accurate and able to lay down impressive fire, giving the American forces an advantage over opponents armed with slower bolt-action types. (Author's Collection)

of the invasion. Mulberry 'A' went to support the Americans at St. Laurent, Mulberry 'B' the British at Arromanches. Four days after D-Day the Mulberries would enclose an area of water the size of Dover harbour, reaching an amazing daily through capacity of 12,000 tons of stores and 2,500 vehicles. The artificial harbours were supplemented by 'Gooseberries', five small craft shelters or breakwaters, one off each main beach, made of blockships.

The air assault

What the direct contribution of Allied air forces should be remained a matter of controversy for a long time. By 1944 bombs had been dropping on Western Europe on and off for roughly four years. Ineffective RAF attempts at the precision bombing of German industrial targets had commenced as early as 1940, and only gradually had intensity and accuracy been built up. Nevertheless by 1943 there were dramatic, if later controversial, successes, such as Operation *Gomorrah*, the devastation of Hamburg by firestorm. Also by this date the United States Army Air Forces (USAAF) had entered the fray, and new and better bombers, capable of carrying much heavier loads, and with better navigational equipment, had been committed. The new B-17 Flying Fortress was in fact supplied to the United Kingdom in small numbers as early as 1941, and the Lancaster entered service with the RAF the

With the might of America behind them, the Allies were able to launch bombing raids on a larger scale than before, using machines such as this B-17 Flying Fortress. (The Granger Collection/ Topfoto)

following year. In their later models these craft were capable of carrying bomb loads of almost 10,000 and 22,000lbs respectively. Cover for these big birds of destruction was also improved by the support of fighters and other smaller craft with progressively longer ranges, notably the P-38 Lightning, the P-51 Mustang and de Havilland Mosquito. The thousand-plane raid became a reality with *Millennium* on Cologne in May 1942. Though both the RAF and USAAF took heavy losses the Luftwaffe was worn down in an aerial war of attrition, while Allied capabilities slowly but surely increased. Indeed according to one calculation the chance of survival was better in the Waffen-SS on the Eastern Front than it was in the Luftwaffe.

Opinion remained divided as to whether the main objective should now be general degradation of enemy air power; the obliteration of strategic industries such as fuel and ball bearings; the mass destruction of all war and industrial targets; or an interruption of the bigger picture to focus – at least temporarily – on the specific objectives of *Overlord* by means of bombing in support of ground forces, and selective strikes against transport nodes such as rail yards, bridges and roads. For Air Chief Marshal Arthur 'Bomber' Harris, head of RAF Bomber Command, writing as late as January 1944, the only option was more of the same, being, as he put it, 'the intensification of attacks on suitable industrial areas in Germany'.[3] Anything other than this would be a diversification of resources leading to less than optimum impact. General Carl Spaatz, chief of the United States Strategic Air Force in Europe, was also dubious about a change of course, preferring instead to continue

Typhoons of 181 Squadron, RAF, returning from an air strike in April 1944. Air superiority, judiciously used, could hamstring both enemy supply and daylight movement. However, what to use tactically in support of ground forces, and when, long remained a point of contention. (Courtesy of W. Grey)

battle with the Luftwaffe, attacking targets that were bound to draw the enemy into air combat, and destroy aircraft production. If there was a change it should be in favour of targeting German oil, within the general parameters established by *Pointblank*. To overcome such doubts required both persuasiveness and arm-twisting on behalf of the *Overlord* planners, and specific directions for the co-ordination of efforts.

In the event, and probably wisely, it was decided that the priority of the air campaign should be to obtain air superiority over the battle zone, ensure reconnaissance, provide troop transportation and supply, and directly support the landing and advance of ground forces while disrupting enemy communication and supply. Spaatz and Harris were subordinated to Eisenhower until the critical early phases of the campaign were complete, and 'tactical' air commands were allotted permanently to be integral parts of the expeditionary forces. As the April 1944 'Overall Air Plan' summarized, the task now was to, 'attain and maintain an air situation, which would assure freedom of action for our forces without effective interference by enemy air forces and to render air support of our land and naval forces in the achievement of this object'. For Eisenhower re-entry to the continent was 'the supreme operation of 1944', and the air forces were to contribute to this mainly by depleting enemy air capability, and destroying and disrupting enemy rail communications, 'particularly those affecting the enemy's movement towards the "Overlord" lodgement area'.[4] How crucial this air intervention would be, especially when supplemented by the disruption created by French Resistance and Special Forces on the ground, was only proved with the unfolding of events.

The role of Allied intelligence

The *Fortitude* deception plan was developed along two lines: in 'Fortitude North' a secondary strand was created, aimed at making the enemy believe that there would be an attack on Norway, but the main effort was devoted to France. To lend credibility to *Fortitude*, a massive shadow formation was created. This phantom was FUSAG – the First US Army Group, theoretically comprising a US and Canadian army together totalling eleven divisions. To make the enemy think that it was a serious threat it was not only given dummy camps, craft, tanks and communications, but also some genuine troops and a real personality as its fake commander in the form of General George S. Patton, a figure already larger than life, and highly credible as a choice to lead an assault. The non-existent onslaught, aimed at the all too believable target of the Pas de Calais, was made all the more plausible by real air strikes. A major strength was that the deception played to the preconceived notion of the enemy that this area was most at threat.

More tricky was the balancing of concealment and deception, for if the dummy assault were too well hidden it would not be discerned by the enemy and therefore become redundant. Too obvious and the subterfuge would soon become apparent. Intelligence and double agents were significant planks in the operations intended to reveal just enough to the enemy to appear convincing. Arguably the Allies started with an advantage since the German 'Enigma' code system had already been broken, and counter-espionage against the Axis forces had made great advances since 1941. And so by early 1944 the British Security Service MI5 had no fewer than 15 double agents in place ready to feed misinformation to the German *Abwehr*. Through these 'Double Cross' operatives was leaked a certain amount of genuine and sensitive information, interwoven with the false. By this means the enemy were able to check part of the story, which they could then determine to be true, lending credence to the source, and to the fabrications. Three of the key characters in the operation were code-named 'Garbo', 'Brutus' and 'Tricycle'. Garbo was Spaniard Juan Pujol, who ran a stable of 24 entirely fictitious contacts; Brutus was Polish officer Roman Garby-Czerniaski; and Tricycle a Yugoslav businessman, Dusan Popov. All three had worked for the enemy at some point, but had quickly declared their missions to the Allies, enabling themselves to be 'turned' effectively.

How well intelligence and security had worked was shown by the fact that as late as the beginning of June 1944 the enemy had no exact idea where, nor precisely when, the blow would fall, though the possibility of Norway appears to have been effectively discounted. Perhaps even more importantly *Fortitude* would continue to be believed for some time after the morning of 6 June, the German High Command, and Hitler in

OPPOSITE
An 'Enigma' coding machine as used by the German armed forces. Conceived by Arthur Scherbius this electrically powered device consisted of a series of wheels or rotors for the encryption of individual letters to produce coded messages. Some of its secrets were discovered by a team of Polish mathematicians, and in 1941 capture of a complete example by the Royal Navy allowed British code-breakers at Bletchley Park to master the German military code system. (Author's Collection)

particular, holding back on committing full resources to Normandy in the belief that this might be only a diversion from a 'main attack'. This hesitancy was further reinforced by Operation *Zeppelin*, a feint in the Mediterranean that suggested – by means of an exercise involving 13,000 men commencing on 9 June – that invasion of the south of France was imminent. *Zeppelin* and its offshoot *Vendetta* may not have been fully believed but the enemy was still not confident enough to draw away forces from the south.

Troop preparations

The other side of the coin of keeping the enemy in the dark, and the details of *Overlord* secret, was ensuring that the vast numbers of troops of the multi-national invasion forces knew what they had to do, and were trained to do it. This was easier said than done, for the operation was of a different order of magnitude to what had gone before, and presented unique challenges. Moreover, though some of those going to France were veterans of earlier campaigns, many were not. Amongst the Americans the 'Big Red One', the US Army's 1st Division, was arguably the most experienced, having fought in North Africa and Sicily. By contrast the 29th 'Blue and Gray' was a National Guard outfit, fleshed out with conscripts, and few in the ranks had seen action. The US 4th Division similarly had plenty of training, but no acquaintance with combat. It was equally true that many of the men in all the Allied armies, whatever the illustrious records of their regiments and divisions, were either young or 'citizen soldiers' who had yet to fire their first shot in anger. For those that had as yet little military experience, simple fitness, skill at arms and orienteering were still at the heart of training that spring. Nelson Horan of the US 29th was just one of many for whom the memories consisted mainly of running and marching. Relatively few of the Canadians had seen action, and while more of the British had seen combat – for example in North Africa or Italy – many were also new conscripts. Highlander Tom Renouf was one of these, recruited in 1943. Taking part in exercises on the 'frozen Yorkshire moors', he was left with vivid memories of a tactical exercise in which he was part of an 'enemy' unit. After two days 'huddled in slit trenches' an umpire came up and announced disconcertingly, 'You're all dead. You've been wiped out by an artillery barrage'. [5] Nevertheless, compared to many of the

Private Martin Schirald of Ohio demonstrates the US Army's M3 submachine gun at Camp Davis, May 1944. Like the Thompson, the M3 fired the powerful .45 cartridge, giving excellent firepower at least at close range. While submachine guns saw extensive use, especially with the American airborne troops and during street fighting, they were not a general issue to the ordinary infantry squad – unlike the Sten gun which was used on a scale of one per section in British and Canadian forces. (Author's Collection)

campaigns that had gone before, the ordinary Allied soldier on D-Day was both well equipped and well trained. Bill Betteridge of the Queen's Own Rifles of Canada felt that he was very well, but rather over optimistically, enlightened, 'They had sand tables, duplicates of where we were going to land, showing every little cabin along the shore … they would say there has been 2ft of concrete put in this hut here, or a machine gun, or a mortar … we thought it was going to be a tea party'.

Some of the most difficult skills to learn without tempering in action were those of the new 'Special Forces', the Rangers, Commandos and Airborne. Sergeant Edward Shames would later claim that the US 101st Airborne was the 'most highly trained unit that's ever been', yet much of the most important work was done in the run up to D-Day. Jan de Vries, with the 1st Canadian Parachute Battalion, had never jumped before reaching the UK:

As soon as we arrived at the Carter Barracks on Salisbury Plain, they took all those that went over there to reinforce the battalion, bring it up to strength… And so there was about 80 of us who were unqualified, so they gave us the pay and the boots and no berets. We had to earn those … the first jump we had was out of a balloon basket in England. And there was a hole, a 3ft hole. And if you didn't arch your back and clear the 'chute off the hole, you'd be tipped forward and 'ring the bell'. Lots of broken noses and bleeding noses. Anyway, I managed to arch myself and clear the pack… You dropped about 180ft, 200ft, before the 'chute opened. Only the speed of your falling body opened your 'chute. You didn't have the prop blast from the plane. I was quite pleased. I remember I was biting or had my hands up to my mouth or face and wondered when the 'chute was going to open and finally I heard this faint rustling, so I knew everything was all right. Then I enjoyed the scenery.[6]

Fellow Canadian Ronald 'Andy' Anderson was also new to parachuting, for though a soldier of some service he had started off in the engineers and been tempted by boredom into a transfer. Feeling 'wonderful' at the prospect of adventure he was moved, via Bulford, north to the paratroop training centre at Ringway near Manchester. Rubbing shoulders with British, Poles and Americans he gained his parachute wings in six weeks. Disconcertingly he learned that while the Americans carried a spare parachute the British did not. The 'airforce fellows at Ringway explained to us that the British had considered a reserve 'chute early on in the war, and found out that it took up too much space'.

In the event Anderson did not drop on D-Day: but then many of the troops, and much of the mass equipment, were needed for the campaign

American infantry pictured with key weapons: the M1 rifle, Browning Automatic Rifle (BAR), M3 submachine gun, grenade and bayonet. The BAR, seen on the right, was far from new having been introduced towards the end of World War I, but was still a useful squad support having a 20-round magazine and full automatic capability. The soldier with the M3 'Grease Gun' appears to have taped two magazines together, so that having expended his first 30 rounds it can be detached and turned. The Mark IIA1 fragmentation grenade, seen bottom left, could be thrown or rifle projected. (Author's Collection)

that followed. For 6 June was just one day of the more than 300 that comprised the campaign in North-West Europe. As Eisenhower described the scene in the weeks leading up to the invasion:

> All southern England was one vast military camp, crowded with soldiers awaiting the final word to go, and piled high with supplies and equipment awaiting transport to the far shore of the Channel. The whole area was cut off from the rest of England. The government had established a deadline, across which no unauthorised person was allowed to go in either direction. Every separate encampment, barrack, vehicle park and every unit was carefully charted on our master maps. The scheduled movement of each unit had been so worked out that it would reach the embarkation point at the exact time the vessels would be ready to receive it. The southernmost camps where assault troops were assembled were all surrounded by barbed wire entanglements to prevent any soldier leaving the camp once he had been briefed as to his part in the attack. The whole mighty host was tense as a coiled spring, coiled for the moment when its energy should be released and it would vault the English Channel in the greatest amphibious assault ever attempted.[7]

GERMAN PREPARATIONS

In early June 1944 the German defenders in the West numbered over 58 divisions. Such a total appears impressive particularly when one takes into account that it was likely that the first wave of any Allied seaborne assault would be limited to about half a dozen divisions, mainly by dint of numbers of landing craft available, with a further three being dropped or landed from the air. Such bald calculation might on the face of it make it appear that *Overlord* was doomed from the outset: but the strategic situation was much more complex, and not one sided. For in the first place the admittedly numerous defenders had to be placed somewhere, and – even if landings in other countries were broadly dismissed – France was a big place with a massive coastline, many parts of which could conceivably be reached by the Allies, most obviously on the channel coasts but also in the south. Commandos had also struck as far west as St. Nazaire on the Atlantic coast as early as 1942. So it was that only half the total German strength was actually located in the

OVERLEAF
The Normandy landings: a 4kg charge of explosive was placed inside the pillbox. This is equivalent to a 6in. shell, an astonishing 25kg charge was in the 16in. shell which were used to destroy much larger bunkers. (Jeremy Llewellyn-Jones)

danger area between Amsterdam and Brest. Moreover, while the initial thrust might appear puny it was but the tip of an iceberg. Given a foothold of sufficient compass, and convenient points to disembark, masses of reserves could be piled progressively onto the continent. Eisenhower's own history mentions 39 Allied divisions ready for use in England and a further 41 that could be sent from the United States to either the United Kingdom or direct to Europe as required. Troops on hand included not only American, British and Canadian, but contingents of Free French and Polish: armour, Special Forces and virtually every form of ordnance, engineer, transport and support formation were represented in the invasion inventory. Most formations were up to strength and adequately supplied, and following protracted struggles over a period of years, the Allies had achieved the upper hand both on the sea and in the air.

The strategic logic was inescapable in that if enough German forces were available early on they could outnumber, and very probably defeat by counter-attack, the small spearhead. Conversely any lengthy delay, accompanied by a loss of territory large enough to accommodate a bigger force, would spell disaster for the defenders who would themselves be progressively outnumbered and inundated. As Field Marshal Rommel put it, 'If we do not succeed in our mission to close the seas to the Allies, or in the first 48 hours, to throw them back, their invasion will be successful'. Yet an even distribution of German forces was no solution, since it has been a military maxim from time immemorial that he who defends everything, defends nothing.

At the start of 1944 much of the German High Command was agreed that a cross-Channel invasion was highly likely that spring or summer, and began to review deployments in the light of possible landings. Both Field Marshal Gerd von Rundstedt, Commander in Chief in the West, and Field Marshal Erwin Rommel assumed that the Pas de Calais and areas north of the Seine were most at threat. Indeed the stretch from Le Havre to Boulogne was identified as the likely landing area. This was logical in that the sea route was shortest, best covered by naval and air forces, and might allow Allied forces, once safely ashore, to head directly for either Paris or the heart of Europe. Being already across the Seine would also put one more potent barrier out of the way of the advance. Against this was set the argument that being so obvious the Pas de Calais was most heavily fortified, and the invaders might therefore be influenced to select somewhere less conspicuous and easier to attack. As early as the spring of 1943 fortress engineer officer Colonel Max von Stiotta had examined the problem, and ventured the opinion that the sector from the mouth of the Seine to the city of Brest was the most vulnerable. Likewise Hitler's own intuition was that the Cotentin peninsula in Normandy, or possibly Brittany, offered the most attractive landing grounds. Despite the accuracy of this prognostication it did relatively little to help, for while in April 1944 he demanded immediate strengthening of the northern coast of Normandy, this was only to be done without weakening the Calais area. In early May von Rundstedt refused Rommel's similar demands for the strengthening of Normandy and Brittany and faced criticism from General Alfred Jodl, Chief of the Operations Staff for the *Wehrmacht*, as a result – but by then it was too late.

DAS ALLES SIND INFANTERIEWAFFEN

Beim Nahkampf, im Waldgefecht, sind Pistole und Spaten dem Grenadier wertvolle Waffen und Helfer

German propaganda and previous successes gave the enemy soldier a reputation for thoroughness and ruthlessness. Yet by 1944 the German Army was degraded and thinly spread: by deception and concentration Allied forces achieved local surprise and advantage of numbers. (Author's Collection)

It could not be assumed that a majority of the German troops to hand were amenable to swift redeployment in the event of a landfall in an unexpected place. Relatively few units were genuinely mobile, and many were under strength, suitable mainly for static fortress defence. While most were sufficiently well armed there was widespread use of captured and foreign produced weapons and munitions, as the latest technology tended to go to units actively engaged on the Eastern Front and a relatively small number of elite formations. Some of the defenders were not German at all, being voluntary, or coerced 'Ost' troops (soldiers or conscripts from the Eastern territories occupied by the German Army) put into defence against the Western Allies as their performance against the Russians was already in question. Transport was neither swift nor plentiful, for the majority of German infantry divisions still relied on horsed transport, and the overwhelming Allied air strength would be in its element hitting road and rail intersections and bottlenecks. This could be guaranteed to cause lengthy delays even if relatively few defenders were actually killed, and the position could be made worse by local Resistance efforts. Although the French underground was rightly wary of pitched battle, sabotage of communications and industry under cover of night and the distraction

OPPOSITE
One of the
four 150mm
guns of the Les
Longues German
naval battery
between Port-
en-Bessin and
Arromanches,
Normandy. Set
back from a cliff
and protected
by concrete
emplacements,
barbed wire,
mines and other
bunkers, its long-
range guns
(salvaged from
destroyers)
threatened
Omaha, Gold
and Juno
beaches. Though
pounded by
bombers Les
Longues engaged
the American
battleship
Arkansas before
firing on British
vessels off Gold
beach on D-Day.
(Author's
Collection)

of the arrival of the Allies was much more feasible. Indeed, the very fear of such activity was prone to introduce elements of paranoia and hesitation.

Nevertheless it would be extremely unwise to dismiss the bulk of the German foot soldiers as impotent, for while the best were undoubtedly fighting, and dying, in Russia and Italy in mid 1944, there were still a good number in France with long experience and skill. Also, though mobility and fitness were sometimes in question, machine guns in particular made potent defensive weapons especially when emplaced in fixed positions.

Coastal defences

The much vaunted 'Atlantic Wall' was both genuinely tough, and thoroughly milked for its awesome propaganda value. The wall was certainly majestic in conception being intended as a 2,800-mile barrier to invasion stretching from northern Norway to the Spanish border – a western bulwark to *Festung Europa*, 'Fortress Europe'. As a building project of such ambition it should rather be compared with edifices such as the Great Wall of China or Hadrian's Wall, rather than the relatively humble battlefield constructions of so many campaigns. Individual strong points and batteries were of impressive strength and construction. Yet in planning, construction and occupation, it was far less monolithic, and has been described with some justice as a 'string of ferro concrete pearls' rather than a genuinely impermeable 'wall'.[8] Its variable quality and diverse elements are explicable in part because it was built over a period of time, and by several different agencies.

Coastal defences had been started as early as 1940, when use of concrete was limited, numbers of troops in France high, and fixed positions seen merely as part of a general scheme in which air force and naval units featured significantly. Some pre-existing French structures were used, but raids and spies were much more likely than invasion. Thereafter the international situation had changed entirely, and, in March 1942, Hitler had issued 'Directive 40' under which various types of permanent defence were selected for construction. Standards of construction were set under which 5m thickness of reinforced concrete was required for the most important weapon sites and headquarters; 3.5m for submarine installations, heavy gun sites and radar positions;

2m for permanent standard defences; and 1.2m for improvised and field structures. The German Navy, who traditionally provided coastal defences, built mainly bigger batteries using more modern weapons with an offensive function in mind, while the army, whose best weapons were reserved for the field, more often equipped its positions with captured guns – drawn from as many as ten different countries. Though it fell to von Rundstedt to implement, the *Organization Todt* was responsible for the bulk of labour and materials, with Albert Speer, Minister of

Armaments and War Production, promising to deliver 400,000 cubic metres of concrete each month. Foreign labour was also recruited – both forced and voluntary. The target set by Hitler was 15,000 works along the entirety of the wall to be manned by 300,000 men, completed by May 1943.

Like many grandiose plans formulated quickly by politicians under pressure of events this was not to be the final word, nor was work finished at the appointed time. Indeed activity increased in early 1943, with a peak pouring of over 769,000 cubic metres of concrete being achieved in April. A fresh Führer Directive, number 51, was issued that November:

> A greater danger now appears in the West... Should the enemy succeed in breaching our defences on a wide front here, the immediate consequences would be unpredictable. Everything indicates that the enemy will launch an offensive against the Western Front of Europe... At the beginning of the battle the whole offensive strength of the enemy is bound to be thrown against our forces holding the coastline. Only by intensive construction, which means straining our available manpower and materials at home and

in the occupied territories to the limit, can we strengthen our coastal defences in the short time which probably remains. The ground weapons which will shortly reach Denmark and the occupied areas in the West (heavy anti-tank guns, immobile tanks to be sunk into emplacements, coastal artillery, artillery against landing troops, mines, etc.) will be concentrated at strong points in the most threatened areas on the coast.

So it was that large amounts of concrete and steel continued to be used in the first half of 1944, and indeed in some places additions were still being made to fortifications a month after the invasion had actually taken place. 'Fortress' ports were designated for special attention within the scheme, and in the last months a range of new and smaller posts were added with just 1m of concrete protection, many of which were intended as air raid shelters, or mounted tank turrets and automatic weapons. Many works were completely buried for concealment and improved protection, others partially sunk into the landscape and camouflaged. It has been calculated that ultimately 28 million cubic metres of earth were excavated and landscaped, and by the time of the invasion it is thought that there were about 700 different types of forts, posts and bunkers in the Atlantic Wall scheme. Armament varied from nothing at all on many shelters, to the mighty 40.6cm guns of the Pas de Calais battery 'Lindemann' whose shells had a range of 42,800m. Co-ordination of army and navy efforts was thrashed out in October 1943 when it was decided that the coast itself defined the 'main battle line' beyond which the navy had fire control, with the army taking precedence from the shore line.

Late in 1944 gunner officer Jack Swaab would get the unsettling pleasure of viewing part of the Pas de Calais defences around Calais from the landward side:

After tea tonight went with the battery commander around the utterly deserted coast defences near here. Everywhere is sown with mines and barbed wire and obstacles, and out of a sea slashed white by the wind rose line upon line of 'Element C', the standard beach obstacle. The Germans have mined the invasion coast and filled it with the most amazing, and I suppose Teutonic, thoroughness. Every field for miles inland is filled with anti-airborne poles on a scale not dreamed of in England … and four long years of preparation are evident.[9]

Construction of the fortifications along the Normandy coast from Cabourg to Mont Saint-Michel was undertaken by Organization Todt's *Oberbauleitung Cherbourg*. This was less prolific than some area building commands but still created 540 significant concrete works in the northern Normandy area. Additionally it built 345 'non standard units' comprising light anti-tank and machine gun 'Tobruk pits', bunkers with recycled tank turrets, and battery positions for smaller artillery pieces. In what would later become the Allied landing grounds were built 30 batteries mounting guns greater than 100mm in calibre of French, Czech and Russian as well as German ancestry, as well as many 'resistance nests' with lighter armament. The heavy guns of the Atlantic Wall were the backbone of the defence and a

It's your job to die!

The daunting task ahead. As one enemy propaganda leaflet put it menacingly to the GI: 'It's *your* job to die'. (Author's Collection)

significant deterrent to invasion from the sea, also creating death traps on beaches. The smaller works protected troops increasing their value against attackers by virtue of both physical protection and concealment and psychological boost to their defenders. The key constructions were supplemented with observation posts, obstacle zones, wire, mines, tank traps, trenches and earth and log works. What is less apparent perhaps is that in many instances the defences lacked 'depth' – they were a tough crust to stop or delay assault on and near to the shore, but usually not particularly deep 'zones'. Initial plans had worked on the basis of three lines, a forward, main and reserve, several miles deep, but later plans stressed the shoreline and beach exits, with the aim of halting the enemy before any foothold could be achieved. For all the effort they took to produce it was clear that only some of the defences would ever face a full scale seaward attack, and that if an initial invasion succeeded many would see no further use. With benefit of hindsight Speer would later venture the opinion that 3.7 billion marks, and five percent of Germany's production, had been squandered. Where the Allies invested largely in mobility, much German effort had gone into the static.

So it was that disproportionate responsibility fell upon the Panzer divisions: the armoured formations that possessed both mobility and power to inflict swift and serious damage against any incursion from across the sea. Nine Panzer divisions and one *Panzergrenadier* division were stationed in the West, but the original purpose of their presence was only partially defensive. Of these ten major German armoured formations in France four were in the south under Army Group G, leaving just six in the north with Army Group B: five in France and one in Belgium. Many of the tank units were brought, or formed, here as a way to equip, train and rest them out of reach of the enemy, before recycling them into the maelstrom of the Eastern Front. They certainly performed deterrent and occupation functions but at any given moment it was likely that a proportion of Panzer units in France would not be up to strength, making them a less potent strike force than might otherwise be the case.

The 21st Panzer Division, which would have a significant bearing on events in Normandy, was an interesting case in that the body reformed near Rennes in France in July 1943 was a reconstruction of, or replacement for, the original 21st destroyed in the fall of North Africa. Initially training with a mixture of older German and captured French vehicles it was still short of full strength in 1944. As of June its commander reported fielding 127 Panzer IV types and 40 self propelled guns. The 2nd Panzer Division fought in Poland, France, the Balkans and the centre of the Eastern Front before rebuilding in France. By June 1944 it was much better equipped, its tank component comprising not only 99 Panzer IV types but 79 of the newer, faster and harder hitting Panthers, plus assault guns. The 116th Panzer had been formed as recently as late March, using the remains of other units as its nucleus and by the time of the invasion had about 150 tanks on its books, roughly half Panzer IV and half Panthers. The 12th SS Panzer was recruited in the latter part of 1943 mainly from former Hitler Youth. Now well trained and aggressive it had a similar tank complement, though a rather higher proportion were the older Panzer IV type. The 1st SS Panzer Division, the elite *Leibstandarte,* had taken heavy loss in the East in 1943 before transfer to the old military base at Beverloo, Belgium, for refitting. It fielded about 80 tanks and a smaller number of assault guns. *Panzer Lehr* was something of an exception in that not only was it virtually up to strength with almost 200 medium tanks but also boasted a few attached Tiger tanks and Jagdpanzer IV tank destroyers.

Where exactly these six vital units should be deployed was a matter of debate, since dubbed the 'Panzer controversy'. The crucial issue was whether the bulk of the armoured units should be placed forward, so as to be individually close to the beaches, or back, in order to make a co-ordinated thrust from a central position. Both scenarios offered advantages and disadvantages. Tank divisions near to the coast would be more difficult to redeploy and vulnerable to the incursion of fighter bombers and even naval bombardment: away from the coast they might arrive too late for decisive intervention. Rommel, now commanding Army Group B, was in favour of putting the armour forward, but General Geyr von Schweppenburg, commanding Panzer Group West took the opposite view, intending that once the focus of the invasion was known it could be hit a massive blow from which it could never recover.

Neither got their own way since the Panzer forces were to be regarded as a decisive High Command strategic reserve only to be committed on the order of Hitler. This accorded broadly with the overarching plan of Führer Directive 51:

> Should the enemy, by assembling all his forces succeed in landing, he must be met with a counter attack delivered with all our weight. The problem will be the rapid concentration of adequate forces and material, and by intensive training, to form large units available to us into an offensive reserve of high fighting quality, attacking power, and mobility, whose counter attack will prevent the enemy from exploiting the landing, and throw him back into the sea.

Three Panzer divisions were placed forward north of the Loire, with only the 21st Panzer Division actually close enough to the Normandy beaches for swift action. The other three divisions were set back: their deployment would remain problematic throughout the later battle for Normandy.

———————

The stage was now set for the largest amphibious operation ever launched and one of the most ambitious military operations ever conceived, truly the last great crusade of World War II.

D-DAY
6 JUNE 1944

" The noise was unbelievable ... to the point where you could hardly hear the screams of men. "

Moreton Waitzman, US 29th Infantry Division, Omaha Beach

THE AIRBORNE LANDINGS

For many thousands of Allied troops D-Day really began before the dawning of 6 June. These included the Special Operations Executive (SOE) and Special Air Service (SAS) teams tasked with harassment and distraction; reconnaissance parties; pilots of bomber craft dropping 'Window' (small metalized strips) to confuse enemy radar as well as the one-third scale dummy parachutists; and naval reconnaissance parties, to name but the most obvious. Yet the largest portion of these so-called 'early birds' were the parachutists and glider troops of three divisions: the British 6th and the US 82nd and 101st Airborne. Eisenhower managed to meet with some of the 101st before they took off. He was greeted enthusiastically, but as he later remarked to his British driver Kay Summersby, 'it's very hard really to look a soldier in the eye, when you fear you are sending him to his death'.[1] Those he addressed looked bold and fully composed, but as Edward Shames recalled, had their own inner demons to wrestle with:

> We were scared. We were scared. We. Everybody. If you weren't scared you were crazy. Course there were a lot of crazy guys including me, but we were still frightened I'm sure. But we knew. We knew what we had to do and we were gonna do it. And … we did it.

Though the paratroops were indubitably a 'special force', designed to strike swiftly, it would be a mistake to assume that they went lightly into battle. BBC correspondent Robert Barr saw some of them just before boarding their C-47 Dakota transport planes:

PREVIOUS SPREAD

A recreation of the aftermath of the D-Day landings, as dead soldiers and discarded weapons littered the landscape. (Impossible Pictures)

> Their faces were darkened with cocoa; sheathed knives were strapped to their ankles; tommy guns strapped to their waists; bandoliers and hand grenades, coils of rope, pick handles, spades, rubber dinghies hung around them, and a few personal oddments like the lad who was taking a newspaper to read on the plane. As they knelt around their padre in prayer, with heads bent and on one knee, the men with their equipment looked like strange creatures from another world.[2]

With the 101st Edward Shames required assistance merely to get his equipment to the aircraft:

The gear weighed about 150lbs that I put on to get on that plane with the parachute. Everything we could possibly have… Weapons, maps and stuff. Smoke grenades. Recognition panels. The whole works. And some guys had mortars. 81mm mortar plates that they jumped with. Machine guns. Everything. Course I had my M1 rifle and all my ammunition and grenades. Grenades. As many as you could possibly carry.

The otherworldliness of the paratrooper's existence continued into the air, where darkness and engine noise conspired to separate man from environment:

In the plane we stand pack to breast, I am jumping one but last of my stick. And as we stand in the plane, for there is no room to sit, we feel the tremendous vibration of the four motors as we start down the runway. All around in the darkness are other great planes and row upon row of gliders. And the plane is airborne and in the fuselage all you see in the pale light of an orange bulb is the man standing next to you.

Arguably glider troops were even more vulnerable, for their craft were tethered to powered planes and once committed to action there was little chance for evasive action, or to regain height.

Paratroopers of the 101st Airborne have their equipment checked by Lieutenant Bobuck, prior to boarding their C-47 for the flight to Normandy. The C-47 in the background has had the black and white D-Day invasion stripes hastily painted on. (NARA)

The Popeye voice on the intercom croaked 'this is going to be a piece of cake'. And so it looked, until just short of the enemy coast we began to run into dense cloud. We went through that and came out facing the coastline. And then there were pretty lights. Hundreds of thousands of them, and all of tracer. The enemy seems to go in for fancy tracer. Maybe it's to keep his gunners amused. There it was ahead of us like the Blackpool illuminations, and when it seemed obvious to us that we should call it a day and go back, the pilot put the nose of the aircraft into it as if it were confetti... We had to skirt belt after belt of this flaming stuff to bring the glider exactly over the zone it was to land on. It was a trying time for any aircraft, but for a tug and a glider linked by a strand of rope it looked to me like suicide... We dived into a cloud. We could see nothing.

Not for nothing did the Americans christen the Horsa glider the 'flying morgue'.

On the Allied left were the British 3rd and 5th Parachute Brigades: the 5th planned to seize the Orne and Canal de Caen crossings and clear the ground for later glider landings, the 3rd was to take the Merville battery and demolish bridges over the River Dives, thus simultaneously aiding the sea landings and impeding the movement of the enemy. First into the fray were pathfinders to set up beacons, and three *coup de main* glider parties. That of Major John Howard's six glider group aimed at the crucial Orne and Canal bridges. A total of 423 RAF aircraft were devoted to the effort of these two brigades. The Air Landing Brigade glider force would reinforce the mission on the evening of D-Day.

Just after midnight, a few minutes into 6 June, Howard's gliders, carrying six platoons of 'D' Company of the Oxfordshire and Buckinghamshire, separated from their Halifax tugs, and swooped almost silently onto the targets. Three landed within about 100 yards of the Caen Canal crossing, then code-named 'Euston 1', but now immortalized as 'Pegasus Bridge', after the winged horse insignia of the airborne troops. Two more gliders landed close enough to the river bridge, and only one, under Captain Priday, went far astray. At Pegasus the enemy were taken completely by surprise: Lieutenant Brotheridge's first platoon clambered swiftly onto the road and rushed the bridge, one of the sentries ran, the other managed to fire a flare before being cut down. Although Brotheridge was killed by a burst of fire from an emplaced MG 42, and some of the enemy escaped, Pegasus was quickly seized with grenades and bursts of Sten gun fire. 'Euston 2', the bridge over the Orne at Bénouville was likewise rapidly secured, and the code words 'Ham and Jam', signifying the taking of both bridges in tact, were transmitted. Within half an hour elements of Lieutenant Colonel Pine Coffin's 7th Parachute Battalion began to arrive, preventing the enemy from making good an attempted counter-attack. This was as close to text book as any of the airborne operations that day.

Glider landing was risky, especially as Rommel had seen to it that many of the Normandy fields were now cross-cut with ditches, or sewn with his famous wooden 'asparagus' spears, capable of smashing a glider to matchwood. Yet glider teams did at least land, if they landed, on one spot. Parachutists were distributed as their transports wove and ducked the anti-aircraft fire, cloud and each other. Adverse wind made canopies flit like so many dandelion seeds in the dark. Such was the story of much of the remainder of the 5th Parachute Brigade, barely two-thirds of which made it to their rallying point. Nevertheless the 12th and 13th Parachute Battalions succeeded in seizing Le Bas de Ranville and Ranville. In the 3rd Parachute Brigade the 9th Battalion and 1st Canadian were also scattered. Canadian Jan de Vries suspected inexperience on the part of the pilots as much as enemy intervention:

The air was full of planes. We didn't, couldn't, see anything because the port holes were too high and the only time I reckon we saw the flashes of the anti-aircraft guns [was] when we went over the coast of France, I think that's what scared the pilots. They were [as] green as we were. And they took evasive action, lost where they were supposed to go and the pilot, [keen] to get back to England, had to get rid of the paras, so he just put the light on and we all jumped out and I remember I was about six or seven miles away from where I was supposed to be, I didn't know it then but I hit a field, and got out of my 'chute and ran over to the edge of the field... I looked through

OPPOSITE
The PaK 38 5cm anti-tank gun. Designed in 1938 by Rheinmetall-Borsig the PaK 38 was capable of penetrating about 90mm of armour at close range, and was one of Germany's key anti-tank guns, remaining in service right through to the end of the war. Though it was used in Normandy to counter the D-Day landings, it was one of the smaller pieces, much of the damage being done by the 75 and 88mm types. (Author's Collection)

the hedge and saw this track and I moved on, there was nobody. And I was hoping to run across a couple other guys from the group – nope, not a sound... I walked towards the coast and eventually it was starting to turn daylight. Now, I'd heard voices and footsteps and I just went under a bush or a hedge, dived under a hedge and lay perfectly still. And I know there were a couple of patrols went by me but I never made a noise and they couldn't see me, it was that dark, and the German patrols were usually quite noisy, very talkative.[3]

Also in the 1st Canadians, Private Joseph Gautreau was with a Vickers machine gun section. This carried with it extra responsibility – and a lot of groping about in the dark, to locate the various parts of the clumsy gun, tripod, water container and ammunition. In the meantime there was also your rifle to worry about:

All at once, geez, the shooting started and I got hit and, and that was it... I jumped in a ditch and the shooting stopped for a minute, and I tried to follow the ditch to get out and there was barbed wire going right down into the ditch and I got caught in that darned barbed wire but I pulled and pulled

Canadian troops and bicycles disembark from Landing Craft Infantry (Large). These vessels lacked wide ramps having gang planks on either side making exit rather slower than from smaller assault craft. (Imperial War Museum, B5261)

and ripped the back of my jump jacket. And then I finally got onto a dike and followed that up and, and got in the bushes there. But I'd got shot in the hand so I wasn't, I couldn't, I couldn't handle my rifle.[4]

With the war 'just three or four days old' Gautreau was back in England, oddly enough, feeling 'robbed' that his time in Normandy had been cut so short.

In theory the 9th Parachute Battalion, supported by jeeps, mortars and anti-tank guns, was supposed to gather and march a little over a mile to the Merville Battery, and, with the added assistance of some gliders crash landing directly on the position, neutralize this threat to Sword beach. Reality was rather different: Brigadier James Hill landed in the flooded Dives valley, and after struggling to extricate himself and some of his men using toggle ropes, had squelched towards the rendezvous. On the way his party was bombed by Allied aircraft leading to further casualties. Lieutenant Colonel Terence Otway, commanding the 9th, waited until three in the morning but was then forced to advance with what he had. As the official 'after battle report' put it:

> The battalion dropped at 0050 hours over an enormous area. They moved off at 0250 hours only 150 strong and having only one machinegun. No mortars, no special stores, no Royal Engineers or Field Ambulance personnel and no mine detectors. The glider borne element failed to arrive; and whilst on route to the battery position it was ascertained that the preliminary heavy bomber attack on the battery had completely missed its objective.

Nevertheless this weakened unit picked its way forward through minefields and wire and engaged the enemy with their only machine gun: then at the vital moment one of the three gliders assigned to the battery appeared, crash landed and disgorged its troops. As the regimental history recorded:

> Hardly had the occupants of the glider joined battle, when Otway gave the signal for the gaps in the wire to be blown. The assault parties then moved against the battery, but slowly, for bomb craters, wire and mines strewed the way. Nothing, however, could stop the indomitable troops whose average age was twenty-one – most of them be it remembered, in action for the first time. In due course they reached the guns and engaged in hand to hand

OVERLEAF
Support troops of the 3rd British Infantry Division assemble on 'Queen Red', Sword beach. This photo was taken at 08.30am while they were under intermittent enemy mortar and shell fire. In the foreground and on the right are sappers of 84 Field Company, Royal Engineers. Behind them, heavily laden medical orderlies of 8 Field Ambulance, Royal Army Medical Corps (some of whom are assisting wounded men), prepare to move off the beach. In the background men of the 1st Battalion, the Suffolk Regiment, and No. 4 Army Commando are being landed. (IWM B5114)

combat with the German gunners. These resisted stoutly until one of them happened to catch sight of the badge on the battle smock of a parachutist. '*Fallschirmjäger*', he yelled, whereupon he and his remaining companions lost heart and surrendered.

Otway now had but 80 of his own men left, plus 22 prisoners. The little party moved off to attempt their secondary objective, the seizure of the high ground near La Plein. This turned out to be held by a greater number of *Ost* troops under German command, so the paratroopers desisted, having to leave this target for the Commandos to destroy the next day.

Towards the western end of the invasion zone the American parachutists of the 101st began to land at about 01.30am. Their vital mission, 'Albany', was to seize the landward side of Utah beach, securing the area between St. Martin-de-Varreville and Pouppeville, thereby facilitating the exit of the 4th Infantry Division from what might otherwise prove a cramped death trap. Many yelled a battle cry tumbling out into the night sky. What this morale boosting shout actually was depends on who you speak to, and what regiment is under discussion. The orthodox version tells us that 'Currahee!' was the war cry of the 506th: others mention 'Geronimo!', or 'Bill Lee!' (in honour of a former leader). The division's commander, Major-General Maxwell Taylor, jumped with his men:

> As the plane roared away, I was left floating to earth in comparative quiet, broken only by occasional bursts of small arms fire on the ground. Since we had jumped at about 500 feet, to shorten the time we would be floating ducks for enemy marksmen, there was little time to try and select a point of landing. At the last moment, a gust of air caused me to drift away from my comrades of the stick and only by a mighty tug on the shroud lines did I manage to avoid becoming entangled in the top of a tall tree. Then I came down with a bang in a small Norman field enclosed by one of the famous hedgerows which compartmented the countryside… Many a parachutist that morning found himself suspended from one of those tall trees, from which he could only hope to lower himself by a rope before a German rifleman found him. At last on the soil of Normandy, I began to struggle out of my parachute, expecting that one of my men would appear to help me. But looking around I saw not a single soldier, only a circle of curious

Norman cows... I was still trying to extricate myself from my chute when a German machine pistol opened up in the next field with the tell tale sound of a ripping seat of pants which energised me to frantic struggles to free myself. In the wet morning grass, it was a terrible job to unbuckle the many snaps, and I finally gave up and used my parachute knife to cut my way out. Then, reluctantly abandoning my leg bag and its contents, I started out, pistol in one hand and identification cricket in the other, to find my troops – a lonely division commander who had lost or at least mislaid his division.[5]

At first everything looked unpromising, even unfamiliar, for large portions of the 502nd Parachute Infantry had been liberally scattered around the countryside in small packets. The 506th and 501st may have fared a little better, but even so some came to earth miles from their intended drop zones. According to one calculation the total area covered by the 101st when they hit the ground was 15 miles by 27 miles. Quite a few of the 'Screaming Eagles' therefore spent much of 6 June walking to where they were supposed to be. Of the 433 aircraft involved, 13 were lost and 81 damaged, most of them by the enemy flak that, together with cloud, had scattered the formations. Sergeant Ed Shames managed to gather about him a small squad composed of the random selection of men who happened to land nearby, several of whom had adopted Native American war paint and Mohican haircuts for the drop. Although he now had troops Shames had little idea of topography, and decided that the simplest thing to do was ask a local:

We had to take a chance. I discussed it with the five and they said OK sarge, maybe you're right. Let's try it. So I said OK. Three of you guys hang around the house; you and you come on with me, and let's go and wake this farmer up, which we did. We knocked on the door. And the farmer came to the door with his wife. She started screaming. I grabbed her and put her down and we told him it was an invasion. And course we forgot what we looked like. Most of these guys had blackened faces. Crew cut haircuts. Scalped, you know ... like the Indians.

Fierce and confused, if sporadic, fighting broke out as parachutists now attempted to join their companies. In at least one instance Americans and Germans were so much on top of each other that bayonets were used – an unusual event by 1944. The 2nd Battalion of the 501st was heavily engaged around Les Droueries where they bumped into an entire German battalion. The 3rd Battalion of the 506th Parachute Infantry was amongst the last to land and was caught when a ready enemy set light to a wooden building, so illuminating the battlefield that the parachutists made easy targets, and the commander of the battalion was killed. The experience of Donald Burgett was by no means unique:

> Small private wars erupted to the left and right, near and far, most of them lasting from 15 minutes to half an hour, with anyone's guess being good as to who the victors were. The heavy hedgerow country muffled the sounds, while the night air magnified them. It was almost impossible to tell how far away the fights were and sometimes even in what direction. The only thing I could be sure of was that a lot of men were dying in this nightmarish labyrinth. During this time I had no success in finding anyone, friend or foe. To be crawling up and down hedgerows, alone, deep in enemy country with a whole ocean between yourself and the nearest allies sure makes a man feel about as lonely as a man can get.[6]

Second Lieutenant Frank Gregg was another who jumped into the unknown with the 101st – only to float down through the darkness into a flooded area:

> It was dark and of course you heard the engines of the plane when you went out, and the prop blast from the wind, you heard all of that. And then maybe 30 seconds later all you could hear was machine-gun fire … the anti-aircraft artillery didn't bother us very much, because we were only about 600ft off the ground when we jumped – the shells burst above us so they didn't bother us. But the machine-gun fire was something else. It was criss-crossing the whole area. In fact I could hear some of 'em hitting our plane in the wings or some other parts of the plane which were not too crucial – but we didn't suffer hits in vital places. But I was standing in the door looking out, trying to keep my bearings and everything, and saw one of the planes in the formation burst into flame and went down and I didn't see where it hit... That was the first time I was shot at... I didn't have any problem coming down. But my problems started when I hit the water. I could see flashes – reflections – and I knew I was coming down in the water, so I started getting ready to be sure I could get to my trench knife to cut the harness off...

And anyway when I hit the water, the water was about knee-deep …
everything was wet. I mean, my carbine was wet. I had a 45 pistol – it was
wet… The water was cold, my hands were cold and I wasn't being very
effective in unfastening this stuff. I got the left strap undone and had the
right one to go, and I could not get that one undone. So I reached in my
boot where I carried my trench knife, and slid it under the strap of my right
leg, gave a tremendous pull on it, and felt a rush of cold water going in my
crotch area, and realized that I had slit my pants, about 3 or 4in, with that
sharp knife. It went in under the fly, and cut the fly and about a 3 or 4in slit
in the leg. But I got the parachute off then no problem, and then started
listening closely, to see if I could hear any of my men around. And I couldn't
hear a thing except the planes leaving, and then the machine guns firing,
and the anti-aircraft shells still going off. So I took about two or three steps
and dropped into a drainage ditch… I didn't know what I was stepping into.
But it was about 8ft deep anyhow, and I went over my head. I scrambled out
of that, and then started out again not knowing which way to go, because
I didn't know whether we were on our drop zone or not. And so I took a few
more steps – and dropped in another drainage ditch … then I finally I picked
up one of my men… And we went a little further, picked up two or three
more – and I think I had 19 by the time I reached land.

Major General Matthew B. Ridgway's 82nd Airborne, on mission
'Boston', were supposed to come to earth with one regiment around
Ste-Mère-Église and two on the other side of the River Merderet, quickly

A C-47 of the
90th Troop
Carrier Squadron
takes off from
Greenham
Common with
a Horsa glider
in tow on 6 June
1944. (NARA)

securing important bridges. In fact they were even more scattered than their comrades of the 101st. Of the 378 aircraft eight were lost and 115 damaged. Jack Schlegel of the 3rd Battalion, 508th, was in one of the aircraft hit:

A line of tracer bullets cut through the length of the fuselage of the C-47 causing men on either side to pull their feet in closer. No one was hit, but it got their attention fast so that everyone was alert for the next surprise – a direct hit on the left engine. Immediately Lieutenant John Evans yelled, 'Stand and hook up!'… No sooner were we in place when a third hit took off part of the right wing. The plane tilted down and to the right. Lieutenant Evans shouted 'Go!' and led the way. That was the last time anyone ever saw or heard from Evans. I recall I was the 24th man and last to leave the plane, and remember how the plane was going down. I moved as fast as I could to get out, and after baling out, saw the plane going down in a ball of flame.[7]

OPPOSITE
The church at
Ste-Mère-Église,
around which
American
paratroopers
fell right onto
German
defenders in the
early hours of
6 June 1944. The
stick that fell in
a concentrated
pattern in the
town centre
was 2nd Platoon
mortar squad,
of F Company,
505th PIR, 82nd
Airborne. The
dummy dangling
from the tower
represents the
hapless Private
Steele, who was
lucky to survive
the action, and
was cut down
and captured
later. (Author's
Collection)

Even 48 hours later the entire 82nd would only be able to count 2,100 'effectives', out of a total start strength of over 6,000. Some men, overshooting the drop, fell into flooded areas and were drowned. Even Lieutenant Colonel Vandervoort, commander of the 2nd Battalion, 505th Parachute Infantry, broke an ankle and was forced to command his unit from the back of a small ammunition cart.

At Ste-Mère-Église a stick fell right into the middle of the town, and several men were shot in the air. Sergeant John Ray landed in the square, and was shot dead, but not before he had mortally wounded the German who hit him. Another man came down in a burning barn, and more were hung up on trees. Privates John M. Steele and Kenneth E. Russell snagged their 'chutes on the church, and while Russell was able to cut himself free and escape, Steele hung there during the course of the battle, before being rescued and taken prisoner over an hour later. Eventually the 3rd Battalion of the 505th managed to gather about 180 men and stormed the town – mainly with grenades, knives and bayonets – killing or capturing the remaining enemy. A strong German counter-attack later in the morning saw the 91st Division troops, the 795th Georgians and some Stug III assault guns attempt to wrest the town back. This failed as by now the defenders had been substantially reinforced. At La Fière the 82nd fought a running battle that eventually lasted three days. On the afternoon of 6 June the enemy mounted a counter-attack towards the

La Fière causeway, through the flooded ground, led by captured Hotchkiss tanks and supported by artillery and mortars. Both sides suffered heavily, but the defence held.

One of the few people where he was actually supposed to be was Ridgway himself, who, with just 11 officers and men, set up his headquarters in an orchard. Yet the enemy were all around:

> Sometimes within 500 yards of my command post, but in the fierce and confused fighting that was going on all about, they could not launch the strong attack that could have wiped out our eggshell perimeter defence. This was in a large part due to the dispersion of the paratroopers. Wherever they landed, they began to cut every communication line they could find, and soon the German commanders had no more contact with their units than we did with ours. When the commander of the German 91 Luftlande Division, Generalleutnant Wilhelm Falley, found himself cut off from elements of his command, he did the only thing left to do. He got in a staff car and went to see for himself what had gone on in this wild night of confused shooting. He never found out. Just at daylight, a patrol of paratroopers stopped his car and killed him as he reached for his pistol.[8]

As it turned out Falley's division did not last much longer. Despite the 'Air Landing' name the 91st was actually an army unit formed as recently as January 1944. It was disbanded on 10 August, and despite being reformed later it disappeared entirely by November.

Given that the day had begun looking like a disaster it was a mixture of irrepressible fortitude and luck that turned it into success. For expensive as they were, and though not all objectives had been met, the Americans' parachute actions had done the really vital things they set out to achieve. The enemy had been confused and prevented either from pushing reserves up to Utah beach or stopping the 4th Division

from getting off the landing ground. Although casualties were significant many of those missing on the morning of D-Day would later turn up, having covered many miles to rejoin their units. Those coming ashore by sea at Utah had much for which to thank the 82nd and 101st. As Sergeant Shames put it, 'the Canadians and the Brits did better than we did', and the American divisions were, 'messed up', but, in the final analysis, 'accomplished our mission one hundred percent'.

THE AIR AND NAVAL ASSAULT

The airborne assault was just one of the ways the main amphibious force was supposed to be supported ashore. The others were bombardment from air and sea to neutralize – if not destroy – enemy positions that overlooked the beaches and blocked passage inland. Bombing of transport and other targets had gone on for weeks, though organized in such a way that Normandy was not attacked in isolation to avoid revealing the Allied landing grounds. The final air onslaught began at 03.00 in the morning of 6 June, with heavy raids aimed at batteries including those at Longues, Mont Fluery, Merville, Ouistreham and elsewhere. Charles Owen, a Lancaster pilot with the RAF's 97 Squadron took part in the attack on Pointe du Hoc:

> We thought the briefing sounded a little odd for this trip and sure enough when we broke over the French coast the Channel was full of ships. The army had pulled its finger out at last and D-Day was on. We bombed at 05.00 just as it was getting light, and had a grandstand view of the Americans running in on the beach. First class prang on the battery, but saw Jimmy Carter shot down by a Ju88 over the target. Marvellous sight coming back as the sun came up. We were on the way back and the Americans were on the way out. Landed back in time for breakfast, but very disappointed there was nothing on the eight o'clock news.[9]

The US Eighth Air Force put all its bomb groups into the air during the morning, many of the planes marshalling over England before massive streams headed out over all the landing beaches. They dropped more than 3,000 tons of munitions on enemy positions, and effectively overwhelmed the air defences suffering only modest losses themselves.

Enemy radar appeared to be much degraded, and the opposition terrified. As one war correspondent put it, 'the beaches shook and seemed to rise into the air, and ships well out at sea quivered and shook'.[10] However weather conditions were imperfect, and often the decision was made to err on the side of caution, bombing further inland rather than risk hitting Allied shipping or troops. The result was therefore much less effective than planned. Equally, although British efforts had damaged batteries, they had not silenced as many weapons as was hoped – at least partly because quite a few had been dismounted and transported to the rear. According to one calculation a total of just 18 of the 50 major enemy guns deployed in the 'Neptune' area, the area designated for the first day's landings, were put out of action by air attack.

Now it was the turn of the navies – not just battleships and destroyers, but special vessels designed to deluge the beaches rapidly with rockets and bombs. The *Neptune* plan saw ship-to-shore support in three phases timed around 'H-Hour' when landings took place. First came the pre-'H-Hour' bombardment, designed to 'soften' beach defences and 'knock

In late May through most of June 1944, the Eighth Air Force was diverted to missions over France to support the Operation *Overlord* invasion. Here, a weathered B-17 of the 100th Bombardment Group bombs coastal defenses near Boulogne on 5 June 1944, the day before D-Day. (NARA)

the spirit out of the defenders'; secondly the static defences were hit to aid passage of the first wave of the assault; and thirdly the reserves were landed. All this was juggled with the movement of 7,016 vessels of all sizes and several nationalities along ten major sea lanes, through a previously mined area, to the landing grounds. The orderly array of vessels underway was impressive indeed. To British tank officer Ian Hammerton it looked 'as if a giant had pulled ropes with them all attached' – dragging them inexorably towards the coast of France. Naval fire against land targets was both 'drenching' and specific. In the British sector the second bombardment phase co-ordinated with the actions of the 'Funny' tanks of the 79th Armoured Division as the naval 'battle summary' made clear:

> In this phase, tank landing craft with tanks specially equipped for beach obstacles, preceded by assault landing craft equipped to project 60lb bombs intended to blast a lane through wire and anti-personnel mines, were to beach at H-Hour, followed immediately by a wave of assault infantry and obstacle clearance teams. The whole were to be supported by close range fire from gun craft, warships and DD tanks.

The capital, and many of the other significant warships, were initially divided into five 'Bombarding Forces', each of 16 or more vessels, in support of the Eastern and Western 'Task Forces'. The biggest guns were the nine 16in pieces of the Royal Navy battleship *Rodney*, but there

were many other awesome gun platforms, like the *Warspite* and *Ramillies* with their 15in guns, and the USS *Nevada* and *Texas* with 14in pieces. Pre-arranged 'fire plans' were commenced when either the landing vessels came in range of shore, or the light was judged sufficient that the enemy would be able to spot the fall of shot from his own batteries. Programmes of 35 to 45 minutes were allotted to specific targets, though flexibility was maintained to allow 'impromptu shoots' throughout the day. Interestingly, while the British plans tended to focus both heavy guns and air power on selected batteries and strong points, American ones were more decentralized, and on Omaha, 'spread evenly over the whole length of beaches'. The naval bombardment was impressive indeed, and in many areas did precisely what it was intended to do – stun the enemy and keep his major guns from being used on the vulnerable ships committed to the landings. British tank gunner Peter Davies was underneath the flight path of some of the biggest shells, which 'sounded just like a train going over your head'. Staff Sergeant Lewis of the US 116th Infantry also heard the cacophony:

> I remember the battleship *Texas* firing broadsides into the shore while we were close by. It was God-awful, terrible explosions – muzzle blast in our ears… The smoke ring passed by us and it looked like the funnel of a tornado, growing larger and larger and finally dissipating… I don't believe we should have been that close because we actually felt the muzzle blast… All the ships did a great job except the LCT rocket ships which didn't get close enough to hit their targets. Destroyers came within a thousand yards of the shore and let go their five and six inch guns… The flash of the big guns was blinding and the explosions from the muzzles deafening.[11]

Yet Allied vessels did not have everything their own way, as Rear Admiral Arthur Talbot on HMS *Largs* could see:

> As we approached the lowering position, HMS *Warspite*, HMS *Ramillies*, HMS *Roberts* and HMS *Arethusa* were already anchored in their bombarding positions to port of us. Our own aircraft streaked low across the eastern flank at about this time, and laid a most effective smoke screen to shield the force from the heavy batteries at Le Havre. Unfortunately, three German torpedo boats took advantage of this to carry out a torpedo attack and, though engaged by the bombarding squadron, were able to make good

OPPOSITE
HMS *Warspite* of the 'Eastern Task Force' seen here bombarding the Normandy coast. Her 16in guns gave a range of 32,000 yards, allowing her fire to reach well inland. At first concentrating fire on enemy positions around Sword beach, she later moved onto other targets in support of both British and American land forces. By 1944 the *Warspite*, which had been commissioned in 1915 and was a veteran of the battle of Jutland, had earned the nickname 'Grand old lady'. (Author's Collection)

OPPOSITE
The 1944
memorial on
Utah beach
topped with an
'LCA' or 'Landing
Craft Assault'.
Attacked by the
US 4th Division
on D-Day the
beach was no
easy nut to crack
being backed by
grassy dunes, and
assault craft were
pushed away
from their
intended point of
landfall by strong
currents and
mines. However,
more than
23,000 men
were landed
on the first day
with relatively
light casualties.
General
Roosevelt, a
supernumerary
with the
4th Infantry
Division, was
posthumously
awarded the
Congressional
Medal of Honor
for leadership in
directing troops
off the beach.
(Author's
Collection)

their escape in the smoke. Two torpedoes passed HMS *Warspite* and HMS *Ramillies* and at 05.30 one hit HMNS *Svenner*. The shot appeared to have hit *Svenner* immediately under her boiler room. There was a burst of steam amidships and her funnel fell aft as the whole ship seemed to lift out of the water. The ship's company was seen to fall in on the forecastle and quarterdeck and, as she broke her back and started to sink rapidly, they began to jump into the water.[12]

Shells from shore batteries also fell closer, watched by an anxious Peter Davies: 'I was on the top deck looking across, I could see little landing craft and there'd be a huge plume of water and the landing craft would disappear from sight. And you'd think it had been hit. But then suddenly it would appear out the other side and sail on quietly. And we'd think, well, that one's got through.' The young Bill Ryan was less lucky: 'my boat was hit, was blown up in the air: all I remember was hitting my head against the bulkhead. It sounded to me like an explosion, an "88". That's what did most of the damage... I cracked my skull and I had a bit of shell fragment in my shoulder.'

THE BEACH LANDINGS

By the time amphibious assault forces arrived off the beaches many troops in landing craft were already heartily sick – sometimes quite literally – of the entire venture. Hal Baumergarten was just one who had no idea whether he could kill a man, and now made up his mind that he would never be coming back. Fellow American Donald McCarthy was just one of many praying that he would. Some admitted to premonitions of death to their comrades-in-arms, and were quickly proved correct. Matters were made worse for all by the fact that D-Day, originally scheduled for 5 June, had been postponed by 24 hours due to bad weather, and the men kept cooped up shipboard overnight. There were still 5 or 6ft waves in the Channel on 6 June. As Beach Master Petty Officer Ken Sturdy observed, a rolling sea and the flat bottomed craft needed to get onto beaches were no easy mixture. Canadian medic Roy Armstrong recalled bobbing about in the Channel and getting on and off ships for a period of about three days, before appearing off the beaches next to some of the biggest guns firing:

Didn't eat for about three days. And didn't eat for four days after. That's why they called it the longest night, the longest day … people didn't have time to eat or sleep … only one or two bathrooms … lotta men. Man could stand on the edge, relieve himself into the ocean… Rough, rough, rough. Sick as a dog. I didn't care whether I landed in France or not… And every time the battleship guns fired, the recoil sent about a 20ft wave, and that little barge went 20ft up 20ft down. I was so glad to get that jeep on the land…[13]

Fellow Canadian Chan Katzman also felt the weather, but imbibed some 'Dutch courage':

June 5 and June 6, the sea was rough. Some of the waves were almost as high as the ceiling. Your boat went down and came up and when you were down and started up your stomach was still down when you were going up. We had bottles of rum and it was passed along both sides. Everybody took a swig and when that one was empty another came on. I don't want to use this word but we were more than half-pissed when we hit the beaches. We'd go through a wall, not because we needed a drink, but we were trained that way.[14]

Donald McCarthy of the US 116th Infantry, who had come most of the way on a British destroyer before transferring to a bumpy landing craft, parted company with his breakfast at an early stage: 'We were cold and … were soaked almost immediately. So cold bitter shaking and sea-sickness took us over. And I think I tossed whatever I had because we weren't too crazy about the Brit food on board.' McCarthy put the quality of his Royal Navy food down to some grudge over the War of Independence. Ian Hammerton was 'continuously sick all the way over, until I could be sick no more'. For many the mere suggestion of food was too much. Charles Scott-Brown, a Canadian officer on loan to the

British, had only to produce a bully beef sandwich for fellow soldiers to beg him to throw it away.

At 06.30am the first troops swarmed ashore: Americans at Utah, followed almost immediately by their comrades at Omaha. Just under an hour later the British beached at Gold and Sword. Last to begin landing were the Canadians at Juno at about 07.45am. Despite the impressive array of equipment there were problems from the start. On Juno the armour simply was not where it was supposed to be. Much of it was adrift for some time because of navigational problems, but choppy seas also meant that many DD swimming tanks had to be released later, and closer inshore. The perils of launching further out in poor conditions were dire, as the Canadian 6th Armoured Regiment discovered to its cost. One moment Shermans and crews were there, the next they were gone:

> Now, on that landing craft tank, there were four, five, other tanks and we presumed that they all went down on account of the rough water. I didn't actually see them eye to eye but what I did see was one tank on the beach and there should have been five others. So you have to believe these are off the craft and they didn't get onto the beach … mass drowning you might say, they all went down, not to be heard again really. It's one of the feelings that you have in warfare, you have to give and you have to take and you have to do a lot of things that you wouldn't normally do in say peace time or, or just training for instance.

Canadian troops hug the side of a building during the battle for St. Aubin. The roadblock of logs and steel uprights protected approaches to enemy 'resistance nests'. (Imperial War Museum, B5228)

Adrenaline and shock sometimes caused men like Chan Katzman, Royal Regina Rifles, not to realize they were actually casualties until a few seconds after they were hit:

> When we were on the beach, I couldn't get the Bangalore or anybody to help me. I went to grab a machine gun because they shot our machine gunner. I used to instruct them, that's all. I went to grab it and as I was reaching a guy from behind me, I couldn't see, reached over top grabbed the handle and just about lifted it and he got a bullet right square in the front. Just about in the centre. He was killed instantly. He's the guy that got the bullet instead of me. So I have always felt he saved my life. Don Warhead. He used to be a good runner. We used to run 15-mile area races and 5-milers. He was a bit of a cowboy... After my buddy got shot I took off to the left and I ran about maybe 20 steps when I got machine gunned and every time I went to get up I fell down and I didn't know why. But I had a machine gun [bullet] that went through my leg. At the time when you get hit, it's more of a shock. It doesn't hurt but I couldn't stand up. I couldn't run. I couldn't walk. The only way I could manoeuvre was crawl or wait until the tide pushed me up a little. The tide was coming in all the time. That was after I got hit here and then I crawled on to the beach further on and the guys that made it over the top started going and they were shelling with 88s coming across on the beach. Our Spitfires and bombers had made big craters – and the 88 cannons. I was going in for cover to get into that hole and by golly, I had just about made it when a big shell burst and I got a piece of shrapnel that landed in behind my eye. It knocked me cold.[15]

Late arrival on Juno had serious consequences, for not only was the armour not close at hand but the tide meant that the landing craft often touched the ground amongst the beach obstacles, rather than ahead of them. Alex Adair was headed for the sector near St. Aubin code-named 'Nan White' with the Queen's Own Rifles of Canada, when disaster struck:

> My craft hit an obstacle out in the water, and it blew the whole front of the landing craft up in the air... I was towards the back thank God. Jumped over the side in about 7 or 8ft of water. Our little life preservers held us above the water. You'd go to the bottom and back up to the top... Bouncing up. Well right away I get rid of the mortar bombs. I said to hell with them:

I'm supposed to hang on to them, and the guy that's carrying the 2in mortar, he's relying on me for ammunition, and I'd dumped them. I dumped them and I've got my rifle only. Just paddled my way in – not going very fast – when I got knee high in the water, and then I thought well I can make a run for it now. And I ran and fell down… Somebody looked back and thought I'd been hit, but I immediately get up and on my feet again and started to run again. The sea wall was out in front of us at least 75 yards. It was far away enough. All you wanted to do was get there because that offered some protection from the rifle or machine-gun fire that was obviously headed our way.

At this point Adair was momentarily torn between self-preservation and desire to help his comrades:

Ankle deep in water and coming up the sand, I looked back, and one of my guys, MacDonald, he'd lost his helmet when he went over the side, and he's coming in bare headed. And just as I looked back he was hit, and he went down and disappeared in the water… So I ran back and grabbed him. We weren't supposed to do this by the way. They told us don't stop for anybody. But … I'm not going to leave the guy to drown in the water there if I can help it. So I ran back and dragged him up the beach, but he was badly hit.

Up at the sea wall the Queen's Own Rifles finally had an opportunity to take cover. Adair remembered seeing 'the reassuring figure of Norman Hoare', up at the wall gesticulating and shouting at him to get down. Adair needed no second bidding, so 'flopped down on the sand' and crawled the last few yards: he was now well behind his team and 'a lot of bad action had already taken place'. Around the sea wall Canadians bobbed up and down attempting to return fire, but there were other figures, lying there, not moving. The wounded were wrapped in blankets along the comparative safety of the face of the wall. One of these he recognized as 19-year-old Rifleman Russell Adamson, of Midland Ontario, 'I talked to him for a minute or two, and he wasn't talking at all. He was an awful colour, almost purple. I thought, "my God that guy doesn't look good". Well he didn't make it. He passed away on the beach there, "killed in action". He survived for a little bit, then he died.'

Canadian Bren gunner Tom Settee also had a 'wet landing' a little further west, with the Regina Rifles near Courseulles-Sur-Mer:

We jumped off the small landing craft, came up to our waist in water and we had to wade in. You had to hold your Bren gun up and wade in. These guys were peppering us. Boy, I don't know how I ever made it. Guys were dropping here and there. Big Corporal Dunfield ran in front of me and down he went. I kept running.[16]

Bill Halcro had to step over a casualty even to get off the landing craft:

The ramp went down. The first one got hit and fell off into the water. The second guy got hit in the arm and laid on the gangplank and then I was number three. He said 'number three' and I was kind of hesitant to move. He hollered again. I had to go. I got up and stepped over this fellow who was laying there and jumped off into the water and made my way to shore.[17]

At least the navy had done some good – Settee felt that they had 'really plastered the place'. One of the nearby emplacements containing a 75mm at the sector code-named 'Mike Red' had already been knocked out, and others had suffered hits causing temporary cessation of fire. What remained however were smaller concrete pillboxes from which still emanated a 'brrrt, brrt, brrt' noise that Settee quickly recognized as a 'fast, fast, fast belt-fed gun', the deadly accurate MG 42.

A Canadian bulldozer, tanks and infantry on the crowded shoreline at Juno beach. The casual attitudes and high tide suggest that this is after the initial landing. Reinforcements continued to be brought in via the original landing grounds for a long time after 6 June. (Imperial War Museum, MH3097)

Mines

The mine was a key part of fixed defences and the Germans deployed many different types to counter the Allied advance. Most effective when covered by other weapons and combined with obstacles such as wire, mines could be laid in definite patterns in defined 'fields', or irregularly as a nuisance factor beyond or between 'main lines of resistance'. Minefields were not marked on the enemy side but usually indicated on the 'friendly' edge with corner posts, fencing, signs or other devices. Although engineers searched for mines with electronic equipment, infantry were often required to 'prod' for them with bayonets. Dummy minefields complete with fake markers were also used to slow the Allied advance.

A sequence shot with a high-speed camera showing an anti-personnel (AP) mine explosion. While larger mines often killed outright, typical small AP mine injuries included loss of feet or legs and multiple shrapnel wounds which would hinder any advance. (Impossible Pictures)

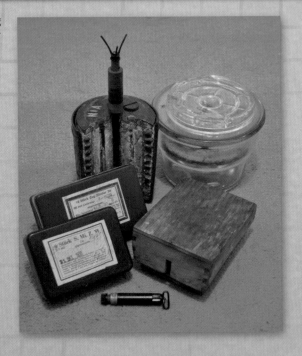

Typical German mining equipment. Back left: a sectioned example of the 'S' mine, or 'Bouncing Betty', showing the internal arrangement of the detonators within the TNT main charge and the shrapnel balls around the inner cylinder. The boxes are for igniters. Back right: the *Glas* mine. Front right: the *Schü* mine, shown in the closed position. Foreground centre: the *Zugzünder* 42 (ZZ42) pull igniter. These could be used with a variety of mines and booby traps including the *Schü* mine, the anti-tank 'box mine' and the *Riegel* mine. (Author's Collection)

Anti-tank *Teller* mine with anti-lifting devices. The mine is buried just below the surface in the normal way, but has been rigged with wires pegged into the ground so that attempting to remove the mine activates a switch setting it off. Notice that one of the anti-lifting devices is right underneath the mine, so that a wary technician who discovers the more obvious booby trap mechanism and disables it may still be caught out. As American engineer Captain Frank Camm related, one other way round the problem was to, 'tie a rope around it and then back off about 50ft and then pull the mine to see if it would explode or not … and we had two or three of 'em explode on us'. (Author's Collection)

Usually 'S' Mines had a ZZ35 igniter, requiring direct pressure to set off the mine but were made more effective with trip wires. Here mines have been fitted with the ZZ35 igniter and 'Y adaptors', and wired unobtrusively to pegs a short distance away. A stumble against any of the wires exerts a pull, setting off a mine – even though the mine itself has not been touched, and, being just below the surface, cannot be directly observed. (Author's Collection)

The 1943 type *Glas* mine. Made almost entirely of glass this particularly vicious AP mine was difficult to detect. The thick 'pressure plate' on the top rested on a thin 'shear plate'. Downward force of c.20lb caused the shear plate to give way, applying pressure to the lever of the igniter setting off the detonator and then the main charge. The entire mine then exploded into shards. (Author's Collection)

Detail of the *Schü* mine seen with lid open. This AP mine was easy to manufacture in small workshops as it was simply a small wooden box with hinged lid. The ZZ42 igniter was positioned through the hole in the front. When trodden on the lid depressed, pushing the pin from the spring-loaded igniter. This snapped back, setting off the detonator and main charge – not shown in the deactivated example. *Schü* mines weighed little more than 1lb and were highly versatile used alone, or in conjunction with anti-tank *Teller* mines and obstacles. (Author's Collection)

At 'Mike Green' the Royal Winnipeg Rifles were making better progress. Naval gunfire helped smooth the way, and an attached company of the Canadian Scottish Rifles managed to get right off the beach, through barbed wire and the minefields at Vaux. The second wave was coming in, and although Juno was still under fire, some forward movement was now possible. What would really make a difference was whether the armour, late as it was, could do the specialized jobs it had been planned for. In one spot Churchill AVRE tanks arrived and did succeed in bridging the sea wall, but as the first tank crossed it hit a mine. A bulldozer was called up, and was beginning to clear the obstruction, when it too was mined.

Ian Hammerton's arrival on Juno in command of a troop of flail tanks was thus a very welcome sight, both for infantry looking for support and anybody in danger of mines – and that was pretty well every Allied soldier yet on shore. As his landing craft bumped in and the first tank in his group nosed its way off, the vessel rose and surged forward on a wave. The ramp struck an underwater charge and was partly blown off – but the first two tanks were undamaged and drove off, followed by Hammerton in the third. In theory they should now have crossed the sea wall, but the bridging team they had been relying on was hit on the way in, so they cast around for other options as Hammerton explains:

> I found a concrete ramp leading up to the top of the sea wall sealed with two gates made of welded railway lines, or steel bars, all knotted round with barbed wire, and fixed at the top of the ramp, and of course the top of the sea wall had very dense barbed wire entanglements all the way along. So I got my two flails to move off to either side, give me covering fire, while I moved to the foot of the ramp, which was about 25ft from these steel gates, and we were so close the gunner couldn't use his telescope, because it's 21in off to the side of the gun. So it meant unloading the gun, and I had to look through the barrel [known as 'bore sighting'] aiming at each of the gates... It's amazing how big a 75mm barrel is when someone is firing at you from the other side. Anyhow it was a slow process, because I had to aim, load, fire, eject the empty case... In the end we demolished these things, and then it was a question of getting the debris out of the way and one of the engineer tanks went up the ramp and tried to do that but unfortunately he got one track over the side of the ramp and tipped over. So [we] drove up close, the water was now, incidentally, up to the end of the ramp, and I got out and

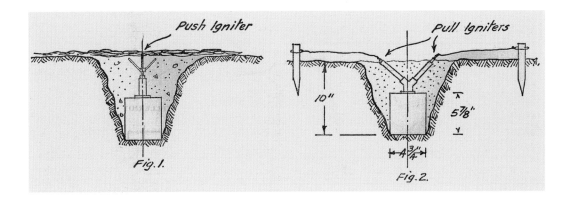

attached our tow rope to the wreckage, and towed that out to the sea. We cleared the exit, and I got my other two tanks to come round and go up the ramp and start flailing and they immediately started blowing up mines. As soon as they started up there I said to my drver 'advance'. He said, 'well I can't, the engine's just stopped, I have got water up to my chest.' So I said, 'right, bail out'. We dismounted the turret machine gun, seized as many boxes of ammo as we could, and stuffed our pockets with grenades, and we had to do a balancing act along the beams of the flail, and drop off...

British manual illustration showing the deployment of the German 'S' Mine with the basic pressure igniter (left) and the ZZ35 pull igniter and wires (right). The American nickname for the 'S' Mine was the 'Bouncing Betty' as the inner casing was projected a yard or more into the air before exploding, scattering fast moving shrapnel balls. (Author's Collection)

Hammerton and his crew then walked up to inspect the work of the rest of the troop who were busy flailing clear another lane through a minefield a few hundred yards away. On route they passed many dead and wounded as he later recalled: 'One of the most vivid memories I have is of seeing a Canadian soldier who'd been hit in the face, and had most of his face blown away. The padre was comforting him, and he wanted a cigarette – but there was nowhere to put it.' Hammerton found his sergeant still working on a beach exit. A Canadian carrier, blown upside down by the blast of a mine was mute evidence of the need for the job. A second set of flail chains were needed to complete the work, but eventually this path was also opened.

Fighting for Courselles continued for some time with each house having to be separately assaulted by men of the Regina Rifles, but here too tanks joined the fray.

By midday it was clear that the Canadians were in France, and prepared to stay. The Mike and Nan sectors linked up, thus creating one front on the western side of Juno. At the eastern end St. Aubin and Langrune remained in enemy hands, but it was hoped that Commandos

could clear these. German soldiers were now surrendering, and many were rounded up, but as Ken Duffield recalled it was not possible to take prisoners in every case:

> We had been firing at this pillbox which kept the enemy busy enough that we could get on the beach and come in behind and clean the pillbox out so the next wave could come in and they would have no resistance. The thing was, you know it's a hard thing to say, they said there was no way we could take prisoners because we had no way to dispose of them. So what do you do? You know if you can't take a prisoner? Well, we didn't have any choice and if a German would come out, it didn't matter, you disposed of him. That was just it because you had to clean everything out of the way so the next wave of soldiers could come through. And that's the way it was.[18]

Many of the casualties from Juno were ferried straight back from the beach and onto transports bound for the United Kingdom. On one of these young Royal Naval medic George Dangerfield helped look after them. In many instances it was easy to see what had done the damage:

Shrapnel wounds could be very, very, ugly. They could take a limb off or masses of muscle tissue, and leave great holes in the body. A bullet – providing it was normal size – could enter cleanly and go through the body. You got used to knowing the difference between the two... You could put a sterilized dressing straight through a bullet wound, provided it hadn't got defaced, hit a bone, major artery or anything like that... Worst were shrapnel wounds and explosions. I well remember one army major that we brought back to England. To look at him as he was standing up you wouldn't think there was a thing wrong with him. But he walked over an anti-personnel mine, and from the top of his head to his heels, he was actually shredded, the whole of his back, arms and legs.

Later counts suggested that although the total number of casualties was higher, about 355 Canadians were killed or died of wounds at Juno. This was little more than a third of the number who died in the disaster of Dieppe two years earlier.

While Juno was hard fought, and errors of timing and navigation undoubtedly cost lives, compared to Omaha it was a highly successful operation. Donald McCarthy landed with the US 116th Infantry:

As we rolled in we swung into a V formation, probably about maybe two or three miles out. Daylight started to come on and you could see the outline of the French coast. And I'm saying, my God, there's France. Wow, we're gonna be there. We're gonna go in ... we saw the patrol craft, the British patrol craft, and a minesweeper, I believe, pulling some of the guys out of the water. But as we went in ... within about a mile and a half ... we could see them shell flashes on the beach. The bombers that flew over didn't help us at all. On the other hand the one thing that we were promised before we left Blandford in Dorchester was that the navy will take care of you. They'll dig all kinds of holes for you. You won't have to worry – there'll be plenty of places to hide. Yeah, I'm saying to myself, doesn't look that way. In any event, we were heading for the Dog Green section. There were four sections on the [West] beach, Easy Green, Dog Red, Dog White and Dog Green... As we were going in we started taking in mortar fire and artillery fire, and some machine gun fire. The coxswain, bless this guy, realized that we couldn't get in because there were two LCVPs that were burning, just in front of us: 88s blew the ships right apart. There were nothing left ... he yawed, he turned the boat to the port side and took on more water. As he

OPPOSITE
A dead American soldier on the shore, still wearing his life belt. 'Bloody Omaha' cost the Allies over 2,000 casualties – of which about a third were fatal. This was considerably more than any other beach. However this was only a fraction of what was lost in the ensuing Normandy campaign. Moreover the psychological impact of Omaha appears to have been magnified by the fact that so many of the casualties were suffered in the first wave, and in a relatively short period of time attempting to cover a few hundred yards. (Author's Collection)

took on more water, we started to yaw and finally we broached probably about two boat lengths from the beach. When the boat broached, all the guys who were on the port side went in the water. I was on the starboard side … probably 15 of us that went in about the same time. We just rolled over into the water. I went under the water but I came up… I got rid of everything. All I've got on is my little 29th Division jacket, that's it. The combat jacket is gone. The rifle is gone. My camera's gone. I'm saying, son of a gun, my Dad'll kill me, because I lost the camera. I was originally wanting to take some photographs on the beach, that was the whole idea of this thing. I'm saying to myself, God, come on God, if I ever believed in you it's right now. And I yelled up at him and I said, God, please, please, please get me off this beach and I'll do anything you want in my whole life, if you just do this for me now. And the smoke came over. That was the miracle.

On most of the landing grounds the word 'carnage' would have been an exaggeration. On Omaha it was not. Men were hit on landing craft, in the water and on shore. Nowhere was truly safe. Morton Waitzman was witness, 'I think always particularly of one man who was dragging through the sand with his intestines all hanging out, begging for someone to shoot him, and a few of us did shoot him … we had syrettes of morphine and, and we emptied those syrettes into him to help put him out of his misery … and we proceeded as best we could under those conditions.' Also with the 29th Infantry Division, Bill Doyle's experience was equally traumatic:

Dead bodies all over the beach … when the ramp went down it almost fell on a soldier, a dead soldier there. I noticed there was something wrong, didn't look natural, and then it just dawned on me that he had no head, he only had a piece of bone sticking up… We started walking in, inland and I think the first thing I saw was a German self-propelled gun that had been knocked out, it had a big hole in the front of it and there were dead soldiers laying all around it, around that gun. I looked inside and there were two men in there, what was left of them. One of them wasn't anything left of him but his hips down [to] his legs … the rest of his body was gone.

Donald McCarthy's prayers for survival had been answered, but he was still in the water:

Now there's a kid next to me and I thought he had just come up with me, but later I found out he had drowned. But I was talking to him, as close as I am to you. I'm talking to him in the water, I'm saying, 'come on, swim, swim, swim'. And he's not saying anything to me. And I grabbed him on the shoulder and I pulled him along with me. Initially I was pulling him because I was using him as a safety net. I wasn't doing it out of any favour for him, I was doing it out of favour for me. This bothered the hell out of me for a lot of years...

Part of the enemy advantage was that they had been sitting on this coastline for years – long enough not only to build fortifications but to gauge every distance and field of fire. As Sergeant Nelson Horan of the 29th Division put it:

> The Germans had everything figured out. They knew the range of everything, all they had to do was fire for effect. And us, we didn't know what the range was, we had to guess ... artillery had to fire and see where the shell landed and then fire again – whether it was over or under or what. But they had the advantage ... they were always on the defensive ... you know, which always makes it a little harder for the people that are attacking.

A German operator demonstrates the use of the man pack flamethrower. It had been recognized as useful as part of the combined arms team for attacking fortifications as long ago as 1915. During D-Day and the ensuing battle for Normandy the Allies would turn them on German defensive works. (Author's Collection)

GI Hal Baumgarten quickly caught the wrong end of a shell:

> An 88mm shell landed in front of me … it's used to knock out tanks and
> stuff. I got hit by a fragment of that 88 which hit me in this side of my face.
> My cheek, as described by a medic later, was laying over my ear. The upper
> jaw was shot away on the left side of the maxillia. I had a hole in the roof
> of my mouth, I had teeth and gums laying on my tongue. Couldn't spit 'em
> out, couldn't swallow them.

One would have imagined that this would have been enough to put him
out of action for the rest of the day – if not permanently; but while he
was waiting for medical help further agony was piled on.

> I saw Sergeant John Fraser on the beach laying parallel to the wall, and the
> shells were starting to land around him. I saw his eyelids moving… I ran
> out to get him. It was just an impulse you know, he was one of my guys. Just
> then a mortar went off and I got three pieces of shrapnel in my helmet, into
> my scalp and I reached in with three fingers, came out with blood. Blood
> came over my ear and down the back of my neck.

As he watched a flamethrower team nearby was also hit – the fuel tank
burst into flames, and the team were 'cremated'. It was possible not to
look, but impossible to avoid the reek of burning flesh. Eventually
Baumgarten managed to crawl away, only to be wounded a third time.
He was under the impression that he had set off a mine. In any event it
felt like, 'a rock hitting my left foot'. There was now a 'clean hole'
through his foot. Having applied a dressing he had at least now got off
the top of the beach. Here he was caught in a burst of machine-gun fire.
This time the round whizzed through his lip taking a lump out of the
right upper jaw and he fell, 'on top of these guys, who didn't matter
anymore because they were just about gone'. Lying in a ditch he stuck
himself with a syrette of morphine and simply hoped for the best. Much
later when a medic reached him this served only to attract sniper fire.
Baumgarten was wounded for a fifth and final time in the right leg. This,
he said, 'wasn't a bad wound, believe it or not'.

What had gone so badly wrong at Omaha was not just one thing:
but an accumulation of many. This may have started with German
increases in troop numbers from March to May, but ineffective aerial

bombardment, poor sea conditions, navigation issues and less than accurate fire from rocket launching landing craft also contributed. In addition, there were severe problems with getting the tanks ashore. Swell prevented the 743rd Tank Battalion launching its DD tanks off-shore, and instead most were carried all way to the beach: 40 of 48 made landfall, but were confronted with heavy anti-tank fire. If anything the 741st made a worse, if brave, decision, to launch their swimming tanks 5,000 yards out. Some sank immediately as their canvas screens collapsed, and many crewmen drowned. Another tank landing craft struck a mine with the loss of three more vehicles. Just 18 of the 48 tanks of this unit got into action, and three of these were quickly knocked out by anti-tank guns. At 'Easy Red' sector there were just five viable tanks. Meanwhile, only some of the luckless 'Gap Assault Teams', designated with clearing beach obstacles, managed to actually clear lanes through the obstacles, leaving significant areas intact and posing a very real threat to the later waves of assault troops. The infantry, now very vulnerable, were further hampered by the fact that many craft grounded on sandbars 50 or 100 yards from shore. They now presented excellent targets as they struggled through the water and up the beach, looking for the largely non-existent bomb craters that might otherwise have given them welcome cover. In places, as at 'Dog Green', the German defences now functioned exactly as intended with enfilading fire from adjacent 'resistance nests' creating zones of interlocking fire. The 116th infantry

Official sketch of the Sherman DD or 'Duplex Drive' swimming tank, dated 10 June 1944, showing front, armament and exterior stowage. Brainchild of Hungarian engineer Nicholas Straussler the DD system used power from the tank's engines to drive a propellor when the tank was in the water. The canvas skirt, seen here in the lowered position, gave buoyancy when raised around the vehicle. Although prone to swamping in rough sea, those that did get ashore on D-Day gave a valuable boost to the power of the landing and to the morale of their infantry comrades. (Author's Collection)

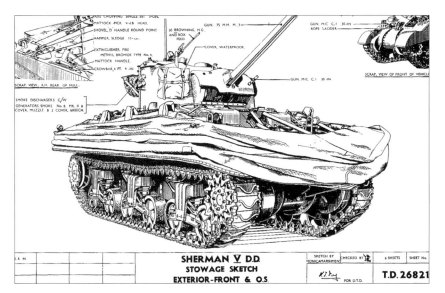

SHERMAN V D.D.
STOWAGE SKETCH
EXTERIOR-FRONT & O.S.

T.D. 26821

lost three of four company commanders – and 16 other officers – even before attempts to get up the beach. Even what was arguably the most courageous feat of arms at Omaha, the scaling and capture of the Pointe du Hoc by the 2nd Rangers under Lieutenant Colonel James Rudder, was somewhat deflated when the men who captured the gun casemates discovered them to be empty. Only by extreme tenacity, repeated attempts and the good fortune that the commander of the 352nd Division, Generalleutnant Kraiss, had decided to divert part of his strength to confront the British, was a narrow toe-hold at Omaha retained. Interestingly of the 214 Distinguished Service Crosses awarded to American troops taking part in the invasion nearly three-quarters went to men who landed at Omaha. Of the remaining 61 the vast majority were won by parachute troops.

Had all the landings been like Omaha the course of history might have been very different. Happily they were not, for while Utah and the British beaches had many tribulations, success of these enterprises was not long in doubt. At Utah the invaders also suffered fire from German batteries, and due to current and poor visibility the 8th Infantry and the 70th Tank Battalion were actually landed more than a mile south of their intended target. In addition, the tanks were delayed and came in just after the troops they were supposed to lead. These problems were quickly overcome, however, as it so happened that landfall was made on a less well-defended sector where the key enemy strong point had already received several direct hits. Although harassed by artillery fire, teams set about destroying beach obstacles, and on their arrival the tanks were directed to confront surviving bunkers. Rather than move along the shore to the original exit points General Theodore Roosevelt Jr., a 4th Division 'Supernumerary General Officer', set out to reconnoitre alternatives. A causeway was located and although a German anti-tank unit managed to put up some stiff resistance this was finally overcome and many Germans were captured. Aided by disruption caused by air landings, and the good work put in by both the 82nd and 101st Airborne in preventing German reserves reaching Utah, the infantry were able to get across the causeway. Eventually more causeways were opened. Though it did not get as far as initial plans had hoped, the US 4th Infantry Division achieved a secure hold at a total cost of about 200 lives. The 8th Infantry performed exceptionally well – something that many of its veterans would later attribute to thorough training. Later that day Sergeant Orval Wakefield

surveyed the scene, 'By middle afternoon the beach had changed from nothing but obstacles to a small city. It was apparent that we Navy 'Construction Demolition' units had done our job well because as far as I could see to one side the beach was opened, there was nothing holding the landing craft back. We figured our day was well spent.'[19]

At the extreme eastern end of the landing grounds Sword beach was held by one German division, the static 716th, composed of older men from the Rhineland and Westphalia. However they were led by veteran general Wilhelm Richter, and, perhaps more significantly, Sword was dangerously close to the positions of the 21st Panzer Division – and potentially presented an open flank to the enemy. Despite losing nine of 40 DD tanks, and arriving late, a good deal of the armour got to shore, and the 'Funnies' of the 79th Armoured set to work. However enemy machine guns as well as 88mm and 75mm anti-tank guns in enfilading positions had survived, and these now fired down the beach knocking out tanks and causing casualties. The helmsman carrying Ken Sturdy's Beach Master team steered for a church steeple that he knew lay behind the landing ground, and his passengers, amongst the first ashore, were beached 'hardly getting our boots wet'. Since the shoreline was raked by fire it was vital to clear everybody as quickly as possible. Sturdy remembered one of the Beach Masters had, 'of all things, a bulldog on a lead, which made one think of Churchill of course, and he was yelling "Get off the beach!", his instructions of course as beach master, was to clear the beach and get people over the sea wall, because the Germans had the range of the beach'.

On the way to Utah beach. Task Force U sets sail for Normandy on 5 June with a flotilla of LCI (landing craft, infantry) ahead, as seen from the bridge of an LST (landing ship, tank). (NARA)

The 1st Battalion South Lancashire Regiment came in on the 'Queen White' sector at 07.20am, in front of the unsuppressed strong point code-named 'Cod'. Amazingly they carried with them three flags in regimental colours, each emblazoned 'XL' in memory of their predecessors of the old 40th Foot, providing visual rallying points and a marker for the second wave of their craft. They attacked through fire from 88mm guns, mortars and machine guns, and though the commanding officer Lieutenant Colonel R. P. H. Burbury fell, flag in hand, and the unit took more than a hundred casualties – about a quarter of these fatal – 'Cod' was stormed and the South Lancashires were able to press on all the way through to the beach exit and the village of Hermanville before the morning was out. Here they rewarded themselves with a drink, it being claimed by their regimental history that they were the first to brew tea on this side of the Channel. They were, as General Miles Dempsey, commander of the Second Army, put it, 'a terrific lot of chaps'. Much the same could be said of the other assault units in the 8th Brigade, the East Yorkshires and Suffolks.

Private Richard Harris was with the 1st Battalion, the Suffolk Regiment, immediately adjacent to the South Lancashire's landing:

> Trembling, my rifle tightly clutched, I crouched awaiting the dreaded shout of 'Ramps Down!'. We seemed to inch in, inbetween craft already beached, some of which were burning... This was it – I was determined to present myself for a minimum [amount] of time as a target ... and being one of the first off I had a clear run. On the order to go I leapt up, bounded down the ramp and landed in about 4ft of cold sea water ... and waded as quickly as I was able to the shallows and the beach. My impression of the scene was a complete shambles. Had the whole thing failed, was it a gigantic cock-up? Against a backcloth of smoke and gutted blazing buildings were several burning knocked-out DD tanks and strewn about from the water's edge to the sea-wall were sodden khaki bundles staining red the sand where they lay... But there was no time to be staring at my first experience of corpses, a mad dash up the beach ... to gain the shelter of the sea wall. Find some sort of hole. Keep your head well down and try to locate a beach exit.[20]

John Cloudsley-Thompson was a County of London Yeomanry tank officer in the second wave on Gold. In theory his landing was supposed to be on 'Jig Green' sector, but pretty clearly this was not exactly where he had landed up. Nor were the German defences fully suppressed. In a moment of levity somebody joked that the maps of Normandy with which they had been provided were a blind – for a trip to the West Indies. Making the best of bad start Thompson landed, glad that his tank was sealed against water as his disorientated driver headed along the beach instead of for the nearest gap:

> I thought another few waves and we'll be sunk, and everybody would have to swim – if they could swim with all our equipment on. So I tapped the loader, and pointed … and he indicated by tapping to the driver 'turn left', because we couldn't talk to each other … a sheet of water had come down and hit the earphones or junction box of the driver, and he couldn't hear instructions from me. I suppose he realized when he was tapped on the left shoulder he had to turn left, which put us back on track.

The tank gained the top of a rise, and here the crew stripped off and jettisoned what remained of the waterproofing. Enemy small-arms fire was still coming their way, and another tank commander in the group was wounded. Luckily there was no direct anti-tank fire at this moment, but evidence lay around of those who had gone before, shell holes, and a knocked out German gun. The troop found a path already marked by the engineers and drove off.

The one Victoria Cross (VC) won on D-Day was awarded to a soldier who landed at Gold, Colour Sergeant Stanley Hollis of the 6th Battalion, Green Howards. Having landed on 'King' sector Hollis was passing pillboxes near the weirdly code-named 'Lavatory Pan Villa' when a machine gun opened up. He assaulted the pillbox single-handed, rushing it and poking his Sten gun through the aperture to spray the interior. He then climbed on the roof before lobbing a grenade inside. Other Germans nearby surrendered. Later that day he attacked an enemy field gun with a PIAT (Projector, Infantry, Anti Tank), and was instrumental in helping two of his comrades escape from a dangerous position.

Interestingly the Commando 'Special Service Group' was landed in the second wave of the invasion, with its 1st Brigade, comprising Nos 3, 4 and 6 Army Commandos and 45 Royal Naval Commando toward the eastern end of the Allied landing grounds, and the 4th Brigade, of Nos 41, 46, 47 and 48 Royal Marine Commandos, to come in at the centre. No. 46 RM Commando formed a 'floating reserve', but the remainder

Tough but slow and under-armed the Churchill tank had first been planned as a heavy 'infantry' tank for crossing shelled terrain. While a very imperfect model was rushed into service in 1941, it was several years before it could be revised in the light of experience – such as that of Canadian crews at Dieppe. By the time of the introduction of the Mark IV in 1942, the Churchill was fitted with a 6-pdr gun and boasted 100mm front armour: by 1944 the much redesigned Mark VII was using a 75mm gun and had 150mm protection. (Author's Collection)

would advance from their landing points, through and around the first assault waves, tasked with both moving rapidly to support the British Airborne forces, and attacking enemy strong points and villages from the flanks and rear. By this means they would both bolster the advance with fresh and highly trained troops, and help to dissolve the cement holding together German resistance. Highly useful as this undoubtedly was, it was also controversial, and a significant departure from previous techniques. Formerly Commandos were a vanguard, preferably arriving on a flank, in small numbers, and by stealth. Now they attacked headlong against an enemy very thoroughly alerted by bombing, shelling and the first wave of the armada. With enemy guns as yet unsilenced, the run in for the Commandos was often as dangerous as for those who had gone before.

Vincent Horton was with 48 Royal Marine Commando disembarking in the wake of the Canadians on Juno. In theory this should have been an easy landing, but in practice they landed in the midst of battle:

There was terrific gun fire all round, and mortar fire. When I got off the ship I was carrying the adjutant's map case, and as I got off two ships went down – lost completely. I was starting to run [but] mortars came over and I dived into a bomb or shell hole where part of the sea wall was blown down.

And my rifle cut my left eye open, and I felt some bits go into me. I [thought] they'd finish me, because they used to come in a salvo of about 12. I waited till they'd finished and dashed off to where we had to rendezvous, and gave him back his map case. He looks at this and there's a hole right through it – they dug a few bits out of me, and patched me up. [By now] we'd taken all their strong points [on the way] into Langrune... When we got there they were on the sea front; our objective was a gun and mortar position, that were hitting our ships. The road up to it had been recce'd, a tanker had attempted to go up there and hit a mine and blown up. And when we looked, [we] saw there was a brick wall joined onto houses either side of the road with a machine gun nest in the middle facing the road down. And the only way we could ever get in was through there. So they filled two ammunition boxes with high explosives ... and laid them near to the wall. And when they went up so did parts of other houses, and out came the Germans with their hands up.

As a post battle summary explained 47 Royal Marine Commando landed on Gold in the 'Jig' sector at about 09.30am. In doing so they lost all but two of their assault landing craft, and much equipment including their wireless sets. This, however, 'did not deter them'. But in truth the fortunes of the Commandos were mixed that day, and often dependent on the success, or otherwise, of first waves. On the left Lord Lovat's 1st Brigade made good progress, linking up with the airborne troops and propping up the worrying left flank of the invasion – despite some hard fighting and heavy losses. No. 4 Commando in particular did sterling work in attacking and taking the Ouistreham battery from behind. The 41 Royal Marine Commando had a hard time at Lion-sur-Mer, and though it cleared the sea wall successfully attacking its first objectives, could not reach the radar station at Douvres which was still in enemy hands ten days later. Langrune cost many casualties before the attempt to clear it was abandoned for the day, and had to wait for armoured support the next morning. Port en Bessin also fell to 47 Royal Marine Commando on 7 June in an expensive set piece action commencing with an attack by Typhoon fighter aircraft and naval gun fire.

Arguably the worst moment on the British sector came with the unleashing of General Edgar Feuchtinger's 21st Panzer Division late on the afternoon of 6 June. For this was just what was feared – an armoured thrust, delivered before beaches could be consolidated or troop numbers built up. Two tank battalions and a battalion of Panzergrenadiers struck from the direction of Caen. Part of the force ran headlong into the 2nd Battalion, King's Own Shropshire Light Infantry, and an armoured squadron of the Staffordshire Yeomanry armed with Sherman 'Firefly' tanks with 17-pdr guns, as well as artillery. The Germans were diverted and lost 13 tanks, but the British were halted in their object of reaching Caen. As it was Panzergrenadiers did reach the coast near Luc-sur-Mer creating a dangerous gap in the invasion zone between the British and Canadians, and making contact with pockets of the German 736th Division. This was extremely worrying, and caused the invaders to be more cautious than might otherwise have been the case: but General Feuchtinger's force was damaged and lacked strength for the decisive intervention required to roll up the landing grounds from such a tenuous position of advantage. Frustratingly there was no word from High Command, nor the usually dynamic Rommel, whose wife's birthday – that by strange quirk of fate fell on 6 June – had preoccupied him in Germany. With the arrival that evening of a fresh wave of air landing troops, and in the absence of orders, Feuchtinger decided that to leave his troops where they were could only result in their own encirclement. That night he withdrew to Caen and began strengthening defences north of town that would for so long absorb the efforts of the British and Canadians.

By midnight of 6 June it could fairly be claimed that despite many mishaps the invasion had succeeded in its primary objective. Approximately 155,000 men were ashore, and every beach was occupied. True the toe-hold at Omaha was barely a mile deep, and pockets of enemy resistance remained between the invading corps. Caen and Bayeux, always optimistic targets for the first day, were not taken. Yet this was most definitely a glass half full. The Canadians made remarkable recovery at Juno and created inroads inland, and the enemy was unable to combat progress at Utah. Interventions by tanks had been parried. Only if the opposition could now succeed in marshalling their strength, and particularly the Panzer divisions – into concerted and successful counter-attacks – would the tentative decision of D-Day be reversed. BBC news reports were sanitized of the worst, but essentially accurate. They also gave some hint of the scale of the task that lay ahead:

The part of the coast on which our troops landed and fought their way in land was a good sample… Prior to the operations, it is true to say that you could not have put a pin down on any part of that coast which was not under direct fire from machine guns and mortars, or fire from heavy guns. The wall was breached by bombardment from the Allied Navies and Air Forces, and it was cleaned up by soldiers who went ashore under fire. The Germans knew that no fortification however strong could stop a determined assault concentrated on one sector of the coast. The purpose of the West [*sic.* Atlantic] Wall was to slow down the occupation of the beaches, and therefore to slow down the build up, so that their own build up of troops in that area would be faster than ours. Then they could meet us in the field with superior forces and drive our army back into the sea…

The confusion of Juno is finally sorted out as columns of troops march up a freshly laid track and off the beach. (Public Domain)

NORMANDY
7 JUNE – 25 JULY 1944

> **Each little field [had] one gate ... so each a little battlefield... So the Germans fought in that one, and when they got pushed out they fought in the next one.**
>
> Patrick Delaforce, Royal Horse Artillery, 11th Armoured Division

Allied plans were undoubtedly delayed by failure to take some major objectives on the first day, but the basics remained the same. The beachheads still had to be expanded and joined. In the west, American forces could achieve this by securing Carentan and Isigny, with the British linking with them by the final reduction of Port-en-Bessin. This sounds simple, but many places were fiercely contested. Mines, in particular, continued to be a menace, and had no sense of when to give up. Cunningly, they were not only used to block open fields and pathways, but sometimes planted in just the spots where men might seek cover from other weapons. Marine Commando Vincent Horton, already slightly injured on D-Day, fell victim at Sallenelles:

> There were quite a hell of a lot of dead Germans there … shells coming in. On the front was a gun position to be taken, so we went down to take that out, and when they spotted us they turned the gun around to us, and we ran for a hedge. And that's where the mine was, and I stepped on it and it blew my leg... I was knocked out, and I first woke up three days later in a dugout: there was a surgeon, two women orderlies, and a wooden bed and many wounded. 'You've got gas gangrene', he said, 'that leg has got to come off … but not in your condition'.

So it was that Horton was passed back to the United Kingdom and from one hospital to another – first in peril of his life, then under threat of losing three of his limbs. Eventually he won his struggle to live, but lost both legs. He was 23-years-old and his total time in France amounted to less than a week.

CAPTURING CAEN

PREVIOUS SPREAD

A recreation of a German Tiger tank being hit by a Sherman Firefly armour piercing round. (Jeremy Llewellyn-Jones)

Caen and Bayeux were seen as crucial to the ability of the British and Canadians to enlarge their lodgement and prepare for the advance south. Despite transport bottlenecks and enemy pressure on the Special Forces in the Orne bridgehead, new formations poured in. Bayeux fell to the British 50th Division on 7 June, and over the next few days the US 29th Division broke free of Omaha to link up with the 101st Airborne. After fierce fighting Carentan fell on 10 June, and in the centre the US 1st Infantry Division fought its way forward to Balleroy. Caen was a

American troops receive fresh bread and newspapers, 7 July 1944. Logistics were crucial to Allied success and eventually supply lines had to be established from Britain to France and all the way into Germany. Demand for motor transport was further increased by the German forces destruction of supply lines and rail links as they retreated. Churchill, as well as many frontline combat troops, railed against the apparently extravagant administrative 'tail' of the Allied armies, nevertheless massive investment in logistics remained a highly necessary evil. (Author's Collection)

different matter. For although the enemy remained hesitant to commit all his reserves, and daylight movement was extremely perilous, two Panzer Divisions were nevertheless moved to the defence of the city: the 12th SS *Hitlerjugend*, under the fanatical Kurt Meyer, and the *Panzer Lehr*, under the equally experienced Fritz Bayerlein. Against them from the north came the British and Canadian 3rd Infantry Division. It was also hoped to envelop the town from both sides, and even to drop paratroops. If successful these moves would eventually encircle Caen.

It was at Tilly-Sur-Seulles that the newly committed 7th Armoured Division – the famous 'Desert Rats' – had their first serious taste of action, being counter-attacked by *Panzer Lehr* on the night of 11 June. So hard pressed was the 2nd Battalion, the Essex Regiment, that it was forced to call down artillery on its own positions, hoping that the attackers would suffer more than their own in the British foxholes. There were also other terrors here, as was reported soon afterwards by Frank Gillard for the BBC:

The whole area around Tilly is just a nightmare for anybody who's got to move around up there. There are mines and booby traps everywhere; but this is the story of a stretcher bearer who turned all this mining and trapping to his own purposes. During the battle he found a nest of twelve eggs. There was no time to take them then, and he knew that other people might stumble on them at any moment; so he found a piece of board and scrawled on it a notice which said 'booby trap'. That notice he left propped against the nest of eggs. Well, when the fighting had died down and he had a moment to spare, he went back to the nest and there were the eggs just ready for the pan.[1]

Frank Rosier fought with the Glosters at Tilly:

It was more or less street fighting. I think they had 25 goes before they took Tilly-Sur-Seulles. It was a hell of a fight... You learned pretty quickly never to fire unless you are going to hit the target, because if you fire and miss you give your position away... Hand-to-hand fighting is vastly different; a bit nasty. You're killing a human being, not a target... The SS are not easy boys to fight. I was on my own, and I'd taken the wounded back to join the unit, and out of this hedge – this young German boy, my age, 18, 19 – it was like cowboys, we went for our guns. I carried a Sten gun at that time I was there. And I killed him. And I sat on the ground and was sick. I killed a human being. And as I talk to you now, I can see that ginger-headed boy, some mother's son – you know – and that's horrible ... worse. When it's remote that's nasty, but this is personal.

The battle for Villers Bocage

While the 51st Highland Division advance east of Caen failed at an early stage, the British 7th Armoured Division pushed on south in the direction of Villers Bocage, hoping to exploit a gap in the enemy defences. Led by Brigadier 'Looney' Hinde the 22nd Armoured Brigade stormed into the town on 13 June, scoring a deceptively easy victory. This looked like the beginnings of a breakout, so Hinde pushed out tanks of the County of London Yeomanry towards Point 213, a vantage point on a nearby ridge. However, they were not aware that the enemy had now rushed reserves to the area, most importantly the 2nd Company of the 101st SS Heavy Panzer Battalion, led by Obersturmführer Michael Wittmann. With skirmishing commencing between elements of the Rifle Brigade and a German reconnaissance unit, the tanks of the Yeomanry now ran into six Tigers. As Wittmann himself reported, 'I had no time to assemble my company, instead I had to act quickly, as I had to assume that the enemy had already spotted me and would destroy me where I stood. I set off with one tank and passed the order to the others not to retreat a single step but to hold their ground'.[2]

A sergeant of the Rifle Brigade sent a hasty warning – but too late. Wittmann emerged onto the road and engaged and destroyed a British Cromwell tank. A similar fate befell a Sherman Firefly that attempted to stop him, and this tank was left burning across the road. The other Tigers now fell on the British tanks at Point 213.

Wittmann drove into Villers Bocage where he surprised a column of vehicles, destroying several including two of the three M5 Stuart light tanks that gamely attempted to block his path. John Cloudsley-Thompson was in his Cromwell when pandemonium broke:

We stopped – just on the edge of town… I was rather busy looking at the map and trying to work out what was happening. And then quite suddenly the tank in front of me burst into flames. Big explosion. I was by a slight bend and couldn't see anything… I thought that an anti-tank gun down a side road had fired and hit it. So I said to the driver, 'Reverse, left stick', and we actually backed off the road, up against a wall, blackcurrants growing there – it was a garden – and through a hedge. There was a lot of smoke and an 88mm shot went so close to my ear that, although I was wearing headphones, I was deaf for a week afterwards. Anyway we backed into this position, then through the smoke in front I suddenly saw this huge tank

OPPOSITE
A Sherman Firefly of the 1st Northamptonshire Yeomanry in the Odon Valley near Caen. The Firefly was one of few Allied weapons capable of taking on Panther and Tiger tanks. It was originally an expedient pushed by officers of the Armoured Corps when development of other tanks stalled in 1943. Its 17-pdr gun was initially capable of penetrating about 140mm of armour, but in late 1944 this was upped to over 200mm with the appearance of Armour Piercing Discarding Sabot (APDS) rounds. (Courtesy of the Tank Museum, Bovington)

This top view of a Sherman Firefly shows the length of the barrel, the distinctive egg-shaped muzzle brake; the large locker on the turret rear that housed the radio; the large circular commander's cupola in the right turret roof; and the unusually positioned square loader's hatch. (The Tank Museum, Bovington)

coming along and I gave the gunner the order to fire. He said, 'Um! The travel lock's on'. Well, I couldn't unlock it in time, so I fired the smoke mortar we had on the outside of the tank … and it went way over the Tiger, must have been [no more] than 20 yards away… Some of the other tanks did get shots at it, and they just bounced off. It moved the 88, just like that, and then 'Wham!' – a shot came. I was standing up within the turret looking through the periscope. I ducked down, and felt a tingling between my legs. I thought lucky my legs were apart…

The armour piercing round had gone clean through part of the front of the Cromwell, missing both Cloudsley-Thompson and his troop sergeant, who was in the co-driver position, ploughed through the length of the tank, and landed up somewhere in the rear.

All I could see was a mass of flame from the engine – came [right] over me. In the front we had a can with petrol in for brewing up and cooking, because there wasn't a particularly safer place anywhere else… So that went off, and there was flame both sides. So I said, 'Bail Out!', and the crew bailed out, and I bailed out – and I was still wondering a bit what had happened. Tried looking round. The tank behind me was the adjutant's tank … and he looked at me and waved, and he was bleeding from his head. Machine gun in one of the houses on the far side of the road [had] fired: missed his head and just hit the top of the turret – splinters cut his eyes and things … he went on to try and shoot up the Tiger … but he got shot up.

A while later the rampaging Tiger was itself damaged by a close range strike from a 6-pdr anti-tank gun. Wittmann was forced to make his escape on foot, but the debut of the Tiger tank in Normandy had been a terrible shock. More than a dozen British tanks had been knocked out in about 20 minutes, and most of the advance party at Point 213 were later captured by other enemy units. Though the Tiger had been met in other theatres the psychological impact of the sudden appearance of a vehicle that was all but invulnerable to ordinary Allied tank armament was considerable. As Canadian Malcolm Andrade put it, 'A Sherman tank shell bounces off like peanuts. That's the armour. The only way to get at them in a Sherman tank was to attack from the rear where it's weaker'. The one thing that really seemed able to hit back was the Firefly, a modified Sherman tank mounted with a 17-pdr main gun, which at that stage was issued to one per troop in squadrons equipped with Shermans or Cromwells.

Meanwhile the battle for Villers Bocage continued, and, with the resolve of the British steadied, more German armour pushing into town was ambushed at close-range with PIATs, tanks, anti-tank guns and grenades. Harold Currie was a tank commander in the midst of the action: 'Tanks normally fight each other from a distance but in Villers Bocage we found ourselves engaging with German tanks firing through buildings... Explosions were taking place all over town. Pretty horrifying, because you could see tanks being blown up, and then you think it could be me next time. But then you have to dismiss that from your mind – because that's the way life goes.' Another of the defenders was Sergeant Robert Bramwell in a Sherman Firefly:

> Soon afterwards three German tanks came down the high street, I am sure the one in the lead was a Mark IV – I fired at it and missed. Fortunately a 6-pdr of the Queen's was brought up and they knocked it out. The next along was a Tiger. I had reversed back a bit and I could see it through the windows of a house on the corner, so we traversed our gun and began to engage through the windows, first with high explosive – which made a terrible mess of the house – and then with armour piercing. I don't know how many shots we fired but we knocked it out.

This attack having failed more German infantry was committed, and house-to-house fighting continued against men of the Queen's Royal Regiment. Both sides bombarded various parts of the town with artillery. Losses mounted to defenders and attackers alike, until, under cover of darkness, the British withdrew. Cloudsley-Thompson and his crew had

OVERLEAF
A soldier's grave, booby-trapped. Graves were frequently marked with a rifle and were often booby-trapped by retreating German soldiers using anti-personnel mines and trip wires. During the making of the documentary a trap was recreated using explosive to recreate the devastation. The wire is clearly visible in this image for the benefit of the viewer. (Jeremy Llewellyn-Jones)

A German *StuG III* and its four man crew. The various types of *Sturmgeschütz* – literally 'assault gun' – all mounted a powerful weapon in a turretless armoured vehicle with the primary purpose of supporting infantry and tank attacks. The limited traverse of the *StuG III* 75mm main armament was something of a drawback, but the weapon was compact and had good frontal armour. This vehicle was also cost effective in that it made use of many of the components of the old Panzer III. Production of the *StuG III* eventually exceeded 10,000 units, or approximately 20 percent of all German tracked armoured fighting vehicles manufactured during the war. (Author's Collection)

taken cover, first in a trench, then in a cellar, 'where there was nothing to drink but calvados', but were alarmed to discover an enemy tank parked outside the house. Only later when a Typhoon strafe hit nearby, and 25-pdrs started shelling, did he decide it was too dangerous to remain. Following a personal reconnaissance his crew made their escape, through hedges and across fields, avoiding enemy vehicles. By the narrowest of margins, and on one occasion even feigning death, he made it back to British lines.

Here damaged armour was being collected, and where possible repaired. Cloudsley-Thompson watched horrified as some unfortunate crewmen, burned and broken beyond recognition, were quite literally 'washed' out of crew compartments: 'For the first time in my life I was really frightened … after that every time I saw an 88mm, or heard one, I was thinking, "Shall I have to be washed out of the tank?" And it was a horrible thought, to be washed out of a tank.' As it happened he was not the only one to have such thoughts: accordingly the recovery and maintenance teams were ordered not only to clean out a damaged tank but re-coat the interiors with a thick white paint that disguised both scars and odour. Usually exterior numbers were also painted over and unit designations altered. As one officer working with the Maintenance Battalion of the 3rd Armoured Division put it, 'the new crew never knew its history – and we never told them'.

Over the next few days the alarm generated by the battle at Villers Bocage led to both heavy bombers of the RAF and concentrations of American artillery being called down on the town. However, the ruins would remain in German hands for some weeks to come. As Harold Currie put it, 'we came in the morning – beautiful town, no sign of any damage whatever. And when we left it there were tanks all over town, buildings destroyed … bodies lined up in the square. Young men who had been alive that morning.' Brigadier Hinde's post-battle analysis stressed two tactical errors: the lack of really close infantry and tank co-operation, and the sin of inadequate dispersal allowing the enemy to trap the British vehicles. Rightly or wrongly Wittmann's action became a thing of legend, and much propaganda was made of this highly decorated tank ace. Nevertheless the fight at Villers Bocage was symbolic of the moment at which it was realized that taking Caen would be measured and costly. As Montgomery later admitted, with some understatement, 'our operations had slowed'.

Fighting in the bocage

Yet what made the weeks after D-Day uniquely frustrating for all Allied forces was the terrain – the ancient enclosures of the bocage country. As GI Nelson Horan observed, field boundaries were built up, on walls or banks with trees and bushes:

> … some of them were up 4, 5, 6 feet high, and each field was completely surrounded. So, in effect, what you had to do, you had to fight your way from one hedgerow to the next, the Germans … fought for every, every field. And the roads on the side – you couldn't use the roads because they had 88s there… And the tanks, we couldn't use the tanks because the tanks would go up over the top of them and it would … expose the soft spot underneath the tank.

While the troops had trained for many things, the bocage was not one of them. As Cecil Newton of the 4th/7th Dragoon Guards put it, 'No one knew about it beforehand. No one knew about the deep lanes, the high hedges, hadn't got a clue… It came as a great shock.' For Ronald Titterton, 2nd Derbyshire Yeomanry, 'It was the worst country in the world to fight in, and to us it was even worse because we were used to open warfare in the desert. And to leave the desert to come to fight in country like the bocage … to us it was suicidal.'

Rommel's preferred strategy would have been to move as many infantry divisions as possible to contain the invasion perimeter along natural lines of defence, then crush it from the flanks with all the armour that could be mustered. In this ambition he was overruled. Yet the country offered considerable advantages, even against an attacker strong in armour. As a post-battle study explained, the bocage:

> proved the most dangerous terrain of the whole campaign for tanks in the attack. The bocage was first rate country for the employment of infantry anti-tank weapons and the light machine gun (Bren or Spandau). Here determined infantry, armed with rocket tubes or bazookas can remain hidden until a tank is within fifty yards and can destroy all but a very heavy tank with one shot. By defending Normandy rather than establishing the main line of defence along the Seine, the Germans pinned the invaders down to the shortest possible front and protected the whole of France.

Lieutenant Stuart Hills of the Sherwood Rangers Yeomanry took a professional view of the terrain from his turret:

> The Allied tanks would have preferred to stick to the high ground and better roads, but the Germans held most of the high ground and had their 88mm guns placed to cover the roads with devastating fire. So tanks, in their key role of supporting the infantry, had to go with them into the narrow lanes. They were handicapped by a variety of factors: their vision was limited, as were their own weapons fields of fire, and it was difficult to traverse the turret in such a confined space. If they did venture through gaps into the fields, mortar fire would be brought down, while any hedge could have a German soldier behind it waiting with a Panzerfaust… This was no rigid defence either, as the German's system of slit trenches and gun positions was infinitely flexible, and even when they vacated a position, they could immediately call down a hail of mortar and other artillery fire on the attackers as they moved back to take up another defensive position. Aircraft could do little to help unless enemy tanks and formations were caught in the open.[3]

Peter Davies, a gunner in a British Sherman, gave a typical account of the disorientating experience of a tanker fighting in the bocage:

We knew there was a road on our map … [the driver] went through one of the big high hedges, and the next minute we were airborne – but it couldn't have been [more than] a split second – and we crashed down 8ft into a sunken road, which caused everything on the tank to rattle and move. The two sets went off because the valves had broken. I'd got a spare box at my side. I picked that up, and it sounded like peas in a tin can, and I knew all the spare valves had broken. So we had no wireless communication … the four tanks had a horrendous day. We lost contact with the other three, [they] went into the village, we skirted the village and went round into open country to see what was on the other side. And they got into trouble – met heavy German tanks – George managed to knock out a couple of them… One [Sherman] tank was knocked out and the five men killed, another tank was hit and two men killed. We had gone round the side, and were suddenly being fired upon – heavy shells – coming in close to us, and we knew by the spurts of dust that it wasn't explosive shells. It was armour piercing, so it must have been another tank. We didn't see them, but we were knocked out. We were hit twice … one hit the bogey and spun us out. The second one hit us straight up the backside – in at the engine – smashed the engine. It was running, and [something] landed on my leg; it was still white hot. Ben said 'bail out!'. As we bailed out another shell came whistling over, ran a groove across the top of the tank, and we all got out and ran for cover… We hadn't even seen who was firing on us, but we were knocked out in a matter of about ten minutes before we had got into any battle.

An American soldier examines an enemy field position concealed within a hedgerow. Bocage country offered excellent cover, and the Germans made maximum use of hedges, walls and ditches, improving them or burrowing through them to create machine-gun posts and snipers' lairs. (Author's Collection)

Things were little better for the infantry as Bill Doyle, 175th US Infantry, found out during an advance:

> On each side of this field was a hedgerow, and an opening in each side of it. And the Germans were firing diagonally across that field and there was no way that we could get into that field or do anything there because of those tracer bullets making one green, big green 'X' across the field. So there was nothing else to do but just go back and start all over again. And we went into another field that the Germans had been dropping mortar shells in … that's when I saw my colonel, Colonel Terry, coming up to us from another field. He's coming in our direction and when he got near where I was some of the officers said, 'Get down colonel, get down!' and he didn't pay any attention to them, he just kept on walking and all, then he was hit by a sniper and he hit the ground, his helmet flew off and he was dead. About 20, minutes later – half an hour I guess, I was hit by a piece of shrapnel from a mortar shell and I was on my way back to England.

Ken Duffield was also wounded during the initial battles, as he recalls:

> we were marching … and they were dropping mortars or artillery or shells, I don't know just which, but one landed right beside me. It blew a hole I would say maybe at least eight feet across and three feet deep. When that exploded it knocked you right down… It's a funny feeling. You have to go through it to know. I didn't even realize I was wounded. I guess from the explosion right beside you you're kind of dazed and when I did come to and realize that something had happened, I had lost all my equipment. It just tore it off. It was all I had.

As well as the wounded, the battlefield was littered with dead. As John Cloudsley-Thompson recalled, 'the whole time you were in Normandy you smelt dead things… Animals in the fields around … everywhere people lying about … very unpleasant.' Decay was unavoidable: because it was summer, because there were so many bodies, and sometimes because reaching the dead was simply too dangerous. According to Canadian Bill Stanfield, 'It was terrible seeing all the dead in the wheat fields … When they die they just shove the rifle where he is and leave it there. And then they're left there sometimes a day, two days, and then they had burial parties come along and bury them.' Patrick Delaforce got

OPPOSITE
Troops being prepared for burial in Normandy. Such sights prompted Arnold Whittaker to think, 'A wooden cross with a dog tag nailed to it… Is this my destiny?' No less than eight American cemeteries were established in Normandy by 10 June 1944, but since then quite a few of the dead have been repatriated to the United States and the sites consolidated. The main Normandy burial ground today is the American Cemetery at St. Laurent, containing the remains of 9,386 service personnel of whom about 300 are unidentified. (Author's Collection)

to know one of the padres who looked after a tank regiment, and, 'one of his awful jobs was to go to every burned out tank, immediately. Not just to rescue, because everybody there was dead. [But] piece them together, and give them a Christian burial. Awful, day after day: dreadful job. And he gave them a blessing and often the bits – you couldn't tell who was whom.' Being a tanker himself Cecil Newton took close interest in the technicalities when three crew were practically 'burnt to ash' on 14 June. It appeared that if the main armament was traversed to the wrong position it blocked one of the hull hatches meaning that a fire in the turret made getting out of the top practically impossible. As a result his comrades had attempted to use an escape hatch, but were found, one inside, one underneath the tank, and one draped 'halfway across the engine casing'. This last unfortunate, aged just 20, was identified only by his teeth.

The reek of the battlefield was rarely an occasion for mirth: but for one American soldier there was a moment of black humour. About two or three days after landing in Normandy John McGuire heard a shout in the night, a yell –

The 88mm Gun

The '88' was undoubtedly one of the most successful guns of the war – and according to a survey of American troops it was the most feared enemy weapon. Power, versatility and speed of loading were key features. With an anti-tank hollow charge round it could penetrate up to 165mm of armour at 1,000m. Allied experiments determined that the alternative high explosive round weighing just over 21lbs burst into about 1,250 fast moving fragments varying from a fraction of an ounce to about five ounces. A few pieces would fly as far as 300 yards from point of impact.

ABOVE A sequence recreating the devastating effect of a direct hit on a small assault landing craft. Much of the bow end is blown away, with debris and smaller pieces of equipment raining down in later frames. (Jeremy Llewellyn-Jones)

RIGHT Diagrammatic view of the 8.8cm Flak 18 on its cruciform mounting, from the manual *Handbuch für den Flakartilleristen* of 1936. The first 88s were designed as early as 1916. Interestingly, as the German Army was not allowed to retain anti-aircraft guns under the limitations of the Treaty of Versailles, some were converted to ground-firing roles and retained for motorized artillery batteries. The new Flak 18 L/56 was designed in 1931 with a

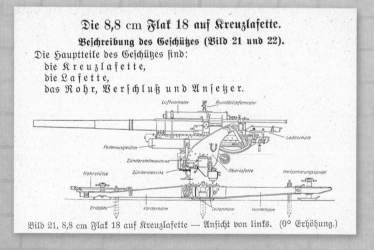

prototype the following year and production starting in 1933. Improvements to the barrel and mounting created the Flak 36 a few years later, and in the Flak 37 the fire control transmission system was updated. Essentially the Flak 18, Flak 36 and Flak 37 had similar ballistic performance being effective against air targets up to 10,000m and all were commonly referred to simply as the '88' by Allied troops. (Author's Collection)

A Flak 37 in the Deutsches Historisches Museum, Berlin. The 88 was deployed in many different ways: with the Luftwaffe in six-gun home defence batteries, or as four 88s protected by two 20mm in field divisions; or with the army as four-gun Flak batteries – or in varying organizations in fixed permanent or temporary defences. (Author's Collection)

The 88 firing at night. In the dark with slow shutter speed the camera catches both the impressive flash and muzzle blast, as well as recoil of the breech. A textbook crew was two gun layers, one each for elevation and traverse; a loader; four ammunition supply numbers; a fuse setter operator; and the fuse setter. The detachment also included a commander and a driver for the gun tractor making a total of 11 personnel. By 1945 many of the gun teams were brought up to strength with teenage auxiliaries. (Author's Collection)

Sitting at a drunken angle on its damaged travelling carriage this image shows an 88 captured on a village street. This example is fitted with the distinctive crew shield. Armour piercing projectiles and the gun shield were developed in 1938 following experience of direct ground fire during the Spanish Civil War. (Author's Collection)

The distinctive British Bofors gun, seen here in action in Italy, left a mark on many of the veterans of the North-West European campaign. (Ullstein Bild/Topfoto)

Or something way off in the distance. I didn't understand what the word was. Then he, or somebody else, repeated the word and it was 'GAS!'. So that put some fear in me because we had seen pictures in our training [of how] the Germans had used gas in World War I and we saw the effects of gas on people. And so we all scrambled around looking for our gas masks, and fortunately I had saved mine; but a lot of guys had thrown them away, because they said they were just excess baggage. But I had got mine and I got it on and we gathered in a group and waited for a while. Then about 45 minutes later a jeep comes through and a guy speaking over a loudspeaker says, 'There is no gas'... What had triggered the false gas alarm was that a lot of dead German soldiers had been collected and placed together in a field, so they could be picked up and buried. I don't know why but the odour of a human being is much worse than that of other animals like horses or cows ... they both smell bad after they'd been killed, but a human being, for whatever reason has just a terrible odour.

Unfamiliar as the bocage might be the men who fought there were soon learning ways to stay alive longer. Looking like an officer was a mistake that had to be avoided if you did not wish to be the recipient of the first sniper's bullet. Lieutenant Scott-Brown made sure that he carried a rifle, just like the men, and that his camouflage smock, worn over the battledress or shirt, carried no 'pips' of rank upon its shoulder straps. New tactics were also evolving – as for example the British 'sniper clearing party' led by an NCO with a Sten gun, who would lead a small group around the flank of a sniper's position while he was engaged frontally. Despite the constricted terrain many, like American Frank

Gregg, were convinced that tanks were vital simply because they had the ability to drive up close to a hedgerow and fire over it. In time tactics were also developed so that a single tank and infantry team co-operated to clear one field at a time. The infantry could creep close, covered by the tank, and then having either ascertained there were no anti-tank weapons, or cleared them, the tank could drive into the field and hose down the hedges. The infantry then advanced along the boundaries and hedges under the watchful muzzle of the tank main armament to root out any remaining snipers.

As always it was artillery and mortars that did the most damage, and of all the guns, as a United States Army survey later confirmed, it was the '88' that was most feared – by both the infantry and tank crews. Bill Evans made its acquaintance just a few days after the landings:

> We were going up a road and there was an 88mm firing and it was coming into the trees, and branches came down … and then '36' Jones was … screaming his head off … shrapnel [in the] cheek bone … blood pumping out. And I couldn't think. Oh good God! [I took a] field dressing and I wound it round his face about three times when this officer yelled out, 'Evans! Leave him for the stretcher bearers, come on, come on'. It was get forward, never mind about this … and I left him there… [Later] I found out that '36' Jones died – bled to death. I wish I could have done more for him.

Troops fighting in the bocage were hemmed in on all sides by thick hedges and high banks. The Bazooka anti-tank weapon was often fired from the shoulder by American infantry directly at hidden German targets just a field away, in what was effectively a direct fire support role. (NARA)

Private Frederick James Jones of the 2nd Battalion, South Wales Borderers, was killed on 9 June. He was later buried in the Ryes war cemetery Bazenville, alongside 987 others – about a third of them Germans. He was aged just 19. The effect of all shells was magnified by noise and numbers, as Frank Rosier of the Glosters put it, 'You could hear them going over the top of you like an express train … and they didn't come in ones they come in dozens … when you heard the shells coming you laid on the ground and hoped to God one did not hit you'.

Interestingly the Germans were not the only ones to turn anti-aircraft weapons onto ground targets. The Americans did this with their .50in Browning quad-mounted 'meat chopper' heavy machine guns while the British and Canadians used the 40mm Bofors. The latter was not powerful enough to damage heavy armour, but it would go through most things. To this day Canadian Bombardier Bruce Melanson still taps his foot to the distinctive 'one; two; three; four' rhythm of the Bofors firing as he relates his story of operating the piece in Normandy:

There were nine people in the truck… The gun employs six people, two sitting down elevating [and traversing], the others firing, passing ammunition, and the sergeant… I did a little bit of everything: I acted as sergeant, sometimes passing the ammunition, sometimes I would be on the firing. There's four shells in a bracket and when they pass that up you've got to put it in and keep firing. You continue to do that as long as they pass the ammunition – one, two, three, four. Empty shells came out at the back – you'd better not be in front of it, which I was one time. One got me right in the mouth, cut my teeth all to pieces. Wasn't funny… The Germans had a good way of trying to hide their troops. Camouflaging with haystacks the houses behind. The Bofors then came in mighty handy because we would fire at those haystacks – right through the haystack into the house. Just 'bang, bang, bang', 40mm shells. Very powerful – soon as it hit there'd be an explosion. After a couple of those were fired, let me tell you a few hands would come up, quite a few. And we would use it for houses, apartments, churches – wherever we thought the Germans were.

Progress to the west

If the Caen sector became a grinding match there was a plus side. For the battle on the eastern part of the Normandy front had drawn in the

OPPOSITE

The *Nebelwerfer* 15cm rocket projector seen here in a camouflaged position. It was capable of creating a brief but intensive barrage of high explosive or smoke rockets out to over 7,000 yards. The *Nebelwerfer* had a distinctive sound causing some American troops to dub it the 'Screaming Meemie', while in Poland it was nicknamed the 'Bellowing Cow'. In Normandy, American infantryman Nelson Horan was convinced that the 'very eerie noise' was deliberately designed to disconcert. The full salvo lasted about ten seconds, reloading requiring about a minute and a half. (Author's Collection) bulk of the German armour, leaving the Americans better opportunity to make progress to the west. Very probably this was happenstance rather than deliberate planning, but now this would be exploited, and ultimately unhinge the defence. By 20 June, the US 4th, 9th, 79th and 90th Infantry Divisions had taken in most of the Cotentin Peninsula: within another week, following intense street fighting, Cherbourg itself was seized. The enemy had carried out a 'scorched earth' policy of demolitions and mining, but divers and crews were immediately set to work to make facilities usable. This would give the invasion a significant port through which ever-more men and supplies could be channelled. It was especially timely given the great storm of 19 June that inflicted serious damage on the American Mulberry harbour, and left much of the US 83rd Infantry Division bobbing about in their transports offshore.

Meanwhile both sides were gathering fresh forces for action around Caen. Montgomery planned to mount a major offensive across the Odon river, seize the high ground including Hill 112, and dominate the west bank of the Orne. By these means Caen might be made untenable. Following delays, and rain that made for boggy ground, Operation

Epsom was finally launched on 26 June. Hard on the heels of a rolling barrage fired by 350 guns, the 15th (Scottish) Division advanced, negotiating the minefields and supported by tanks. The enemy were worried enough, first to call off their own offensive, and secondly, to commit quantities of armour to stem the attack. Heavy fighting continued the following day when the 1st SS Panzer Corps counter-attacked on the right of the advance, only to be halted in its turn on the anti-tank guns of the British 49th Division. The British 11th Armoured Division now pressed forward, but less impetuously given intelligence received through 'Ultra' that two more Panzer Divisions, the 9th and 10th SS, were now in the Odon valley area.[4] On 29 June the British tanks secured Hill 112, but withdrew again in the face of enemy strength. *Epsom* was ultimately terminated in the face of heavy losses – on both sides. The plan had failed in its main objective, but had significant repercussions for the enemy in that reports from frontline generals convinced both Rommel and von Rundstedt that the only sensible course of action was to abandon what was fast becoming the charnel house of Caen. Unwilling to accept such pessimistic decisions from his high-ranking commanders, Hitler dismissed von Rundstedt on 2 July.

As Bombardier Frank Quelch of the Royal Artillery recalled it was said that, 'he who holds 112 holds the battlefield' – and certainly both sides behaved as though this was true. His first notion of what this 'nice countryside' might hold came at Cheux:

We hadn't gone into action yet we were just waiting to go in. And I'm up on the hill, and with binoculars I'm watching a battle that's taken place, you know, a mile or two away, with the old binoculars, and see these little soldiers running through the cornfield and there's tanks burning and suddenly an airplane appeared across the front of me … it was a spotter plane … and he was flying downwards, he was flying along the road. I followed him, you know, I was like, 'What's the matter with him?'… And almost immediately Focke Wulf 190s came across the front and it was as close as you are in my binoculars – I could see his face he had a big moustache, he was enjoying himself shooting down this plane. And then of course they were all gone and I looked at this plane that was shot down, and there was just the burnt remains on the ground … just a patch of black, no sign of the pilot – he was cremated obviously.

Quelch's own moment of truth was not long in coming, and serving with an anti-tank battery his role, and that of men like him, would be crucial in the duels with German tanks throughout the desperate battle for Normandy. Perhaps surprisingly, many encounters with enemy armour were short-range affairs as one tank crew came upon another waiting in ambush, or stumbled into anti-tank guns already in position. The best of the British anti-tank pieces was undoubtedly the 17-pdr, a hefty beast of over 1,800lb but capable of firing a range of rounds including 'APC' – 'Armour Piercing Capped' – and from August 1944, 'APDS' – 'Armour Piercing Discarding Sabot'. The secret of the 'APDS' round was that it contained a tungsten carbide core inside a light steel sheath. The whole was contained within an alloy 'sabot', or outer casing, that split into four parts and dropped away or 'discarded' as it left the gun. The force of the discharge then propelled the smaller toughened shot at far greater velocity. The 'APDS' upped the armour penetration of the 17-pdr from an already very healthy 118mm, to an amazing 231mm at 1,000 yards, a performance calculated to slice through even the frontal armour of the Tiger with plenty of momentum to spare.

British troops of the 3rd Infantry Division engaged in street fighting at Caen. An observer peeps briefly around a corner close to ground level in textbook fashion. The machine gun is not British issue but an obsolete French 8mm Hotchkiss type, fed from metallic strips being served up by the loader. (Author's Collection)

OPPOSITE
The battle for Caen was particularly bloody as the German forces stubbornly resisted repeated Allied assaults. During Operation *Charnwood* a series of bombing raids reduced the city to burning rubble on 8/9 July but even then part of the city remained in enemy hands. Hill 112, to the south-west of Caen, was seized on 10 July but had to be relinquished in the face of heavy losses. Operation *Goodwood* was eventually launched in mid July with the intention of pushing out from Caen towards the Caen–Falaise road. This map shows the position Allied forces had reached by 29 July with Falaise still some distance away. (© Osprey Publishing Ltd.)

Frank Quelch had a less than happy experience of the old 2- and 6-pdr guns, but was more than satisfied with the 17-pdr: 'We moved onto 17-pdrs in 1944: now there was a gun that was almost the equal of the German "88". Everybody was on about the "88", a dreadful thing, because they were anti-aircraft guns and they were very high velocity you see. But [our 17-pdr] could knock out a Tiger tank easy. It was a very accurate gun.' In Quelch's team the gun commander was a sergeant, who stood off from the team to relay his orders by microphone to the gun numbers. By distancing himself slightly from the flash and shattering report he was able to keep a clear eye on the target and observe 'fall of shot'. As 'No. 1' Quelch laid the piece on target, and 'No. 2' slammed the heavy shell into the breech. The 'No. 2' had to be particularly strong and nimble about his work, timing movements to reload swiftly, yet avoid the recoil of the heavy breech as it flew backward on discharge. The 'No. 3' fired on command, and the remainder of the crew hauled shells into the position as 'ammunition numbers', guarded the truck and also provided spares in case of exhaustion or casualties. For just such eventualities the best teams were thoroughly trained to do several different tasks around the gun.

In Frank's recollection the whole thing sometimes took on an air of unreality, as continuous action led first to performing gun drills to the mechanical dictates of training, and eventually exhaustion:

It's funny I never felt scared, and we did take on a tank on Hill 112 in Normandy. I'm afraid we were all asleep early in the morning dawn. Heard all this banging and firing going on and there was one of our tanks, right close, shouting at me because I disappeared down the hole! He says there's a Jerry up the top – and he was ... it was a Panther tank and it was the other side of the hill, in what they call 'hull down' [position]. We came [out of our dugout and] its gun was facing the other way, so while he was busy twirling his gun round our gun was on to him and we got him. It caught fire.

For Bill Edwardes 'Hill' 112 was really a misnomer for some 'rolling' land that was 'just a grid reference'. British VIII Corps had over 4,000 casualties, and dealing with the immediate human cost of attrition were the medics. Edwardes, of the 1st Battalion, the Worcesters, was still not 18 in the summer of 1944, having lied about his age to join up; but was now carrying the bag with a prominent red cross containing

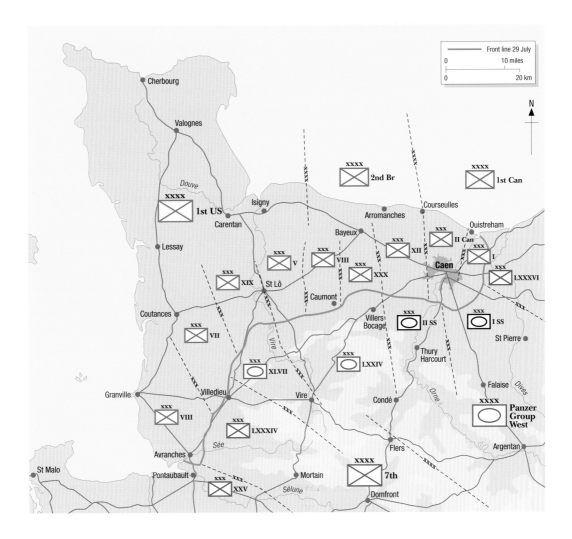

pre-wrapped shell dressings, tourniquet, various waddings, slings, simple instruments and powders that was the mark of his trade. Probably most important, however, was the morphine with which came a 'little indelible pencil' that could never be found because it worked its way to the bottom of the bag. This was 'to mark the forehead, if you gave morphine … if they were pleading for more you'd give them a couple. And then if you did that you had to put "M" with a "2" at the side – we were allowed discretion on that.' He carried no weapon, considering this an advantage since it would have 'got in the way', and provided the enemy with a ready-made excuse to shoot him. It also meant that when a wounded comrade begged to be 'finished off' he could have no truck with the suggestion.

During stretcher bearer training his unit had issued armbands marked 'SB'. Edwardes was glad when these were dropped and replaced with the red cross, as the rest of the troops had taken to calling them the 'Silly Buggers'. Soon they would be addressing them in more respectful terms. The battlefield triage he remembered being taught was the simple mantra 'BBB' – breathing, bleeding, bones. If the man was 'not breathing move on'. If he was, you looked to his bleeding. Neither medics nor stretcher bearers messed about with dog tags, but left the 'not breathing' to those members of the Pioneer Corps who were responsible for collecting the dead. The really demanding and creative parts were getting to the casualty, and what you said to him if he was conscious, 'You have to respond, that's what you're there for, that's what you're trained for, and that's what your mates are relying on. So you get out of your trench and go and find where the call is coming from.' For the badly wounded you 'lied through your teeth', telling them in virtually all instances that their broken bodies were mendable.

In Edwardes' experience the stretcher bearers of the medical platoons attached to the infantry battalions under the Royal Army Medical Corps rarely carried casualties very far. They had to keep up with their unit and so a casualty was tended to as quickly as possible, and the walking wounded set off under their own steam. More serious cases might need to be dragged or carried into cover, but again could usually be left at a collecting point, or aid post, for the ambulance units or pioneers. Rarely then did Edwardes have to carry a stretcher more than five or six hundred yards, something for which he was heartily grateful as he was a flyweight teenager and some of his charges were well built and pushing middle age. One thing that took him a while to understand was that a couple of stretcher bearers were allotted to a company only for short periods, then rotated on to another or the aid post. Edwardes slowly came to realize that the purpose of this was so that they had no chance to become really good friends with those who might soon become their patients: a distraught medic was no good to his comrades, whereas one who was something of a loner was more likely to act with professionalism and detachment. To an extent the system and training worked, indeed, the first time Edwardes saw a man with the top of his head missing his first thought was merely 'not breathing'. Only later, 'when you got back to your own slit trench – that's when the shakes start', did he subsequently recall.

The air campaign over Normandy

Undoubtedly the Normandy land campaign could have been worse, were it not for Allied air superiority and the work of ground-attack aircraft. Of these a crucial type were the British Typhoons flying with the 2nd Tactical Air Force. The Typhoon had first been intended as a Hurricane fighter replacement, and indeed bore a superficial resemblance to its Hawker stable mate. Typhoons were delivered to No. 56 Squadron of the RAF as early as the autumn of 1941, with operational use commencing the next year. However early indicators were unpropitious, for while the new machine was capable of a very healthy 400mph it was not particularly manoeuvrable, with performance dropping off at higher altitudes, and at first it was catastrophically unreliable. Only after more work on the airframe and engine, in addition to experiments to find the most suitable tactical niche, was the Typhoon slotted into a 'fighter bomber' role. Before *Overlord* almost 800lb of additional armour was added to protect the radiator of the plane, and rockets were added to the inventory of possible armaments. Long-range 'sweeps', 'Rhubarb' attacks on enemy airfields, and 'Ramrod' operations in concert with bombers were all mounted well before D-Day. As of 5 June 1944 the Typhoons were deployed in two

Early June 1944 and the rocket-armed Typhoon of Wing Commander Charles Green, 121 Wing, is ready for take off at Holmsley South. Not long afterwards Typhoon ground-attack aircraft would be based on the other side of the Channel. (Courtesy of N. Wilson)

'Groups' (Nos 83 and 84) with a total of seven 'Wings' totalling 18 squadrons in all, to fight over France.

From May of that year Canadian Typhoon pilot John Thompson was attached to No. 121 Wing at Holmsley South:

> I didn't want to fly Typhoons … anyway in those days you did what the hell you were told. The English aircraft were particularly noted for their small cockpits. Yankees had lots of room in their cockpits, but we were in there fairly tightly… But the new aircraft you either loved it, or you hated it. I was quite confident in flying the Hurricane – I could do anything with it… I might have got that way with the Typhoon, but initially I did not get enough hours. I mean five or six hours – I was hardly able to get the thing off the ground and get it back again without crashing. The Wing Commander interviewed me and asked my preference, which would be Spitfires, and second preference for Mustangs. He's looking through my logbook at this time and stops at this one section. I thought 'Oh Jesus!', he's at the page where I had my Typhoon time listed. And he said, 'Well I'm sorry, but I have a request here for an experienced Typhoon pilot for an RAF squadron in the south of England.' I thought I would never see Woodbridge or my mother again…
>
> [My] first combat run was against some big guns dug in on the Cherbourg Peninsula, down below the radar. And then when we got within sight of land the Commanding Officer would call 'Climb!' and we'd put on 'full bore' and we'd climb to about 8,000ft – almost vertical, as fast as we could get up there. And by that time we would be over land … the CO picked out the target, and he'd starboard echelon right. 'Form up', he'd say, 'going down in ten seconds'. Eight [of us] in that particular squadron on that trip, two groups of four, and we'd dive in at 50 or 60 degrees, and get down to 2 or 3,000ft. Then [begin] firing rockets and cannon, and get close to the ground, before pulling out… There's really not much 'G' forces until you get to the bottom… You know it's hard to describe because everything is happening so quickly and you're brand new at the job and you're busy not wanting to make a mistake like run into your number two, or lose the squadron, or do something wrong. But unless you are leading the whole pack its a damn difficult place to be… You're just mainly interested in flying, and shooting your cannon and rockets is incidental. When they are flying in formation we'd be maybe 50 to 100ft apart… I don't care what they say, if you're on ops and you're in a combat zone, the first op is pretty traumatic… Heart's pounding? Everything's pounding!

The British Lancaster bomber took part in the 'softening up' of the German coast prior to the D-Day landings. The bomber is here pictured during Operation *Charnwood* in early July. (Topfoto)

Approximately 400 sorties were flown by Typhoons on D-Day and just seven days after the invasion, three of the Typhoon wings began using airstrips in Normandy itself. More would soon follow. Some missions were chosen deliberately, others were operated on a 'cab rank' system with squadrons launched, and directed to targets of opportunity as they arose. A fresh squadron then took its place on the 'cab rank' ready to be called. Thompson was assigned to targeting tanks, lightly skinned armoured vehicles, flak batteries or even troop concentrations:

> … Anything that was holding up the movement of the Canadian Army boys. We were in radio contact with the advanced units, and they'd say 'we got a target for you', and would put up red mortar smoke on top of it. They'd give us a grid position and we'd hustle to that position on the map and pinpoint the red mortar smoke when it came up. And as soon as it did we'd dive on it… The op trip was only 45 minutes [to an hour and a half] long. That was from the time I went to take off, circle, got the squadron formed up and we were only eight miles away from the German lines, and then we'd fly there and we

had a target immediately... German prisoners would say the noise of those rockets is pretty terrifying ... they say it sounded like an express train coming.

There were various types of rocket, including an armour piercing type with a 25lb head, but in the summer and autumn of 1944 the 2nd Tactical Air Force used mainly the 60lb SAP/ HE round (Semi Armour Piercing/ High Explosive). This was genuinely multi-purpose in that it penetrated, but also caused an explosion capable of destroying a variety of different targets. Against tanks a direct hit, rare as it might be, was utterly devastating. As Thompson observed, it would, 'go right through, then inside the tank, and then explode. And of course it would crucify the crew in there.' Oftentimes multiple strikes from groups of Typhoons, even with only near misses, were good enough to destroy soft skinned vehicles, crater route ways and railroads, and possibly even damage tank tracks.

One of the biggest fears was that the frontline shifted before pilots could be informed, as munitions might fall harmlessly into vacated countryside – or worse onto one's advancing comrades. Moreover aiming rockets was no easy job as it entailed aiming with the whole aircraft – and firing at precisely the right moment. Pilots could see rocket trails, but as Thompson observed, 'very seldom did you see them hit the target because by that time you might have been a little too low. Once you'd fired the idea was to get out of that piece of sky as quick as you could... Get out, get away... Yes I could call it fun. But it wasn't hilarious.' Equal in apprehension was flak, as in contour-hugging attacks even machine guns and small arms were a menace. Thompson was lucky, only ever returning to base with machine gun holes, although this was an all too frequent occurrence.

Operation *Charnwood*

Following a number of more limited actions a new phase of operations began on 8 July with Operation *Charnwood*, a major Anglo-Canadian concentric assault from the north and west towards Caen. Having failed to take the city by encirclement the plan was now to launch an attack on a broad front behind heavy bombing raids, with the intention of both wearing down the enemy and forcing him to disperse his resources. Heavy air raids softened up the enemy during the night, with Bomber Command's heavy bombers dropping more than 2,000 tons of bombs, including many with delayed action fuses, and Mosquitos attacking point targets. Next came the artillery barrage of more than 600 guns, backed by shells from the major ships of the navy fired from off shore. Canadian Alex Adair got a clear view of Caen, with approximately 80 percent of the city destroyed: 'they blew the place to rat shit – pardon the expression. We had a front row seat to watch the city blown to hell, and then they couldn't get their armour through the streets.' Although the bombers aimed well behind the German frontline some ordnance still came down too close for comfort as was recorded by Canadian stretcher bearer Arthur Haley, 'I heard this sound and looked up – and here comes our bombers. I thought "Oh boy! Give it to them". So I just took off my helmet and waved and yelled … next thing I knew, bomb doors open, these things are shrieking down. I headed for a little hole in the ground and dove in there fast.'

Opinion varies as to how effective the pummelling actually was. Some Germans undoubtedly died, and many more were shocked or cut off from support although the bulk of the bombs were aimed beyond their frontlines. On the other hand, as Patrick Delaforce observes, 'We weren't sophisticated enough to know that the bombing actually suited the Germans. It's easier to defend a ruined town than a normal town as the debris gives you marvellous cover.' Before 5.00am the ground attack was underway with infantry and tanks advancing behind the barrage. The Canadians wrested Buron, a small town on the outskirts of Caen, from the enemy, combating the armour of the 12th SS Panzer with Achilles self-propelled guns and 17-pdr anti-tank guns. The prize of Carpiquet airfield fell the next morning, and British and Canadian units met in the centre of Caen having taken the northern part of the city. Alex Adair was in the Canadian attack at Carpiquet:

[It] was a rather dicey affair. We had to leave a village 1,000 or 1,500 yards from the airport … nobody shooting at us thank God. They always let you [have] lots of room to get well out, and then they started shooting at you when you had no place to go but forward. So we got out and our sergeant said, 'Well I'd rather not postpone this – let's start to run, and make the airport as quick as we can.' So we all thousand-yard dash and away we go. And then they started to shell us – air bursts and all sorts of crap … it's set so that it explodes above your head, and the shrapnel is flying through the air every way. We had some guys hit … we're on the run, so we just left them where they were.

General Sir Bernard Montgomery with his army, corps and divisional commanders in Normandy, including Major General Thomas (43rd Division) and Lieutenant General Dempsey. (IWM B5916)

I don't know whether they were killed or wounded, but we made it. Made it to the edge of the airport and then things quietened down again.

There have been a number of criticisms of the performance of the infantry and its tendency to 'lean on the barrage' to get forward. Yet to have such a valuable asset as strong artillery and not attempt to use it to the full, in concert with other arms, would probably have been more reprehensible. Part of the motivation behind such techniques was to make shells and logistics do some of the job that might otherwise have to be done with blood, as there was a limit to the amount of death that could be sustained without damage to morale, manpower shortages, or a waning of support at home. In mid 1944 such concerns were very real. The Canadians, who had hitherto relied on volunteers, would soon be forced to introduce conscription. The British were already under strength, and in July Montgomery received a visit from General Sir Ronald Adam, the British Army's Adjutant General, to inform him that if infantry casualties continued at the present rate it might be necessary to 'cannibalize' units in order to bring the remainder up to strength.

In truth, advancing on the battlefield was never easy, and indeed it may be argued that this required just as much courage and detachment from the possible consequences in 1944 as it did in 1914, as always it was the infantry who paid the lion's share of the 'butcher's bill'. Yet done well battlefield movement was carefully choreographed, and executed according to well-rehearsed procedures that had been honed and considerably improved since the outbreak of war. These aimed to get the soldier where he was needed swiftly, but without avoidable loss, so seizing objectives and defeating the enemy. At the heart of small unit tactics was 'fire and movement' as outlined in the Americans' new battalion and company *Field Manuals*, and the British *Instructor's Handbook* of 1942 and the latest *Infantry Training* of 1944. There were several versions in which, for example, the basic 12-man American squad might be broken down into three elements, 'Able', 'Baker' and 'Charlie' and one or two would be down and firing, enabling the remainder to manoeuvre under covering fire. British sections likewise could be divided into a 'Bren' team and one, or even two, 'rifle' teams that would keep 'one leg on the ground' as the other rushed forward.

This performance could also be operated on platoon scale, as was explained by Charles Scott-Brown, a Canadian infantry officer then on loan to the Gordon Highlanders, 'You do what we called "leapfrogging" or "pepper potting". That is you work with one section moving and one section as a firepower section, and one section in the rear in case you hit something, and you keep them leapfrogging forward to do it.' Bunching was a cardinal sin, men had to be close enough to support each other, and hear, or see, a signal from their officer or squad leader but no closer. Cover and safety demanded that this be the case. Dispersion was an art to be learned, but not one always easy to picture as Scott-Brown explains:

Infantry soldiers are never closer than five yards, they're invariably five yards apart. They are trained athletes from the word go: so if anything lands there, you may have one killed, you do not have five killed. Unfortunately I've talked about this to media people, as for most people that are trying to do movies or anything like that a battlefield is very difficult for them. The one way they can take pictures where they get the maximum of people and activity is if you do them from a flank, but if you are doing it from the front you only see one or two soldiers because they are yards apart. If they're any closer there's a corporal busting their butts saying 'why don't you hold hands sweetie?', they say all sorts of 'nice' things! Stay apart and stay alive, it's just that simple… You don't hang around.

One of the more unusual devices – a booby trapped wheel barrow. When the barrow is standing upright there is nothing unusual to see, except a very fine wire attached to the axle. However if the barrow is moved the wire is pulled as the wheel turns, setting off a charge concealed underneath. Booby traps were a common feature throughout Normandy as the retreating Germans desperately tried to halt the Allied advance. (Author's Collection)

Scott-Brown should know, having had to learn his craft the hard way, collecting no less than four wounds during his service – though one of these he now dismisses as 'insignificant'. The other three were somewhat more serious. One was a 'chunk of shrapnel' during a canal crossing. On another occasion he unwisely stuck his head up on the arrival of a 'moaning minnie', as German rocket artillery was nicknamed by Allied troops, 'thought I was playing golf I guess', and the third was downright embarrassing – clumsy patrol work by someone to the rear and a 'friendly' round went through his buttocks. All this was taken in remarkably good humour, but to his family it was a nightmare, as military bureaucracy was utterly unable to keep up with the pace of events. They received, in no particular order, a barrage of messages ranging from 'returned to active service', to 'missing' and 'wounded'. He was however sent home in vaguely one piece.

Operation *Goodwood*

Arguably the most famous – and controversial – of Montgomery's offensives in Normandy was *Goodwood*, begun on 18 July. As before the bombers appeared before dawn. This time there were 1,850 of them, both British and American, smashing 11 different target areas east and south-east of Caen, including the villages of Colombelles, Cagny, Troarn and the Bourguébus ridge. What the Allies did not realize was that the day before these massive raids a lone Spitfire had already achieved a very significant result. Patrolling over Sainte-Foy-de-Montgommery the

A training illustration showing an enemy method of booby trapping, with a tyre bursting device attached to an anti-personnel 'S' Mine. The tyreburster, which takes the form of a box with projecting metal spikes, is buried in a track with only the tips of the blades being visible above ground. Wheeled vehicles passing this way will have their tyres punctured, but sooner or later the burster device will be discovered. Any troops who attempt to move the burster will set off the mine. (Author's Collection)

pilot had spotted a staff car, dived and attacked, riddling it with bullets. Field Marshal Rommel was badly wounded and was forced to return to Germany rendering the enemy temporarily leaderless. What the British had started, Hitler would soon finish. Rommel was not directly involved in the subsequent 20 July plot to assassinate Hitler, but a growingly paranoid and vindictive Führer offered him the option of trial or suicide. He died by his own hand on 14 October.

General Dempsey's instructions from Montgomery for *Goodwood* were to 'engage the German armour in battle and "write it down" to such an extent it is of no further value'. The objective was not total breakthrough, but enough of a dent in the enemy lines to create a 'firm bastion' for future operations. Accordingly, in one of the biggest tank actions of the war, three whole armoured divisions were employed – the 7th, 11th and the Guards, initially on a comparatively narrow frontage. As instructions to General Richard O'Connor, commander of the British VIII Corps, expressed it: 'what we want over there are tanks. It doesn't matter about anything else.' Nevertheless, *Goodwood* also saw the employment of infantry divisions including the Canadians, the 3rd and the 51st Highland. Again a creeping barrage was used, and the operation initially met with success as the tanks burst through Cuverville and Démouville until the enemy launched counter-attacks and the attackers came up against the Bourguébus ridge where anti-tank positions had survived. Fighting continued until 21 July with heavy losses.

In one of the most celebrated tank actions the 2nd Armoured Battalion of the Irish Guards ran into heavy German armour at Cagny, and got close enough, quite literally, to exchange insults. Lieutenant J. R. Gorman encountered three concealed tanks at barely 100 yards – one of the new King Tigers, a Tiger and a Panther. As his Military Cross (MC) citation explained:

> Lieutenant Gorman fired three 75mm rounds at the leading [King Tiger]. Seeing that these had no apparent effect and despite the fact that it was still covered by the other two, he charged the leading tank with such force that it was unable to fire and the crew baled out. Lieutenant Gorman and his driver then ran back to where they had seen a ditched Sherman 17 pdr [Firefly]. He found the commander dead and having removed him with the help of his driver and having told the gunner to get back in the tank again, Gorman returned to stalk [the enemy tanks]. He scored several hits.

A photograph taken the next day showed that Gorman's tank had smashed into the rear track of the *Königstiger*, which was then too close to turn its barrel to fire. Another Sherman, that of Sergeant Harbinson,

A Canadian machine-gun team in action near Carpiquet, Normandy. The Vickers machine gun may have been a relic, having first been introduced into service in 1912, but it was a powerful and reliable support weapon with a cyclic rate of about 450 rounds per minute. (National Archives of Canada)

attracted the attention of the remaining enemy and paid the ultimate price, being hit three times and incinerated with the loss of three crew. Accounts by other members of Gorman's team added the detail that they had tried a high explosive round as a penultimate resort, suspecting that they would be unable to penetrate the monster with armour piercing, and that finally their gun had jammed. Guardsman Agnew in the bow machine gun position had been trapped because his hatch was blocked, and had to worm his way back out of the Sherman turret. Dropping to the ground he quickly joined four men running for a ditch. As the regimental history explained, 'They were the German crew. After an exchange of cold stares, being a punctilious sort of man, he saluted smartly and disappeared into a cornfield'.

What the 5,000 British and Canadian casualties during *Goodwood* really achieved has been subject of considerable argument. General Dempsey acknowledged flaws in the operational plan but also claimed value in terms of the bigger picture:

> The attack that we put in on 18 July was not a very good operation of war tactically, but strategically it was a great success, even though we did get a bloody nose. I don't mind about that. I was prepared to lose a couple of hundred tanks. So long as I didn't lose men. We could afford the tanks because they had begun to pile up in the bridgehead. Our tank losses were severe but our casualties in men were very light. If I had tried to achieve the same result with a conventional infantry attack I hate to think what the casualties would have been.[5]

Dempsey was correct, up to a point. German tank production was already outpaced by the Soviets, now attacking successfully in the East. The Western Allies, and particularly the American 'workshop of the world', could build machines faster than the enemy could now destroy them. Conversely, although Albert Speer, the German Minister for Armaments and Production, had worked miracles with German manufacture, enemy losses were becoming serious. The German High Command was also becoming increasingly convinced that von Rundstedt's gloomy prognosis might have been correct after all. However it all depended on perspective. As tank man Cecil Newton put it, 'all I saw was the dead, they were just dead people. The whole time that I was in Normandy.'

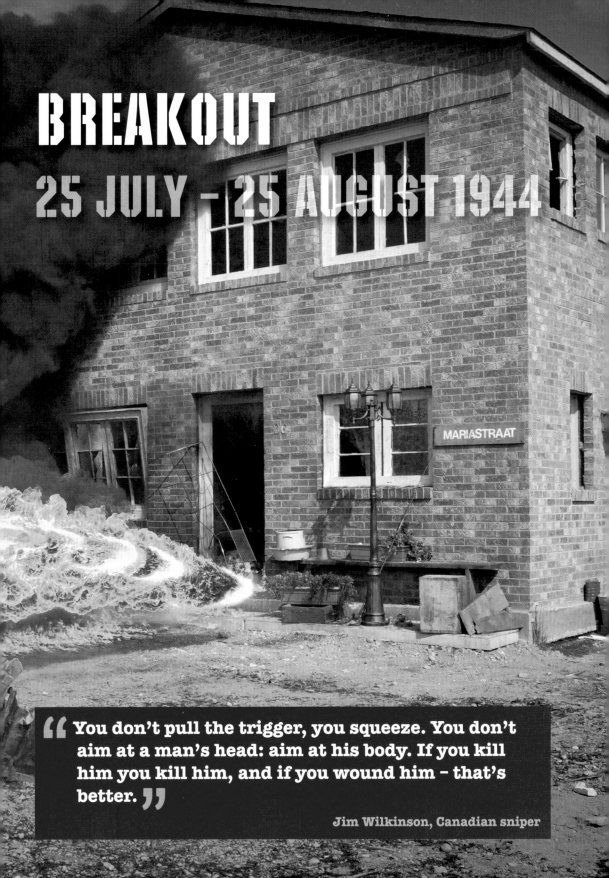

BREAKOUT
25 JULY – 25 AUGUST 1944

MARIASTRAAT

> " You don't pull the trigger, you squeeze. You don't aim at a man's head: aim at his body. If you kill him you kill him, and if you wound him – that's better. "
>
> Jim Wilkinson, Canadian sniper

OPERATION *COBRA*

Operation *Cobra* was designed to swing an overwhelming, and final, right hook against German defences in Normandy, taking advantage of enemy pre-occupation with the British and Canadians around Caen and allowing American forces to make the breakout. Various commanders claimed to have been the brains behind the scheme but Eisenhower was generous enough to share credit with both Montgomery and Bradley. A crucial precursor to the advance was the capture of St. Lô. This was finally achieved on 18 July, by which time the town had virtually ceased to exist with the destruction of her buildings estimated at over 90 percent. Not for nothing would the town be dubbed 'Capital of the Ruins'. The battle that began *Cobra* should have started on 24 July, but was stymied by weather conditions. A massive air onslaught by approximately 2,000 Allied aircraft, intended to help clear the path for ground forces, ran into poor visibility. Many planes were turned back, but some bombed blind, leading to friendly casualties. *Cobra* was postponed for 24 hours, but then the bombers returned. Again some loads fell short – a problem that might have been obviated by directing the bomber streams along the front rather than across it – and there were more friendly fatalities, including Lieutenant General Lesley McNair, the highest-ranking American soldier to be killed in Europe. This time, however, it was the Germans who took the brunt of the air assault, and there was no postponement. As Montgomery later recorded:

> The air plan for the assault phase included bombardment of an area 6,000 yards wide by 2,500 yards deep on the frontage of VII United States Corps by 1,500 heavy bombers of the Eighth United States Air Force, together with an attack by some 400 medium bombers on an adjacent target area. In order to strike the foremost enemy defenders, the American troops were withdrawn 1,200 yards to the north of the heavy bomber target area. Zero hour for the assaulting infantry was 1100, and it was hoped that the assaulting troops would regain their start line before the enemy had time to recover from the air attack. At 1100 hours the infantry of VII United States Corps moved forward, and it quickly became apparent that the results of the air bombardment had been devastating. Enemy troops who were not casualties were stunned and dazed, and weapons not destroyed had to be dug out and cleaned before they could be used; communications were almost

PREVIOUS SPREAD

A recreation demonstrating the power of the flamethrower tanks, which became vital weapons in the battle for Europe throughout the last year of the war. (Jeremy Llewellyn-Jones)

OPPOSITE

American infantry work their way through the ruins of St. Lô, July 1944. The capture of the town by the US First Army was a vital precursor to the subsequent breakout. Much of the early work was done by the 29th Infantry Division, but the 9th, 4th and 30th led the way west and south of the town at the start of *Cobra*. (Author's Collection)

completely severed. By the end of the day American troops had advanced some two miles.[1]

Many GIs watched the unfolding aerial drama awe-struck. George McGuire was one of them:

> One thing I will certainly never forget was the bombing of the German entrenchments near St. Lô... It was a nice clear sunny day and about ten o'clock I was standing on high ground about a mile away from where the German position was. Our first wave came in – and it seemed there was about 100 in [this] formation. You cannot imagine how proud [we were], it was a magnificent sight. And it went on wave after wave: they encountered a lot of ground fire... Eventually it was just a great huge cloud of dust. Can you imagine? Just one huge cloud. The objective was to just totally pulverize this German position and open it up so that our infantry and our army could pour through there... Everything on the ground was destroyed – I mean just totally pulverized.

General Bayerlein, commanding the *Panzer Lehr*, was horrified, describing the result as 'hell'. He later recalled that 'the planes kept coming like 'a conveyor belt', the 'fields were burning and smouldering. The bomb carpets unrolled in great rectangles... My front lines looked like a landscape on the moon.'[2]

Don Marsh was another American spectator:

> Those on the ground were not the only casualties: as we watched a B-17 Flying Fortress had been hit. He was coming down with all four engines dead ... one sight I can never forget. He was losing altitude and the props were not turning. Then they popped out red flares... The pilot was doing all

he could to glide the plane over our lines and crash in friendly territory. We didn't see the exact spot he came down although they made it inside our lines. There was a hell of a lot of air activity that day. We were watching from our foxholes and pulling for our guys to make it, knowing full well some of those flyboys would not make the 25 missions to return to the USA.[3]

Advancing American infantry were amazed to see enemy tanks turned over or blown into shell craters 'like children's toys'. The first two-mile push was hardly spectacular, and even then some of the enemy, including remnants of the *Panzer Lehr* and the 5th Parachute Division, fought back hard. Yet it was enough to crack the crust of the German defences, and over the next two days momentum built. On 26 July, the US 2nd Armoured and 1st Infantry joined in the attack, as did the 8th and 90th Infantry Divisions from Lieutenant General Troy Middleton's VIII Corps. Two days later the 4th US Armored Division entered Coutrances. Spirited German counter-attacks failed to stem the tide as inexorably the American Army worked its way through and around the enemy left flank that had encircled the Normandy bridgehead for almost two months. The western sector of the German defence was finally unhinged as the Americans now pushed on towards Avranches, a town that would also open the door into Brittany. General George Patton's Third Army now took the lead on the right, breaking out and around the enemy, entering Brittany, then turning towards the heart of France.

Operation *Lüttich*

Yet the Germans were still far from spent: for while some counselled caution, or even tactical retreat, Hitler was bent on a counter-attack intended to split the Allied foothold in two, using the bulk of his available armoured strength. Cryptographers at Bletchley Park discovered the plan just before the blow fell, but this was not sufficient warning for the Americans to make counter preparations. It did however inform Bradley of the strength and main axis of the thrust even as it was unfolding. On the night of 6/7 August, three Panzer Divisions counter-attacked at Mortain in the American sector. The aim of Operation *Lüttich* was to break through towards Avranches and the sea. If successful this would pinch off Patton's supply line and isolate American forces in Brittany causing a massive setback, and perhaps restore the line in Normandy.

Much of the blow fell on the 30th Division, a National Guard formation, but the Americans clung like limpets to the key high ground, including Hill 314, the dominant terrain feature around Mortain. The stand of the 120th Infantry, which lost 300 men during the course of the Mortain battle, would become a thing of legend rewarded with a Presidential Unit Citation. As the fog cleared American tank destroyers, artillery and Allied tactical air forces joined the fray, with the Ninth Air Force alone flying 429 sorties on 7 August. The German armour succeeded in pressing west of Mortain, but an attack which had started with such promise was blunted. Perhaps even worse Hitler ordered von Kluge to continue the action with 'daring' and 'regardless' of risk. Sustaining the fight for almost a week would leave key German armoured units deep in the nose of what was fast becoming a large 'pocket'. As General Omar Bradley succinctly expressed it after the event, 'In his reckless attack at Mortain, the enemy challenged us to a decision, the most decisive of the French campaign. It was to cost the enemy an army and gain us France'.[4] Patton was elated: on 8 August he was able to write home to his wife that on this 'big day' St. Malo, Le Mans and Angers were all secured, moreover he declared the enemy, 'finished' – 'we may end this in ten days'.[5]

British and Canadian gains

Perhaps even more significantly Hitler's gamble at Mortain, and the staunch American resistance there, helped to relieve the pressure on the hitherto bottled up British and Canadian corps. Earlier the British had been held in check around Caen by the strongest German forces, now, as these attempted to parry the Americans, it was possible for the Allies to advance elsewhere. So it was that while the hammer of the American armoured thrust swung around from St. Lô and the pivot of Mortain, the northern jaw of a giant pincer was formed by British and Canadian forces grinding their way south. On 25 July, the 2nd Canadian Corps began an advance down the road towards Falaise and Allied troops were soon fighting for Tilly la Campagne, which they first took, and then lost. From 30 July the British and Canadians made further progress, albeit far less spectacular than the American sweep, with the commencement of Operation *Bluecoat*. Montgomery's intention for the coming weeks, as announced on Sunday 6 August, was to 'destroy enemy forces' west of the Seine and north of the Loire rivers.[6] That day the British 43rd

American troops 'mouseholing' during street fighting in Brest. A large charge is inserted into a small basement window, the team retire and blow a hole through the wall. The attackers then enter quickly to outflank or overcome stunned defenders. This technique was used throughout the battle for France and into Germany, where house-to-house fighting was a common feature. (Imperial War Museum, HU94979 and HU94980)

Division secured Ondefontaine, and the 129th Brigade with the 13th/18th Hussars began the attack on Mont Pincon.

Yet for many this remained a soldier's war – of modest progress – in which there was as yet little inkling of the bigger drama unfolding on the generals' maps. As Ted Roberts recalled the infantryman's battle remained a deadly game of cat and mouse in which reliance on comrades was vital: 'You walked when you could, you crawled when you couldn't. You walked if you think its safe, but all of a sudden you may come up against a small group of Germans: it might be a machine gun, it might be a sniper – then you get down. If you are in an open field you try and get to the nearest possible place where … it's a bit safer, like a hedge. As you see the others move forward, you move forward as well, you move as a group.'

The Sniper's War

The sniper in particular remained a scourge of the infantry as to move forward usually meant exposure to an often fatal first shot. After just two weeks on the battlefront Canadian Stan Matulis made a serious mistake:

> The place was being splattered by German mortars, and the days were dry, and the dust that came off those buildings and the cement, and the rocks, well it was like a fog… So you're in line behind guys, and when they go down, you go down with them – behind – and wait your turn, and you wait for the command 'let's move', but these things were getting very serious. I said, 'fellows we're going to get hit sooner or later, lets go into that house across the road'… So there's about three of us [which] went into that house and there was a window. I guess I crossed it twice and that's where the wisdom of the battlefield comes in. You don't do these things: all I knew was I'm twirling and swirling when I hit the ground. I'm cut in half – that's what I felt in my body. I can see all my pouches, but I can't see the rest of my body. So there I am lying and dying, and I thought … of God you know, because I'm a Catholic. And I said, 'Gee. Am I friends with the Almighty?' And I thought of my mother. And this guy comes up to me and he says, 'Hey, you're hit in the neck.' And he put this field dressing on my neck, and one took my arm and one took my shoulders and they carried me out into the street. And these mortars were falling down around us, and they would drop me down and lay beside me. Take me another ten feet, fall down and lie … and finally we saw a military flat truck and they carried me in – they dumped me in – and away we went.

British signaller Jim Holder-Vale was putting up a camouflage net when he was engaged by a sniper:

The Sniper

'The sniper's finger presses the trigger and the bullet passes through the helmet, scalp, skull, small blood vessels' membrane into the soft sponginess of the brain... Then you're either paralysed or you're blind or you can't smell anything or your memory's gone or you can't talk or you're bleeding – or you're dead.' Combat medic from the US 30th Infantry Division

ABOVE A sniper of the German 97th Jäger Division in action with a captured Russian Moisin Nagant 7.62mm sniper rifle. The old Moisin Nagant bolt-action rifle with five round box magazine owed its name to the designers, the Belgian Nagant brothers and the Russian Colonel Moisin. It was fitted with a number of different telescopic sights from the 1930s, including some produced by the German Zeiss Company. (Author's Collection)

RIGHT Filmed experiments soon demonstrated what the veterans already knew: the American steel helmet was easily penetrated by the sniper's bullet. However, steel helmets were designed with small fragments in mind, and snipers were usually taught to aim at the 'centre of mass' of a human target. (Jeremy Llewellyn-Jones)

A British sniper takes aim with the No. 4 Mk I (T) sniper rifle with No. 32 telescopic sight. This effective combination was the most common sniper equipment in both British and Canadian service during the latter part of the war. The No. 4 Mk I (T) was an example of the ordinary infantry ten-round magazine rifle selected from the best on the production line, then modified by the addition of a sight bracket and cheek rest. Typically this sniper wears the camouflage printed Denison smock – often teamed with a face veil, camouflaged robe, face paint or other types of concealment in combat. Often British snipers worked as two-man sniper and observer teams, with one man in each infantry section as a designated sniper. (Author's Collection)

Diagram from the American manual *Scouting, Patrolling and Sniping* showing the essential shooting technique of the sniper. Adjusting telescopic sights in battle was impracticably slow, as combat required snipers to take rapid and often single snap shots at fleeting targets. The answer was to leave sights zeroed at a likely range of engagement, in this case 400 yards, and varying the aim to match distance and movement by 'holding off'. So it is that at 400 yards the aim is at the centre of mass – the opponent's chest. When the target is closer the firer aims lower; further away and the aim is progressively higher. About 600 yards was often the maximum practical against a target of opportunity, with the shot being directed more than 4ft above the point where the bullet was intended to strike. (Author's Collection)

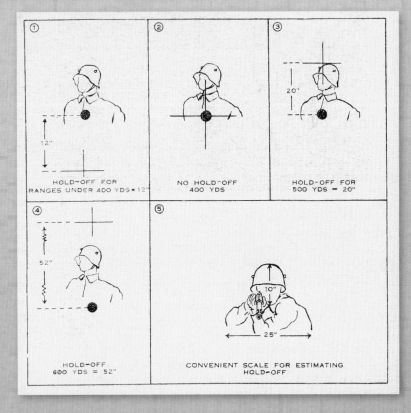

A bullet thudded past my head. It didn't whistle. It didn't whine. It thudded. And I knew that I'd been shot at. So I dashed to cover. The cry went up there was a sniper in the church tower. And Jack got our Bren gun out of the truck: put his glasses on, got down in the middle of the road, took aim at the church tower, pulled the trigger, and it misfired. So he gave that up… Eventually it was decided to use one of our guns to blast the church tower. I didn't see what happened but I gather a young sniper came out with his hands up and he was taken away.

Ted Roberts was hit at a place called Le Bon Repos, a small village south of Hill 112. His first impression was that somebody had cracked a whip close by – enough to make him drop to the ground – before rising again to zig-zag rapidly away. Yet not fast enough, 'two cracks over your head and then a bullet hit me [*sic*] arm and I fell out on my back … tin hat one way, my rifle went somewhere else … 6in further it would've gone through my side and through my heart and I wouldn't be talking to you now… I've never been so scared before and don't think I'll ever be so scared again. Well from then on I daren't move a muscle.'

Just who the enemy snipers were, how well they could shoot, and what their techniques might involve, remained the subject of much speculation. British sniper trainer Captain Clifford Shore took a close professional interest, finding that many operated from what he described as 'hides', 'often inter linked by ditch-ways etc, and in one or two cases it was apparent that one hide had been used as domestic quarters, and the other for the serious job of life. These latter always commanded excellent fields of fire and in the neighbourhood of some of them British and Canadian graves, surmounted by steel helmets which had a single hole through them, were silent, but sufficient, testimony to the efficiency of a real German sharpshooter.'[7] Interestingly, though he concluded that many were not simply 'ordinary infantrymen', only some were equipped with telescopic sights.

Indeed, enemy sniping equipment varied considerably. For while the majority of enemy snipers used bolt-action Mausers, with or without one of a number of different telescopic sights, some were equipped with semi-automatics. Prominent amongst these were the G41 and G43 rifles, both firing the standard service round, and having ten shot magazines and gas-operated systems, albeit of two different designs. The Walther G43 was by far the most numerous of the two and was actually fitted to

An American soldier pictured with two of the enemy's most advanced infantry weapons: left the MG 42 and right the *Sturmgewehr* 44. While the MG 42 was essentially an old concept perfected, being a multi-purpose rapid firing machine gun, the *Sturmgewehr* was a genuinely new and radical concept. Its secret was the 'intermediate' short 7.92mm cartridge. This was powerful enough to kill at most battle ranges, yet compact and manageable enough for full automatic fire with its user on the move. (Author's Collection)

take the ZF4 telescopic sight. Although an effective weapon, it was also something of a curious choice for a sniper arm, as seldom did a sniper fire many rounds from one position. To do so gave away his location – and invited retaliation. Shore regarded the whole notion of an automatic sniper rifle as 'sacrilegious'. At least a few Germans in the West carried 7.62mm Moisin Nagant bolt-action rifles captured during campaigns in the East. Shore eventually got to see a short scope-mounted 1930 type, courtesy of a Dane who had taken it from an enemy occupier. By now it had been through at least three hands in different armies and was in a far from pristine condition. Nevertheless, Shore declared it 'a really workmanlike job' altogether appearing close to the 'ideal sniper rifle'.

One thing that pretty well all snipers had in common was the desire to remain unseen. As one German maxim put it, 'camouflage ten times, shoot once'. Though British methods had improved considerably, Shore retained a grudging admiration of some of the German equipment:

The majority of the men we took in Normandy wore camouflage jackets, and in some cases full suits of camouflage, complete with cowl or hood, but then the ordinary German soldier was much better equipped from the camouflage point of view than our own. Late in the campaign, factories were taken which were filled with the excellent padded camouflage jacket, with hood, with which thousands of the Wehrmacht were equipped. These jackets were very well made and, in winter, ideally warm. They were reversible, one side normal German camouflage design, brown and green in varying tones and geometric pattern, and the other, white, for use in the winter snow.[8]

Even if seen, and captured, the enemy was much happier to remain unidentified as a sniper. So it was that although a sniper's badge was introduced, few wore it in the frontline. How understandable this was is explained by the experience of Patrick Delaforce, 'Snipers … if we caught them, they were shot. I remember I was with a battle group: it was 3rd Tank, 4th KSLI [King's Shropshire Light Infantry], and we caught some snipers who were being "naughty"… "Pat", they said, "you don't have to be part of this, but we are going to shoot this gang". So I watched it being done, that was life.'

German snipers could – and sometimes did – shoot from tree hides: but how effective this could be was subject to debate. As Shore observed:

In Normandy, and throughout the campaign, there was a good deal heard about snipers in trees. I am quite sure that the majority of riflemen will share my doubts as to the efficiency and effectiveness of tree shooting. There certainly were Germans in trees, but I am of the opinion that they were acting as observers rather than snipers. There are comparatively few men who can shoot with sniper accuracy in the offhand position, let alone the far more difficult position which arises from almost any stance in a tree. The Germans used slings for these 'Tarzans' and, of course, such a contrivance captured the attention and fired the imagination of war artists and correspondents, with the result that a most graphic, if not entirely factual, portrayal resulted. The most notable tree merchant I saw – smelled would be more fitting word since there was little left of him but the smell – swung lazily in his sling in a large tree near Crisot in July. He reminded me of highwaymen's remains swinging from the gibbet… A burst of machine gun fire and the hot sun was responsible for this excrescence. When speaking of this monkey business it is only fair to mention that, according to German small arms manuals, training in tree shooting was practised.[9]

While machine guns, clearing parties and artillery were all part of the answer, arguably the best antidote to enemy snipers was more snipers. Canadians Bill Betteridge and Jim Wilkinson were just two of them. The majority of British and Canadian snipers worked in pairs using No. 4 Mk 1 (T) rifles and binoculars or telescopes for observation. Betteridge described his weapon as pretty much 'a regular .303 Enfield rifle' but with scope mounting and a built-up butt piece, 'so you could lean your face against it' while taking steady aim. Peering through the telescopic sight was essentially like 'using one barrel of a binocular'. The magnification on all military rifle scopes was relatively low, typically from about two to five times, but practically this was enough for most scenarios, for as Betteridge realized 'the more the power it is, the less is the width of view'. So it was that a powerful telescope, well rested and used systematically, was a useful spotting tool, but not practical as a rifle sight that needed to pick up a target rapidly. For covering wider areas the observer turned to binoculars, usually relaying sightings to the firer by reference to predetermined landmarks – as, for example, between 'the dead tree and the prominent rock'. A good shooter would not search slowly and laboriously through his sight, but respond immediately to directions by turning his head straight to the target and raising the scope. When this worked well the rifle needed only the slightest adjustment to bring the barrel to aim. As Betteridge put it, you looked through the sight and, 'there's a horizontal line and then a post going up through the centreline with a point, and you just put the point where you wanted to hit'. Despite the adrenaline the best shots did not jerk the trigger, but as Wilkinson said, 'aimed and squeezed'. Naturally accuracy was highly significant, but arguably speed of aim and reaction was more vital still as on the battlefield all but the doomed and intellectually challenged realized that exposure had to be kept to the absolute minimum, and as fleeting as possible. Betteridge's team certainly had quick reactions – but it came close to costing his life during street clearing when his partner fired a snap shot that narrowly missed his head: 'I gave him a little talk after that.'

The good sniper was a master of the art of not giving away his own position. As Jim Wilkinson related, 'we wanted to be as well hidden as possible. We were always with camouflaged jackets on and camouflaged nets. You don't shoot if you don't think you're going to hit him. You're only giving away your position, and they'll get you.' While many might have disagreed Captain Shore did not think the sniping game one of the dirtier aspects of the war, being 'a great game of skill and courage'. Nevertheless, a degree of coldness was to be positively encouraged. As he rationalized:

> the average American and Englishman is averse to killing and many, having been forced to kill, suffer from remorse. But it is a fact that a sniper can kill with less conscience pricking than a man in close combat. Personal feelings of remorse or questioning of motives will slow down a man's critical killing instinct and the sniper who allows himself to fall into such a train of thought will not last long. It is imperative to look upon the killing of an enemy as swatting a fly, an unthinking, automatic action. Two things only should interest the sniper – getting the job done and getting away unscathed.[10]

Actual 'killing' was not however as important as the 'hitting'. As Jim Wilkinson explained, aim was, wherever possible, at the mass of the target for best chance of a strike:

> You don't aim at a man's head: aim at his body. If you kill him you kill him, and if you wound him – that's better. When you wound him you've got hospitals to look after him, people there are busy… You don't feel the slightest bit of animosity you know, you don't feel it, because you're living with [your comrades] for five years. They're your brothers. They are your family, so if you catch one of those [enemies] in your sights … it's a wonderful feeling. It's a terrible thing to say, but it's a wonderful feeling.

Doubtless the enemy felt much the same, and one day they caught Jim at his own game: 'I said I better check this gas can and fuel the vehicle. I'm pouring the gasoline and "BANG!" this bullet hits the Jerry can, falls out of my hand and I'm smoking, and I catch fire. So they get me on a stretcher and another bullet comes and hits the stretcher bearer and kills him, right through there and the bullet landed up in my boot – broke a toe in my boot.'

While British sniping before D-Day had been summed up by an *Army Training Memorandum* of January 1944, knowledge and techniques were honed throughout the campaign in North-West Europe, leading to new codification in the form of a pamphlet in 1946. Each battalion was to have not only the ability to field one designated man per ordinary section but a special 'sniping section' comprising four NCOs and four

OPPOSITE
Canadians of the Regina Rifles during street fighting in Caen. The section Bren gunner is on the right, others carry the No. 4 bolt-action rifle. Note the 'spike' or 'pig sticker' bayonet: these cheaply made pieces were calculated to be the minimum length required to penetrate and kill an enemy in winter dress. However, their lack of a grip made them useless for any other practical purpose. (National Archives of Canada, PA115028)

privates, and, as 'for all other specialisms', a '100 percent reserve' was to be trained. These were not merely to replace losses, but might also be required to act operationally when reliefs were required. Accordingly, 16 camouflaged smocks were needed. Eight pairs of snipers could be fielded at any one time, one with a sniper rifle and scope, the other acting as observer and close protection with a 'machine carbine' (usually a Sten gun) or ordinary rifle. Every rifleman in a sniping team was to go lightly equipped, but would carry 50 rounds of 'ball' ammunition and five rounds of tracer, a water bottle, two grenades and an emergency ration. While these specifics were open to variation as to circumstance the camouflage smock was pretty much indispensable, having the added advantage that its 'ample pockets' eliminated the need for web equipment. Interestingly there are even one or two surviving pictures from the latter part of the war showing Allied troops making use of captured camouflage equipment. Certainly Andy Anderson stated that he had 'a German smock … because my own was destroyed, and we didn't have a quartermaster to resupply us'.

Other Infantry Weapons

The soldier and his Sten gun had something in the nature of a love-hate relationship. For, as Canadian Jan de Vries observed, it was built like a 'plumber's nightmare', yet was powerful for short-range jobs, and had been manufactured, quite literally in millions, to meet the crying need for a submachine gun that had been so entirely neglected before the war. The Sten cost barely a tenth of the price of a Thompson – and looked as though it was worth even less – but it was also true that its very crude simplicity was a virtue in the right circumstances. Almost anybody could be taught to shoot one – if with little accuracy – and it was one of the few weapons that even the unskilled could dismantle and reassemble in short order, and with only a modicum of prior instruction. Amongst the veterans who had to use the thing criticisms were many and varied. Len Mann recalled that even dropping the Sten could set it off – with disastrous consequences. Ron Titterton found the rudimentary safety

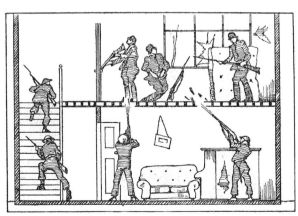

catch a serious worry, being afraid that he might 'shoot the bloke in front' when marching. Edwin Bramall was indeed nearly shot by his own platoon sergeant when his 'wretched' Sten gun went off as they were charging forward. Jan de Vries also remembered that it was a bad move to leave the box magazine charged with the full 32 rounds, as to do so weakened the spring and might lead to a failure to fire.

Andy Anderson remarked, with no apparent irony, that the Sten was 'very dangerous' once loaded. In his recollection, it was 'an awkward thing to use' appearing crude against its German equivalent the MP 40. The latter was popularly known to Allied soldiers as the 'Schmeisser', but this was something of a misnomer as in fact the German weapon was not produced by the well known designer Hugo Schmeisser, but by a team from the Ermawerk using the patents of Heinrich Vollmer. Side by side the comparison between the German 'machine pistol' and the 'machine carbine' was stark, one of them being 'beautifully machined' and 'easier to carry', the other 'roughly stamped out of metal'. Like quite a few others Anderson got rid of his issue weapon at the first opportunity, and,

> carried a German Schmeisser, as many of us did. And when we got close to the Americans of the 101st in Germany some of the men in my platoon, and with encouragement from me, got the American Garand rifle, which was a beautiful machine, or the American lightweight carbine… So there were times when half the men in my platoon were carrying German weapons, or the odd American weapon. It wasn't until somewhere around Minden in Germany that we were in a rest area for the first time and the colonel called an equipment parade… He tore a strip off me and told me to get rid of all the foreign weapons.

Captain Shore compared enemy weapons with professional detachment. Examining the MP 40 he described it as:

> A thoroughly well designed weapon for its job, and although inclined to be heavy it was delightful to use even if only on account of its finish. Frankly it was no more destructive that its most humble progeny, the Sten, which the British produced when a machine carbine was needed most urgently. In general the design of the German weapons was good, and the workmanship in all early models was excellent, but this trailed off progressively as the war continued, and towards the end it was possible to find certain German weapons which fell below the danger point. But the Schmeisser continued to be a perfectly well turned out job right to the conclusion of the war in Europe. On 7 June 1944 I picked up a 'Schmeisser' carbine and a Walther pistol, and it was interesting to see the difference in the steel of the two weapons. The Walther was, or had the appearance of, a very new job, and yet though it had lain on the side of a ditch probably only for the matter of a few hours the barrel was in poor state, and did not respond at all well to cleaning; but the 'Schmeisser' which bore signs of hard usage on 6 June, was in perfect shape despite having been in a similar spot, and cleaned up as bright as a new penny.[11]

OPPOSITE TOP
British manual illustration showing a useful street fighting technique – breaking through the internal wall of a house and throwing a grenade before the enemy can react. (Author's Collection)

OPPOSITE BOTTOM
Illustration from a British manual showing how to attack an enemy in upper rooms during a street fight, firing through the floor before tackling the stairs. (Author's Collection)

THE FINAL BATTLES FOR FRANCE

Even as the Americans were embroiled at Mortain Montgomery's new offensive – Operation *Totalize* – committed the Canadians to a new attack south towards Falaise beginning on the night of 7/8 August. If successful this would eventually enable them to dominate key high ground north of the town and begin the closure of a trap that Patton was fast creating to the south. Yet German resistance remained stubborn, and losses mounted. One unit again pushed into the action was Wittmann's Tigers. Around midday on 8 August the ace, mounted in command Tiger '007', moved north from Les Jardinets not far from St. Aignan. They were soon under artillery fire, and at a range of 1,800m began to engage Canadian Shermans. In their turn the Tigers came into the sights of the Northamptonshire Yeomanry and battle was joined from another direction. At approximately 12.45pm a British Firefly, commanded by Lieutenant James, got a flank view of an enemy tank and at 800m the gunner, Trooper Ekins, drew a bead on the side. He fired, and for a moment the target was obscured by a flash and smoke. A few seconds later there was a sudden and more massive second detonation as the Tiger's ammunition exploded. For some time nobody on the Allied side would realize that Wittmann, the greatest of the so-called 'tank aces', had been killed.

Perhaps this should be little wonder, for *Totalize* included many a confused action. One battle group, 'Worthington Force', lost in the darkness of a night advance, took Hill 140 but were promptly counter-attacked and all but annihilated. Montgomery's later summary was as positive as possible, but the difficulties were very clear nonetheless: 'On 9 August [the] Canadian Army made appreciable advances, [the] 4th Canadian Armoured Division secured Brettville-le Rabat after bitter fighting, and the Poles captured Cauvicourt and St. Sylvain. Repeated attempts, however to make a clean break through the enemy anti-tank gun screen met with little success and our armour sustained heavy casualties'.[12] Quesnay Wood was assaulted on the night of 10/11 August unsuccessfully. Endeavours to advance recommenced a few days later under the title Operation *Tractable*. Yet for Bill Betteridge, as for many others, it was a moment of very personal tragedy that stood out from the

OPPOSITE
Photograph showing the impact of a mortar shell, one of the many weapons the Germans used to hold up the Allied advance as they were retreating.
(Jeremy Llewellyn-Jones)

fast moving canvas of mid August rather than a list of place names or the lines on a map:

> This time we were moving up to take over a position from the front troops so we're not under fire. We're not hurting nobody. All of a sudden Sergeant Browne, one of the nicest guys you'd ever see went down... And I can just see his mother, his brother and sister saying 'Killed In Action'. He's killed with one bullet through his jugular vein. You can't stop the blood – and his buddy is trying to stop the blood: couldn't stop it so he goes crazy, just lost all his nerve. In that [sort of] case they send them back to England for a rest, and you know, get cooled down again. I got him in my platoon later because he was a friend of mine.

OPPOSITE
The German 8cm medium infantry mortar, from the British manual *Enemy Weapons* (Part V). Infantry mortars were quick to set up and relatively light for the size of the projectile. The mortar bomb was launched at a high trajectory and it was often possible to put more than one bomb in the air before the first landed. Aim was achieved by adjusting the elevation and traverse. But to those on the receiving end it always seemed accurate enough. As Canadian Andy Anderson remembered, 'It got to be a standing joke that if you got out of your trench and rattled your mess tin the Germans would put a mortar in it'. (Author's Collection)

The death of Sergeant James S. Browne of the Queen's Own Rifles of Canada was undoubtedly a tragedy for his parents, William and Catherine of Sturgeon, Manitoba. But his sudden death on 14 August was perhaps all the more shocking to his comrades as he was seen as both a leader, and, at 29, a man of experience. The temporary mental collapse of his best buddy was certainly no isolated event, as by now the idea that every man had his limit before onset of 'battle fatigue' was well established. As one officer put it, 'everyone cracks up in the end of course'. The regimental historian of the East Lancashire Regiment subsequently identified that there were obvious advanced signs for those who knew how to read them: slower reactions and lower standards of efficiency being just the most obvious. Perhaps, indeed, there was an increasing carelessness about oneself, eventually a sense of inevitability – what one commentator called being the 'walking dead'. The American Army actually conducted a survey and discovered that about a quarter of their men 'almost always' had the feeling that it was just a matter of time until they were hit. More than half had this worry 'usually' or 'some of the time'. Only about one in seven were stupid, or confident, enough for it to rarely cross their minds. American psychiatrists also picked up on other potential tell-tale signs: 'phobic-like' reactions to shell fire or specific weapons such as the '88'; 'impotent' anger and frustration; anxiety; distrust and guilt; grief; and the generally cumulative wear-and-tear of continual exposure to the elements and the battlefield. Maybe the real surprise was that escape, by means of desertion or 'self inflicted wounds' (SIW), was not more common. Between mid 1944 and the end of the war the total number 'absent' in the entire British 21st Army Group was a little over 10,000. The 'SIWs' were only into three figures, but often difficult to evaluate with precision. These relatively low totals were more remarkable still since the British no longer shot anybody for infractions of discipline, and the Americans, who had a comparable record, had only one recorded instance where the firing squad followed through on a death sentence. Perhaps expectedly research revealed that the majority of deserters were young, in the infantry, below average intelligence, and had some previous problem or difficulty which had been exacerbated by war.

By mid August the US Third and First Canadian Armies were struggling to close the neck of the Falaise Pocket, while the Second British and First American Armies constricted the bag containing the remains of the enemy mass of manoeuvre. Yet, despite many frustrations, it was now just a matter of time. For on 15 August came long awaited news from the south. Operation *Anvil*, the second wave of Allied landings and invasions in southern France, had finally been launched, and by now Allied troops were landing on the French Riviera. The better part of 100,000 men were quickly ashore between Toulon and Cannes, and were soon making good progress. Late on 16 August the Canadians took Falaise: the tantalizing 'Falaise–Argentan gap' separating them from the Americans was now just 15 miles. Within three days Lieutenant General Guy Simonds' armour from II Canadian Corps succeeded in contacting the Americans at Chambois, only to have the enemy – realizing the extreme peril of their situation – break through with elements of the II SS Panzer Corps. Perhaps as many as 40,000 Germans managed to get away, but much precious equipment remained behind.

As Doug Vidler put it they 'lambasted us' at the closing of the Falaise Gap, 'being shelled so bad' that it made it

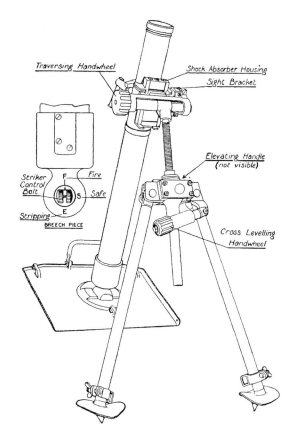

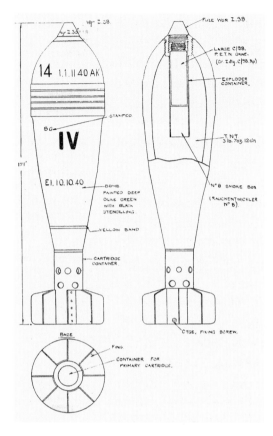

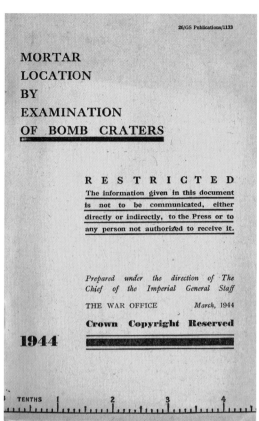

26/GS Publications/1133

MORTAR
LOCATION
BY
EXAMINATION
OF BOMB CRATERS

R E S T R I C T E D
The information given in this document
is not to be communicated, either
directly or indirectly, to the Press or to
any person not authorized to receive it.

*Prepared under the direction of The
Chief of the Imperial General Staff*

THE WAR OFFICE   *March,* 1944

Crown Copyright Reserved

1944

TENTHS   2   3   4

ABOVE
British diagrams
of German 10cm
high explosive
mortar bombs
from the
*Handbook
of Enemy
Ammunition.* The
bomb entered
the mortar tube
tail first and was
launched by the
ignition of the
cartridge at the
base. The slightly
smaller 8cm
bombs for the
medium infantry
mortars, were
similar in
appearance but

impossible to get a secure position for his team to set up its mortars. Some notion of the ferocity of the action was given when a badly wounded despatch rider he knew was loaded up for transportation. Vidler was sure that he had lost his leg:

> We had the stretcher on top of the Bren gun carrier and he was laying there, and I went over and said to him, 'Skip, Jesus, that's too bad, I'm sorry'. And he said, 'What are you talking about? I'm going home... You've got to keep going'... I didn't envy him... But I wanted to get a million dollar wound that would take me out of the action, but without losing a limb... He was just so bloody glad he's getting out of this thing!

Shortly afterwards Vidler was in another carrier when the driver was killed by a shell splinter. He is candid about his feelings, 'I was scared shitless ... shelling was the worst thing'. Walter Balfour had a surreal experience standing at the side of a road with his Bren gun as lorry loads of enemy soldiers 'rolled past' before he could react. Realizing what was happening, he then, 'slung the gun round and opened up on the back end of a truck… I guess I hit the truck and two or three of them.' The vehicle came to an untidy halt as the remainder spilled 'out of the trucks into the ditches on both sides of the road, and of course they opened up on me… I could hear a few zings going past my head before it hit.' Happily the enemy were too intent on making their escape to come back to find out the condition of the wounded, and mightily surprised, Canadian who had just fired on them.

Right in the thick of the fighting were a company of the Canadian Argyll and Sutherland Highlanders with a tank squadron of the South Albertas. Arriving on high ground giving a 'panoramic view' of the Dives valley early on 18 August, they were amazed to see a huge column of the enemy. Now they were given the difficult assignment of advancing to St. Lambert further constricting the main artery of the enemy retreat. This effort was crucial since St. Lambert controlled crossing points over the River Dives. The mission was not made any easier by the fact that nobody appeared to have told the RAF what they were doing, and, like the hapless enemy around them, they too were subjected to attack from the air. Part of St. Lambert was seized, but the remainder was occupied by at least one 88mm gun and enemy tanks and vehicles that first beat off a Canadian attack, then threatened to overwhelm them. Luckily artillery support was acquired during the following day and 4.5in shells now rained down on the German position. Everybody took cover. As Major Currie related in the after action report:

> We were lucky and suffered no casualties from our own guns, but it had a very devastating effect on the Germans and gave us a much needed respite, as the tanks were running low on ammunition… Pressure from the Germans mounted again near dark, and as we were pretty well spread out, I was afraid that we would be chopped up piecemeal. I decided to draw the force in tighter for the night, so we gave up part of the village. All weapons were given fixed lines of fire, to cover all approaches, and everyone was warned to stay put … in the morning we found that we had inflicted a considerable number of casualties on the Germans during the night.

By lunch time on the next day all the officers of the battle group, except Currie, were wounded or dead. That evening the enemy advanced again,

also contained an 'ejection charge'. This had the effect of causing the body of the bomb to 'bounce' up 5m or so before the main charge exploded causing an 'air burst'. This was not very effective on soft ground but increased the effect of the bomb considerably on hard surfaces. (Author's Collection)

OPPOSITE, RIGHT
The British manual *Mortar Location by Examination of Bomb Craters*. It was realized that mortar bomb craters were not usually perfectly circular, nor of even depth: the irregularity of the impression was a function both of the type of bomb and the direction and angle of descent. By determining the direction and angle of impact the approximate firing positions of enemy mortars could be located. (Author's Collection)

but a lucky round hit one of their ammunition carriers resulting in a 'tremendous explosion'. The Argylls and Albertas would hold for another 36 hours before being withdrawn, Currie was awarded the Victoria Cross for his own personal efforts to hold the position.

Between 19 and 22 August the Allies again slammed the pocket shut as the US 90th Division met Polish armour. Polish troops holding what was effectively the little island of Mont-Ormel, in the midst of the stream of alternately attacking and fleeing Germans, fought off the last assault on their position during the early evening of 20 August as the Canadians linked with the Poles the following day. This time it was final, and for many Germans, fatal. What was amazing about the Falaise Gap was not merely the amount of death and destruction but its concentrated nature in both time and space. For, in contrast to the general nature of a war in which the enemy was only infrequently seen, this soon became the richest of 'target rich' environments. One British soldier explained the scene from his vantage point:

The floor of the valley was seen to be alive … men marching, cycling and running, columns of horse drawn transport, motor transport, and as the sun got up, so more targets came to light… It was a gunner's paradise and everybody took advantage of it… Anyway on our left was the famous killing ground, and all day the roar of Typhoons went on and fresh columns of smoke obscured the horizon… We could just see one short section of the Argentan–Trun road, some 200 yards in all, on which sector at one time was crowded the whole miniature picture of an army in rout. First, a squad of men running, being overtaken by men on bicycles, followed by a limber at the gallop, and the whole being overtaken by a Panther tank crowded with men and doing well up to 30mph, all with the idea of getting away as fast as they could.[13]

The corridor of death at Falaise offered an unheard-of opportunity for ground attack aircraft – and the

The underside of the stubby but powerful looking Typhoon. This particular craft JR128 arrived in France on 7 August 1944, but was shot down by Flak at Falaise. (Hawker)

Typhoon squadrons knew it. Pilot John Thompson was caught up in the spirit of the moment, 'Our Wing Commander, Green – South African chap – went out one morning, early on a recce, and to see whether the weather was suitable for the rocket-firing Typhoons. And he came back and landed – practically taxied into the intelligence tent he was so excited. And he said, 'God! There's thousands of tanks lined up out there', and all kinds of light armoured vehicles and men, all heading eastwards. [They weren't] very far from where our camp was… So we just flew constantly that day attacking the German armour and the army and whatever.' For several days the sky was thick with British and Canadian planes, Typhoons being seconded by Spitfires with cannon and machine guns, and on occasion such aerial congestion was reported that targets could no longer be properly observed. More cynical airmen would refer to what they could see on the ground as 'the bank holiday rush'.

On the ground the horror was seen close up. As Jim Holder-Vale recalled, 'the most horrific thing I saw was after the battle of Falaise … concentrated in an area that was pounded by artillery from all sides, and aircraft from all sides. Constantly rocketed and bombed. And afterwards

American troops being welcomed as liberators by the French population. Most of the towns and villages captured in the early fighting had been bombed to rubble, but as the German Army began to collapse, whole areas were seized without a fight, much to the relief of the French population. (NARA)

OPPOSITE

The 'Jerrican' – originally 'Jerry can' – was so called because these flat-sided liquid containers were first used by the Germans for fuel or water. The Jerry can was a good all round useful piece of booty, but not such an unusual find as to arouse any suspicion. This one might well be picked up without a second thought: the result would probably be death, as it is wired to a buried 'S' Mine. (Author's Collection)

we went through there and the whole area was a mass of debris and death, and it stank terribly … they lost so many, and that was really horrendous to see. The real carnage of war. It was horrible.' Sergeant Wally Caines was with a reconnaissance team of the Dorsets, 'near Falaise massed slaughter had taken place by Typhoon fighter-bombers. The recce party passed through this area. We travelled one road and actually our vehicle travelled over the top of many crushed German dead bodies… How that lot looked and stank, dead bodies were running over with maggots and flies – it was indeed a ghastly sight seeing these dead Nazis bursting in the blistering heat of the day… Never before had I seen or smelt anything like it.'[14]

Roughly 10,000 Germans died in the Falaise Pocket, upwards of 50,000 were captured. Perhaps even worse, it appeared that the proud Panzer Corps in Normandy, already severely denuded at Mortain and a dozen earlier actions, was now virtually annihilated. Within 'the shambles', the British Operational Research Section found 187 tanks and assault guns: more would be accounted for as their fuel ran out, or they were caught in the ensuing retreat. Also in the pocket were almost 2,500 other motor vehicles and 252 artillery pieces. According to the Canadian *Official History* the horse-drawn transport could not even be counted since 'the stench of dead horses' was 'so bad that the area had to be passed with all speed'. It was even said that pilots caught a whiff when flying low over the ground. An American officer and veteran of World War I, described the scene as worse than that of the Argonne and Marne – names synonymous with the destruction of war. As late as 1947 damaged vehicles were still being auctioned off from a French government depot established for abandoned equipment at St. Lambert.

Yet, even as the slaughter at Falaise was being played out, Allied forces freed by the encirclement battle were ordered eastwards. The advance was at a cracking pace. On the morning of 24 August, the 2nd French Armoured Division entered Paris. The US 4th Infantry Division headed for the east of the city. Though there was fighting and the Grand Palais burned, many of the occupation force had already fled, and the Resistance were out on the streets. France began to experience what one historian has called the 'delirium of liberation'; as Eisenhower would later remark, 'even doubters began to see the end of Hitler'.[15] Field Marshal Montgomery has been criticized for many things: hubris and plain speaking to the extent of rudeness being only two of the most

JERRICAN
BOOBY-TRAPPED TO 'S'MINE.

obvious. However, the idea that the campaign in France in 1944, for which he was largely responsible, was somehow a failure because timetables or 'phase lines' created during planning were not strictly adhered to is pure nonsense. The ultimate objective was to be within striking distance of Paris in about 90 days. In fact, most of France was liberated with the Americans reaching Verdun by the end of August, and the British in Brussels, deep in Belgium, on 3 September. The road to victory was seemingly clear. But it is an old military maxim that no scheme long survives contact with the enemy, and as many a soldier on the ground had already discovered, the Germans were not about to let any plans run smoothly.

ARNHEM AND THE SIEGFRIED LINE

17 SEPTEMBER – 15 DECEMBER 1944

> " The German gunners were operating their ack ack guns and firing in front of us. Then, shortly afterwards, a cry went up from the back of the glider, "The tail's coming off!". "
>
> Johnny Peters, Border Regiment

OPERATION *MARKET GARDEN*

Amazingly the victorious liberation of Paris and the debacle at Arnhem in the Netherlands were separated by approximately three weeks. The same confidence that the enemy, if kept off balance after the campaign for France, might be beaten, that would inspire American forces to rush against the Siegfried Line, also contributed to a yet more daring plan championed by Montgomery. For while Eisenhower's general inclination was for a multi-pronged advance into Germany, effectively precluding the gathering of significant enemy forces in any one area, but he was soon persuaded that in the northern sector a rapier-like 'single thrust' should be attempted through Holland. Such a bold move, capturing vital river crossings, would effectively outflank the Siegfried Line, bringing the heart of Germany, and the end of hostilities, within reach. It might also trap enemy forces still in the Western Netherlands. With hindsight the idea may seem audacious to the point of folly, but at the time it appeared perfectly plausible. British forces had just advanced from the Somme to Brussels, a distance of 120 miles, with total success and scant regard for any flanks, and in the United Kingdom an under-employed Allied airborne force of more than three divisions was ready and champing at the bit following a succession of cancelled operations. The main reason for these aborted assaults was not any great reverse, but the simple fact that events were unfolding so fast during August 1944 that ground advances were overtaking preparations for the dropping of paratroops. As Major Tony Deane-Drummond of British 1st Airborne summed it up, 'Everybody in the Division wanted to get on with the operation after all the cancelled ones. There was no doubt that risks were taken by everybody with eyes wide open. The feeling was we had to get there before the German Army packed up.'[1] So was born Operation *Market Garden*.

Building on groundwork laid for cancelled assaults, plans for the largest airborne operation of the war were drawn up extremely quickly. Under the 'Market' part of the scheme a series of obstacles would be taken from the air over a period of three days: behind the existing enemy front the US 101st Airborne was to seize the canal and stream crossings at Eindhoven, Zon and Veghel. Further into enemy territory the US 82nd Airborne would hit the bridges over the Maas at Grave, and over the Waal at Nijmegen; while, far behind the German frontline the British,

PREVIOUS SPREAD

The destruction caused by a German flying bomb, the famous V-2. (Jeremy Llewellyn-Jones)

Allied armour passing German prisoners on the road to Brussels. The Cromwell, or Crusier Mark V, left, was powered by a Meteor engine, a conversion of the Rolls-Royce Merlin aero-engine, and armed with a 75mm gun. The most numerous of the Cruiser types of World War II, it formed, together with M4 Shermans, the bulk of the British armoured divisions in 1944–45. On the right is the American-made light tank known as the 'Stuart'. Based on a design dating back to 1941 it remained a swift and handy runaround, but was sadly lacking in both armament and armour for post D-Day service. (Author's Collection)

reinforced by a Polish brigade, would take the ultimate target, the Lower Rhine crossing at Arnhem. The dashing Lieutenant General 'Boy' Browning was insistent that he should lead right from the front, being air landed with his headquarters close to the Americans. 'Market' was to be co-ordinated with 'Garden' on the ground, under the scheme for which the British XXX Corps under Lieutenant General Brian Horrocks would lead the charge in what Montgomery described as a 'rapid and violent' movement, through Eindhoven and Grave, and on to Arnhem. At the tip of the spear of the ground operation would be the Guards Armoured Division, followed by the 43rd and 50th Infantry Divisions and copious artillery that it was hoped could be pushed far forward enough to support the activities of the more lightly equipped airborne troops.

The initial assault

'Market' began on 17 September with 1,400 aircraft of the British 2nd Tactical Air Force and the US 8th and 9th Air Forces preparing the way with intense attacks on Flak batteries and other ground targets. The barracks at Arnhem were hit and set on fire by a Mosquito raid, and bombs fell on numerous points including the nearby towns of Wolfheze and Ede. The first wave of parachutes started to land at 12.40pm. For the enemy this was something totally unexpected. Indeed, some, looking up, saw the sky suddenly 'black with aircraft' and simply assumed that these were all bombers on their way to Germany. Others imagined some freak of weather, producing odd clouds, or even a snow storm. Yet as Leutnant Enthammer quickly realized, 'That cannot be. It never snows in September!'. Dropping in broad daylight, in good weather, had many advantages, but also carried with it fear that the enemy could see you equally as well. Some were fired upon, but nevertheless the majority of the troops arrived in one piece. With the 1st Parachute Brigade, the Brigade Major Tony Hibbert thought the whole air armada was 'extraordinary' as he looked backwards and forwards at his own column of aircraft almost 30 miles long – a 'beautiful sight in the blazing sun'. 'When we landed in Holland it was a perfect summer's day, so quiet we all felt that this could only be an exercise, and in fact of course we didn't run into the Germans for the first two hours... Certainly on the flight over, no-one was frightened. We landed with no opposition at all.' Of the gliders almost 90 percent landed undamaged.

Further back along what became known as the 'Airborne Corridor' many American paratroopers also had good landings. Losses were light, and everything was much clearer than in Normandy. Frank Gregg came down with the 101st, 'It was on a Sunday afternoon, about one o'clock, sun was shining, and I landed right on the drop zone, and it was filled with Holstein cows, milk cows. And they panicked of course when all these parachutes started coming down. And I'm thinking, "oh man, I'd hate to have to write home from hospital saying I was severely wounded by a big Holstein cow..."' Nevertheless things were soon looking up, 'The Dutch people came out carrying bundles of flowers. They passed out applejack to all of my troops. I'm trying to get the heck to our objective which was a railroad bridge. And anyway I finally got them separated from the cows and then the people, and then on the railroad and a short ways up to the bridge. It was real nice – I think all operations ought to be like this.'

However, the complacent impression of an exercise in the sunshine was not to last long. Indeed, German forces reacted remarkably swiftly. Near to the drop zone at Arnhem small units such as SS Training Battalion 16 and the tiny *Kampfgruppe* Weber – a scratch force of Luftwaffe signallers – did their best to engage the parachutists. In doing so they followed a standard doctrine of 'driving into the teeth' of an air landing, making the most of the time in which it took airborne forces to organize. Confused news reached Field Marshal Walter Model, commander of Army Group B, during the afternoon, and by chance he was already at Arnhem, close enough to the headquarters of General Wilhelm Bittrich, commander of II SS Panzer Corps, to join him immediately at Doetinchem. Bittrich had already alerted his Corps and it was now ordered that the already weakened 9th SS Panzer Division should immediately take on the British bridgehead north of the Lower Rhine, while the 10th was to take and occupy the Nijmegen bridge. In any event all efforts were directed at preventing a link up between the British airborne contingent and the remainder of the Allied forces. Indeed, something else that Allied planners had not taken full account of was that at least parts of the German major units were much closer to the *Schwerpunkt* (focal point) of the action at Arnhem than was the relief force.

In his position near Veghel Frank Gregg would experience what this meant as the day ended: '[At] midnight that night about a battalion of Germans came down the road and attacked my bridge… I lost a better part of a platoon one side and I had only three platoons anyway – so I am down now to two, and maybe a quarter, platoons. So I had to gather up what was left and pulled them back to the railroad embankment…' More worrying were other developments, for while the American paratroopers achieved much of what they set out to do on what they called 'Hell's Highway', not all the corridor crossings were secured. The canal bridge at Zon was blown in the faces of the 101st Airborne, and time was needed to establish a temporary replacement. Although the 82nd took the important bridges over the Maas and nearby canal, they had not yet secured the vital Nijmegen bridge. Instead, elements of the SS Panzer got there first. Moreover, plans of much of the operation were recovered from a crashed American Waco glider and relayed to German general Karl Student, commander of the 1st Paratrooper Army, before the end of that first day. Nor were there any easy alternatives: for like some accumulator on which the Allied armies were gambling, success of the whole depended

OPPOSITE
A fully equipped British paratrooper ready for the drop. When carrying a Bren gun or other heavy items along with full equipment, a valise or 'drop bag' was used. The parachutist jumped, then paid out the bag on a rope to dangle below. The bag hit the ground first, followed by the soldier, who did not therefore take the additional shock and strain of landing with the extra weight on his body. Unlike American paratroops the British carried no reserve 'chute. (Author's Collection)

on success of every part. The ground relief force timetables soon went out of the window, and just eight of the 64 miles to Arnhem were covered on the first day. Looking back Lieutenant General Horrocks saw the obstacles more clearly than he had done in September 1944: German defenders with the benefit of wooded and marshy terrain; a single good road and 20,000 vehicles to put down it; and a series of bridges, that – even if they were undamaged – offered a succession of time-consuming bottlenecks. What had been predicted as a straightforward advance was now stiffly contested. As delays mounted the situation became graver, and Horrocks became more aware of the disaster that threatened to overwhelm *Market Garden*:

> This was about the blackest moment of my life. I began to find it difficult to sleep. In fact I had to be very firm with myself in order to banish from my mind, during those midnight hours when everything seems at its worst, the picture of the airborne troops fighting their desperate battle on the other side of the river in front. I had had sufficient experience of war to know that any commander who finds it difficult to sleep will soon be unfit to be

responsible for other men's lives. And here I was going that way myself… But if we were slow then the fault was mine because I was the commander.[2]

The difficulties of the relief should not be underestimated. Surprisingly aggressive German forces succeeded in cutting the narrow artery more than once, and had to be cleared painfully from the path. Cecil Newton was with the 4th/7th Dragoon Guards. His tank suffered an electrical failure and had to pull off the road while the driver attempted to rectify the fault. During the halt he noticed his was not the only vehicle nearby: another crew was working, 'they were taking bodies out of a Sherman tank that had been hit, and they were taking the one corpse out absolutely black. It was just like charcoal, but it was in a sitting position and they were pulling it out the turret with ropes. And there was a neat hole on one side of the turret and the exit [hole] was splayed out like a tulip where it had gone out. That was pretty horrible actually to see…'

Not long after this incident his column was 'delayed a little bit' by a German flamethrower, and then an ambush, during which his tank had to be briefly abandoned due to danger from Panzerfaust teams lurking near to the road. Clearly it would be a long, hard struggle for XXX Corps throughout the course of the operation.

Patrick Delaforce was with the artillery element of the relief forces:

We were right flank protection in the ill-fated Operation *Market Garden*. Our centreline road was cut frequently by enemy columns and our guns often had to fire on a 360 degree basis – that is, in all directions. That was in mid September and I was by then a full Lieutenant, two pips, and became a 'Forward Observation Officer'. This meant working with tank or infantry regiments with their leading troops and bringing down our artillery fire on all kinds of targets – often in a Sherman tank, occasionally a Bren gun carrier, depending who I was protecting. I had many nasty little battles in Holland.

Jim Tuckwell with the 5th Dorsets, 43rd Division, put it all down to simple topography, 'It was then just a series of country roads. There was nowhere to go – the tank couldn't go off the road, because he'd sink. Holland was built on water … [and] they flooded the land.' Things would go yet further awry as the timetable for reinforcement from the air also began to falter. In the end Polish reinforcements were actually dropped two days late – and in a different location to that originally planned.

OPPOSITE
A British airborne officer takes aim with a .38 Enfield revolver through a window during Operation *Market Garden*, September 1944. As the manual *Fighting in Built Up Areas* observed, 'the pistol in practised hands is a useful weapon for very close quarter fighting, as when searching a house. In unskillful hands the weapon is more likely to disconcert, if not actually endanger, our own troops.' Revolvers were already old technology, but had the advantage of ruggedness, and continued to function even if one round misfired. (Author's Collection)

Map detailing the plan for Operation *Market Garden*. 'Market' involved the dropping of three airborne divisions along a corridor north of Eindhoven. The 101st US Airborne Division was required to secure the bridges from Eindhoven to Vegel while the US 82nd Airborne hoped to secure the bridges from Grave to Nijmegen and the Groesbeeck Heights. It fell to the British 1st Airborne to secure Arnhem itself and the high ground to the north. Simultaneously, 'Garden' required the British Second Army to drive northwards from the Meuse-Escaut Canal, on a very narrow front to link up with each of the airborne divisions in turn. Replacement air and ground forces would then be brought in. (© Osprey Publishing Ltd.)

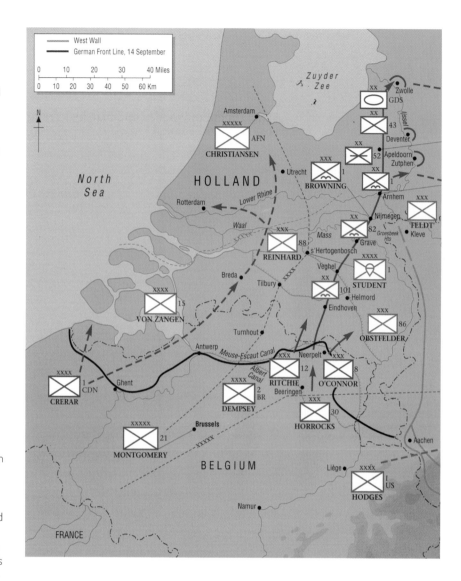

Capturing and holding Arnhem

Meanwhile the British Airborne contingent focused on taking and holding Arnhem and its vital bridge. This was no foregone conclusion since not only did small German units interpose themselves in defensive positions between the British and the bridge, but the landing of an entire division necessitated large open areas. No such places existed in the town itself so the main drop and glider landing zones were around the nearby towns of Heelsum and Wolfheze – well to the west. The paratroopers now advanced along three planned approaches code-named 'Lion', 'Tiger' and 'Leopard'. Though it is difficult to see how else 9,000 men

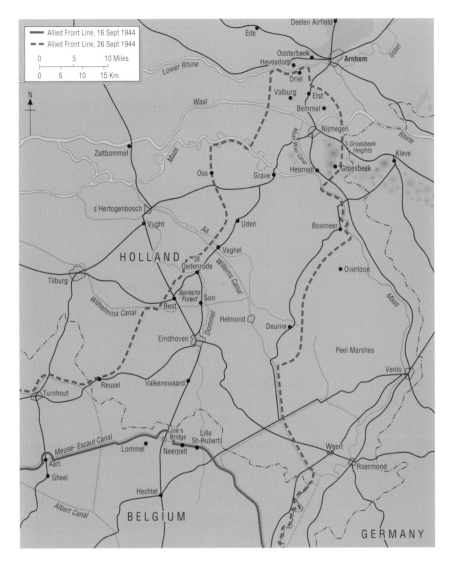

Allied Front Line, 16 Sept 1944
Allied Front Line, 26 Sept 1944

The narrow corridor of land that was secured by Operation *Market Garden* by 26 September 1944. (© Osprey Publishing Ltd.)

could have come down closer to the target, Tony Hibbert regards this as 'one of the first mistakes' of 'Boy' Browning, 'He dropped us 7 miles from the bridge and we were carrying about 80lbs of equipment and weapons, and you just can't run all the way!'. Of the parachute battalions only Lieutenant Colonel John Frost's 2nd made its way quickly around and through the opposition, although even they suffered losses en route. But they did also succeed in inflicting damage on the enemy.

By the time Allied airborne and German forces had converged the British would hold the bridge and part of the town, albeit with a relatively small force, as well as a larger perimeter to the west, including Oosterbeek and most of the original landing grounds. Bill Bloys was amongst the first up onto the bridge when it was raked with enemy machine-gun fire, '... it was coming back off the bridge. You couldn't move. The first four men I think were killed. And quite a few wounded...' The enemy now held the ground between and around the main British perimeters, and much would depend on who could be reinforced first, and in what strength. For much of the time the 'fog of war' now descended over proceedings as the paratroopers' radio communications were poor, and several senior officers were quickly wounded.

On the second day of the battle the bridge defenders were attacked by armoured troops from more than one direction. Before 10.00am the reconnaissance battalion of the 9th SS Panzer made an impetuous charge led by its flamboyant commander Haputsturmführer Viktor Graebner, in an attempt to cross the bridge. He imagined that 22 assorted vehicles, led by armoured cars, would simply overwhelm the defenders who were obviously short of heavy weapons. He was wrong. The paratroopers were able to focus their fire from covered positions at close range. Machine guns, grenades, rifles, PIATS and 6-pdr guns were all effective enough, especially when weapons could be directed from vantage points against open topped carriers. Confusion reigned as one of the German drivers, realizing the impossibility of getting through, jammed his vehicle into reverse and careened into another. Graebner and many of his men were killed, with more than half of the vehicles lost.

The same afternoon the enemy had slightly more success against the western perimeter. Here Johnny Peters, a sniper of the Border Regiment's contingent of glider troops, found himself defending the brick works at Renkum, complete with its chimneys, heaps of clay and wagons for moving stock:

We could hear the barbed wire creaking. Sergeant Tommy Watson was wounded in the head – he fired a Very light, and there were several Germans in that field. So we opened fire on them and then it all went quiet. Sergeant Watson said to me and Eric Borders. 'Get out that trench! Get behind the bogie wheels.' We couldn't dig in. We hadn't got time then. So we stood to during the night. This chappie kept shouting 'Wounded soldier! Wounded soldier!' And Sergeant Watson said, 'If you're wounded get back on the road.' But he kept on, and Sergeant Watson said don't go near him because it might be a ruse and he'll grab hold of you as a prisoner. Anyway he kept on. I think in the end Sergeant Watson had had enough: he got a Sten gun and just shot him. He had no option. In the morning, we looked. We knew this man must have been there somewhere – and he was about 6ft away from the trench we'd vacated. So that was a bit of luck.

But then later on a patrol of Germans came along right in our front, with an officer with about 20 or 30 soldiers, and he was pointing in our direction. Now whether he didn't know we were there, or he was saying we were there, we're not sure. But we opened fire on them and they were just like sitting ducks you know. We killed several of them then. But then the remainder went into the houses opposite and started smashing the windows. We could hear the glass breaking, so [we] fired in there. One chap I could see with [a] machine gun – Sergeant Watson said, 'Get that man!' So I was lucky, I shot him. But then the Germans kept firing from these houses … all day long. And being behind these bogies is like being in a cowboy film. They were ricocheting off – 'pew pew' – it wasn't frightening but it was comical at the time. But anyhow we kept firing at these soldiers. And in the end about 12 o'clock we hadn't run out of ammunition but we were getting low. But the word came round from Major Armstrong that we were surrounded there, and no communication to the rest of the battalion. So then they had to get us out. But we left the rear party behind with a machine gun.

The British had managed to land at Arnhem with 6- and 17-pdr anti-tank guns, 75mm guns, PIATs, mortars and anti-tank grenades. Critically, however, they lacked anything with both firepower and battlefield mobility, and it became increasingly clear that unless resupply was assured ammunition would surely run out. In extremis Ernie Treacher discovered that the light 2in parachutists' platoon mortar could also be turned into a close-range direct-fire weapon, 'One had to cant the thing right over and preferably wedge it against a wall. This was a hair-raising performance to say the least, particularly if the enemy actually saw you.'[3] Nevertheless virtually anything that could be flung at the opposition was tried given the highly unequal balance in heavy weapons. On the second and third days the remainder of the Airborne division continued the struggle to reach Frost's men at the bridge. Gradually, however, the strength of these nine battalions was ground down. So it was that the British could now do little but defend their hard won positions, at Oosterbeek and the bridge, and trust that relief would soon arrive.

A 19-year-old mortar crewman Private James Sims was amongst the paratroopers still holding the bridge perimeter. It turned out he was one of the lucky ones:

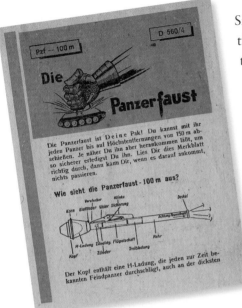

It seemed impossible that the shelling and mortaring could get any worse, but they did. The separate explosions now merged into one almost continuous rolling detonation and the earth shook as though it was alive. My head sang and I was numb to any feeling beyond the basic instinct to survive. I began to realize the full significance of the phrase 'bomb happy'. Yet even in this terrific concentration of fire not one bomb or shell splinter landed in a slit trench or mortar pit: it was unbelievable, little short of miraculous. It is only when one has been through this sort of experience that one can understand how soldiers in the past stood in lines and fired by numbers. With each successive salvo of mortar bombs I screwed my steel helmet further into the comforting earth and clawed at the silty soil at the bottom of the trench... To be alone at the bottom of that trench was like lying in a newly dug grave and waiting to be buried alive.[4]

Arguably the cruellest moment during the battle was when armour was finally heard approaching Arnhem. As Major Hibbert remembered, 'We thought that the tanks were in fact our own tanks coming from the south, the ones that were actually going to relieve us. We were quite extraordinary; as I say we had about 160 people on the bridge and they all took off their helmets and put their berets on and came out to cheer them forward. And of course it was not until they reached up to the top of the bridge that we saw they'd got the wrong insignia on. So they all had to dash back...'

Something unusual about the fight at Arnhem was the continued presence of civilians through much of the battle. Some young Dutch lads volunteered to act as guides or runners for the British, but many inhabitants were simply trapped with nowhere to go when the action started. Bill Bloys relates a moment of comic opera in which the caretaker of one house refused to let him in until it was explained that the paratroopers would be forced to 'blow their way in' if he was not so kind as to open the door. The man relented. Hibbert actually recalled being greeted by Dutch people weeping with joy as the liberators marched in. Later many hid in cellars or behind furniture, and as time passed the mood became grimmer by the hour. More than 450 were killed, others simply broke down. Hibbert was surprised by the appearance of one of them:

> Out of the door came a Dutch woman – really properly dressed with her hat on and so forth – pushing a pram. And she went out and shut the door behind her I could see a child in the back. And with lumps of masonry flying in all directions all around her – she was screaming… I could see her face well and she'd obviously lost her head, and I saw her push the pram out into the middle of the road. At that moment one of our sergeants rushed out of the house and pulled her back. Just one of the things that stick in my memory.

As the enemy closed in Arnhem became a street battle. Houses cheek by jowl offered cover, but meant that uncomfortably close combat was constant. Grenades and submachine guns were at a premium. Also, as Hibbert recalled, 'there was a great deal of hand-to-hand fighting – a great deal of bayonet work. The corporal ordered 'fix bayonets' – and then the Germans ran.' Often such claustrophobic fights were contested one building at a time. As former London butcher Bill Higgs put it, 'When we were in a house … the Jerries started firing at us of course, so we ran out and got into the next one – and they followed up, and let us have it in that one. Well, they had these tank blasters – they blew the fronts of houses right out and they knocked them down one at a time. As we were getting out they were following and letting us have it.'

Private Jack Webb of the 2nd Parachute Battalion described some of the last desperate fighting nearby:

> After we had killed a few Germans near the bridge, well about six, we withdrew and got tangled up in some more house-to-house fighting… Thomson, Woods and myself lost touch with Croucher and Wainwright, and in fact we had lost touch with the rest of the platoon. We got into a house and went about two floors up. The shooting went on and the house we were in had caught fire, again! We became trapped because of the fire and could not

OPPOSITE
Instruction leaflet for the Panzerfaust, or, literally 'tank fist'. The Panzerfaust was a German anti-tank weapon with which armour could be engaged at up to 150m. With distribution down to small unit level, any close country or town became a death trap for tanks unless they were closely protected by their own infantry. Production began as early as the autumn of 1943, and according to Albert Speer's memoirs, 997,000 were made in November 1944, 1,253,000 in December and 1,200,000 in January 1945. (Author's Collection)

British airborne troops defend a weapons pit at Oosterbeek with a Bren gunner to the left and riflemen armed with the No. 4 rifle to the right. (Author's Collection)

get out of the house by using the stairs. As the house then started to blaze Sergeant Thomson decided that we had to jump out of the window. There was no other option anyway. We jumped out of a window and the sergeant and Tommy landed OK. I landed on some bricks and broke my leg. Thomson came up to me and said I would have to stay where I was while he and Woods would see what they could do. Unfortunately, as they tried to move away they were both shot and killed about five yards from me. Then two armed Germans came up to me and were going to shoot me. I pointed to my leg and said 'Kaputt'. Then they put me on a door and took me to their HQ.[5]

Lieutenant Colonel Frost was wounded after four days of fighting at the bridge, having just received news that relief was now unlikely. Parts of the town were on fire, for as Hibbert relates, the enemy were using a brutally effective tactic. A high explosive shell was fired first to break open a building. This was followed by a smoke round, the phosphorus content of which ignited anything flammable inside. In retrospect he described the desolate final scene as 'very beautiful, but distressing – and rather depressing'. Near the end a white flag was produced and German prisoners sent back to their own lines under it with a request for a two-hour cease fire to evacuate the wounded. At about the same time a decision was made that the last of the able-bodied defenders should dissolve into small groups and slip away. As Hibbert relates, 'We decided that, as we could no longer see the bridge, and had virtually no ammunition, we could be of most use if we could get back to the divisional perimeter and get some more ammunition. So we split up into sections of ten men, each under the command of an officer, to try to slip through enemy lines.'

At Oosterbeek, about two and a half miles west of Arnhem itself, Major-General Roy Urquhart continued the defence, and remarkably, at this eleventh hour, artillery from the relief force was able to open fire. More than 3,500 men kept fighting. One of them was Johnny Peters, now tired and hungry amongst the defenders of the high ground at Westerbouwing, on a perimeter that gradually shrank in around the central position of the Hartenstein hotel. Gradually casualties mounted, and Peters still vividly remembers the shock of seeing men he knew struck down by enemy shelling, and now lying in a trench, faces covered by their smocks. On the night of Monday 25 September, with Oosterbeek under armoured attack, the decision was taken to attempt evacuation of the defenders of the last bastion back across the river. This was officially known as Operation *Berlin* – but many just hoped for the

A Sherman Firefly of the Irish Guards leads a column of tanks traversing the bridge at Nijmegen. The Arnhem campaign was not just an attempt to take and hold one bridge but a series of crossings. (Courtesy of the Tank Museum, Bovington)

The Tiger Tank

Following previous experimentation with heavy tanks and experience in Russia the new Panzer VI Tiger was first demonstrated to Hitler on 20 April 1942 – his 53rd birthday. At the time of its introduction, it was the thickest armoured tank, with the most powerful gun, that the world had ever seen. What the Henschel designers had come up with was essentially a massively armoured box, with rolled homogenous nickel steel plate 102mm thick at the front – twice the protection on the bow of the Sherman. Its main armament was the 8.8cm L/56 gun, a version of the 88mm Flak gun. Its 56 ton squat bulk was just over 3m high and nearly 4m wide. Early British reports suggested that the frontal armour of the Tiger was impervious to 6-pdr guns. PIAT weapons were only considered effective if aimed at the 'side and rear of the turret' and 'upper side plate'. The reputation of the Panzer VI was such that many Allied troops were apt to call any unidentified German tanks 'Tigers'.

Artwork showing the side view of the Tiger, showing the sheer scale of the 88mm gun, solid box-like hull and overlapping bogie wheels. In addition to the main armament, the Tiger was mounted with two machine guns, one co-axial to the main armament and a second in the bow. Also visible here are smoke generators on the side of the turret – these were removed from later production. Powered by a Maybach petrol engine, the Tiger was capable of 25mph on roads and had a range of about 120 miles. Narrower tracks could be fitted for rail transport. The Tiger was hardly agile, but its armour and armament suited the defensive missions required of it in the North-West Europe campaign. (© Osprey Publishing Ltd.)

ABOVE For the making of
the documentary a tank mock-up was well
and truly 'knocked out' to demonstrate the sort of impact
created by a Firefly 17-pdr anti-tank round. Confined spaces and stowed
ammunition quickly turns 'Armoured Fighting Vehicle' into 'iron coffin'. The
Firefly was the only Allied tank able to match the Tiger in terms of
firepower. (Jeremy Llewellyn-Jones)

A Tiger I undergoes trials before senior officers: note how the turret has been rotated to the rear to avoid snagging the barrel while negotiating steep slopes. (Author's Collection)

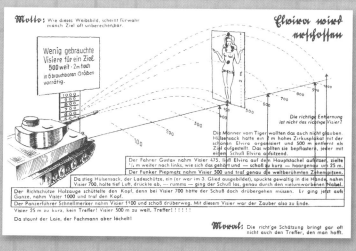

The German *Tigerfibel* cartoon style instruction manual, for platoon commanders and 'Tiger people', produced in August 1943. Many of the pages were made more interesting by the inclusion of suggestive sketches of pretty girls, or other quirky cartoons. Warnings on the dangers of fire, notes on the appearance of enemy vehicles, maintenance data, fuel capacity, track tension and many other subjects were imparted painlessly and succinctly. (Author's Collection)

German tank ace Otto Carius, pictured in his white summer uniform and decorations including the *Ritterkreutz*, or 'Knight's Cross'. Serving in the 21st Panzer Regiment, heavy tank detachment 502 and tank destroyer detachment 512, Carius fought in various types of tank including the Tiger and was ultimately credited with the destruction of 150 Allied tanks on both Eastern and Western fronts. His highest decoration, the Oak Leaves to his Knights Cross, was awarded on 27 July 1944. (Author's Collection)

best, slipped into the water, and swam. For Peters it was 'the worst night of my life', the stuff of nightmares, but in some ways he was lucky, being put in a boat with the wounded to help paddle them out. On arrival he was dished out stew; 'horrible', but he was so famished that he no longer cared. Not long afterwards he was photographed for the press, something for which he quickly remembered to put his helmet on – so as to appear properly dressed. Seemingly such niceties were still preserved to create the correct impression.

For Major Hibbert and a few others the struggle was not quite over. For some time he secreted himself in the ruins of Arnhem, under the coal in a shed amongst the burnt buildings and in the company of war correspondent Tony Cotterel. It was a good hiding place, but after a while he felt 'like a baked potato' due to the heat. It looked as though they had got away with it, but eventually the besmutted Brigade Major and his companion had 'the indignity' of being hauled – filthy – from their concealment. His captors loaded Hibbert and many of his companions onto the backs of lorries, standing room only, and drove off at speed. They were warned that at first sign of trouble the guards would shoot: nevertheless as the vehicle slowed Hibbert and another officer leapt out. A German corporal opened fire with a machine pistol and four British soldiers were killed, two mortally wounded. From this lorry only Tony Hibbert made good his escape, eventually all the way back to American lines. It was a performance to rival that of Tony Deane-Drummond who hid in a cupboard for 13 days, then spirited away. By strange coincidence Hibbert and Deane-Drummond had been at both Marlborough School and the Royal Military Academy at Woolwich, and both are still alive 67 years later. Yet for Deane-Drummond all this was nothing new: remarkably it was his third escape during the course of the war.

Operation *Market Garden* retains a big and controversial reputation in the annals of military history. Yet in the grand scheme of things it was not a massive engagement. The British Airborne suffered about 1,500 fatalities out of approximately 3,700 of all nationalities who were killed. However, when one considers the wounded and many captured, it would be fair to say that virtually an entire British division had been sacrificed.

Indeed, only about one man in three escaped. Understandably several of the Arnhem veterans retain a sense of this battle as almost uniquely in vain. Bill Bloys feels that the whole thing should never have taken place, but the real 'shame' was to have let down the Dutch. Tony Hibbert likewise views it as a 'grave failure' and 'unnecessary disaster'. Nevertheless, there was nothing the ordinary Allied fighting soldier could have done to change the outcome of the battle. Moreover, at other times and in other places the gamble that was Arnhem might have worked. At the time and on paper it seemed all too probable that so hard on the heels of the defeat of the German Army in France this unexpected – indeed for Montgomery uncharacteristically bold – onslaught from the air could have punched a deep hole through the occupied Netherlands. Yet in Field Marshal Model the Allies had come up against the wrong man – Hitler's 'fireman of the Eastern Front' – whose stock in trade had become the parrying of offensives with mobile forces. Very painfully Arnhem also illuminated the fact that the enemy still had some reserves, and more importantly, the will to fight.

INTO THE SIEGFRIED LINE

Strangely, in 1944, the famous 'Siegfried Line' existed only in the imagination of the Allied soldier and the words of a popular song. For the original *Siegfried Stellung* had actually been a part of the trench lines of the Western Front to which the Kaiser's armies of World War I had retreated early in 1917. Yet the name had a great, not to say Wagnerian, resonance – and so for GI, Canuck and Tommy, the Western defence lines of Germany would forever remain the 'Siegfried Line'. To those who manned this defence zone however it was simply the *West – Stellung*, or 'West Position'. Interestingly most of the 'west position' was not new in 1944, but a revitalized and expanded version of the works created here as a bulwark against France, *Der Westwall* – or the 'West Wall'.

The West Wall
The first phase of work began as early as 1936. Slow but steady progress continued until 1938 when Hitler, facing the likelihood that his increasingly menacing strong-arm diplomacy would lead to war, had

ordered that the process be speeded up. The relatively thin line of bunkers facing the much more impressive French Maginot Line was thickened, and German works were extended north along the border with Belgium. In many places lacking natural tank obstacles concrete 'dragon's teeth' anti-tank obstacles, or *Höckerhindernisse*, sprang up. Directives of May 1938 included plans for almost 12,000 bunkers and pillboxes to be completed by October. The so-called *Limesprogramm*, named after the ancient Roman works of the German frontier, also contained provision for an 'air defence zone' behind the ground works under the purview of Luftwaffe Commander-in-Chief Hermann Göring, who was also given a mandate to report on progress of the works in general. Perhaps predictably Göring painted a highly unflattering picture of the efforts of the army, and responsibility for construction then passed to Dr Fritz Todt, and his new Party-sponsored Organization Todt. By August 1938 approximately 200,000 civilian and military workers were toiling on the West Wall, with a hundred trains of construction materials arriving every day, and 8,800 lorries distributing the loads to the building sites. Work continued throughout 1939, the outbreak of war, and on into a fifth construction phase in the spring of 1940, further extending the line northward to the point where the Rhine crossed the German frontier into the Netherlands. According to an American assessment the works as finally completed extended for 350 miles encompassing 22,000

RIGHT
Der Westwall, from an illustration in a German propaganda pamphlet of 1940. Described as 'impenetrable', it was a 'work of peace' ordered by the Führer to prevent incursions from the West, successfully resisting and 'bloodying' British and French troops trying their hand against it. (Author's Collection)

LEFT
Der Westwall, a booklet by Captain Rudolf Theodor Küne of 1939 telling the reassuring story of the 'unconquerable defence zone of concrete and steel on Germany's western border'. (Author's Collection)

separate works in a series of belts with a density of as much as one bunker or turret for every 55 yards of front.

Whether the original West Wall fully achieved its objectives is open to some question, and certainly some senior German officers expressed doubts as to its usefulness. General Siegfried Westphal, for example, later wrote in his memoirs that it was by no means impenetrable:

> The majority of the concrete emplacements had concrete roofs [of] only 80 centimetres thickness which afforded no protection against heavy shells. Many of the positions had loopholes only at the front and were thus at a tactical disadvantage... Because of the short time available it had been impossible to fit the emplacements into the terrain as well as the tacticians had desired. Many of them lay not on the more favourable rear slopes but on the front slopes of the hills. Anti-tank obstacles were only present in comparatively few places. One particularly worrying feature was that some of the emplacements possessed no loopholes at all and could therefore only be used as shelters.[6]

Hitler himself had reservations about how well the West Wall might hold up in the event of concerted action by France and Britain. Nevertheless it did have a deterrent effect while much of the German Army was occupied with subjugation of Poland in the autumn of 1939, and was certainly of great propaganda value. The much trumpeted construction programmes were heeded in the West, and the French High Command did indeed conclude that the existence of fortifications on the German frontier made a military stalemate probable if it was to contemplate serious offensive action of its own.

After the fall of France in 1940 the West Wall slumbered. Focus shifted to the Channel and Atlantic coasts, most weapons were removed, some of the more significant impediments to east–west traffic were cleared, and garrisons reduced to skeleton maintenance crews. The invasion of Europe in 1944 therefore came as the rudest of wake-up calls. In late August Hitler first issued a new directive for the reuse or destruction of parts of the old French Maginot Line, followed on 1 September by the important 'Directive 63', in which he ordered the 'placing of the West Wall in a state of defence', specifically charging Gauleiters with the procurement of labour in their areas. The Home Army rapidly commenced construction of new field works. These included so-called 'Koch' bunkers, which were little more than buried concrete tubes, integrated into trench systems, 'Tobruk Turrets', comprising sunken concrete fox holes often mounted with a machine gun, and tank turrets mounted atop bunkers. With the first Allied border crossings into Germany morale stiffening propaganda reached a new tone of desperate seriousness:

> In the West, the fighting has advanced onto German soil along broad sectors. German cities and villages are becoming part of the combat zone. This fact must make us fight with fanatical determination and put up stiff resistance with every able bodied man in the combat zone. Each pillbox, every city and village block must become a fortress against which the enemy will smash himself to bits or in which the German garrison will die in hand to hand fighting. There can be no large scale operations on our part any longer. All we can do is hold our positions or die.

Such exhortations came none too soon as the Allied assessment was that the disruption caused by the retreat across France, and paucity of German reserves, made it unlikely that the enemy would be able to put more than 20 divisions to the defence of the Western Front in the immediate future. On 6 September Eisenhower's HQ therefore concluded that, 'The enemy is not at present able to defend either the Siegfried Line or the Rhine adequately, in spite of the apparent strength of the former, the natural obstacle of the Rhine will probably offer greater difficulties to our advance. Speed is essential, as the enemy has the capability of withdrawing from other fronts or forming further forces to oppose us. We should advance on a wide front, extending and breaking through rapidly wherever he is weakest.'[7] Characteristically General Patton's encouragement to his men was that the war to date, be it against the Maginot Line or the Atlantic Wall, proved only the 'utter futility of fixed defences' – the only sure defence being offence. So commenced the race to, and hopefully through, the German defences. The spearhead would be elements of the American Army, General Leonard Gerow's V Corps headed towards the Eifel, and General Joseph Lawton Collins' VII Corps to the south of Aachen. But nothing would be as easy as it looked and armies that had travelled one or two hundred miles in the last month, now slowed to a snail's pace. As an American official post-war report put it, 'the Allied drive lost impetus with [the] reaching of the Siegfried Line in the north and the Moselle river in the south'. What this meant from the soldier's eye view was far more traumatic than such a bland statement might suggest.

The difficult road ahead

How a fortified position should be overcome was laid down in January 1944, in the American Field Manual 31-50, *Attack on a Fortified Position and Combat in Towns*. Ideally there were four phases: reducing the enemy outposts; breaking through at the most favourable point; extending the gap by isolating and reducing the emplacements on its flanks; and finally, 'completing the action by moving mobile reserves through the gap' and encircling the enemy. Smoke, night operations, direct fire against fortifications, bombing of lines of communications and the use of special assault squads was recommended. The employment of armour in the 'early stages' was specifically discouraged. What happened in reality could differ for a number of reasons including perceived need for speed, logistic problems in bringing up supplies quickly enough in the wake of the chase across France and the continued absence of major port facilities close to the front. Sometimes the 'wing and a prayer' method worked when it was discovered that the enemy position was not even manned, or defenders simply surrendered when they discovered they were outnumbered. However, fighting over the border fortifications would continue intermittently for months.

With the 94th Infantry Division, Clayton Byrd was witness to a couple of the more lucky outcomes:

> … what you wanted to do was to find some way to get firepower through that slot that they used for shooting … if there was just one pillbox you could do that reasonably well; but when there are multiple pillboxes and one supporting the other, they have ranges of crossfire which makes it extremely difficult. But we found various tactics to do it… Our company was given the assignment one day to take out four specific pillboxes. We approached the pillboxes and there was a white flag hanging out. We went up to the pillbox. They held their fire, and we had conversation with the ranking non-commissioned officer in that pillbox … he said he wanted to go out with his head held high, or in effect words like that. He says if you will put on a display of force, big force, I will surrender the people in this pillbox.

A Panther ausf D at the Wilhelminapark, Breda. Altogether, 842 of the 'ausf D' model of Panther tanks were made from January to September 1943, against a total Panther production figure of approximately 6,000. Even before the war it had been realized that sooner or later the main workhorses of the armoured divisions, the Panzer Mark III and IV, would need replacing – but it was events on the Eastern Front that hurried this remarkable new design into production. (Author's Collection)

The Americans were more than happy to oblige, and let rip with some hundreds of rounds, many of them harmlessly into the air. Not only did the first pillbox then give up, but so did two of the others. The final position, now isolated, capitulated the following morning. Dozens of enemy soldiers were taken prisoner without loss: as Byrd put it, 'we were very fortunate. And we liked it.'

Seymour Rosen, another American infantryman, helped to forge a path through the obstacle zone, and where he was the Germans were far less co-operative, 'Our job was to get through the "dragon's teeth", and the engineers to blast the dragons teeth, so that our tanks could get in and give us support… It took us almost two days to get through the dragon's teeth. They were embedded into the soil, about 4ft high, and staggered so that the tanks couldn't get over them, and without tank support you couldn't get very far…'

Often it seemed that every new tactic, would, in time, be met with a counter-measure. In particular, once the Germans became familiar with Allied bunker clearing methods, they began to pre-register their own positions with artillery, then give up the pillboxes and retire as soon as the American troops closed in. They could then hit the spot with everything they had – a truly unnerving experience. As Rosen remembered:

We managed the fear. It's always there, and you begin to assign levels of fear. For example, in the infantry, small-arms fire wasn't really anything to worry about, but what you worried about were artillery and mortars. The Germans were very effective mortar people and their 88 artillery piece was a particularly deadly weapon … what they used against us was air bursts where the fuse was set on the shell to burst about 50ft in the air and shower down shrapnel. So even if you dug a foxhole that shrapnel would just come down like rain on you.

Another serious issue was that even if concrete was fallible, its combination with minefields created a new problem. This required a judicious approach, as was explained by engineer officer Frank Camm:

The first thing we would do is try to determine whether or not there is enemy fire covering it … so that if when we went out there to try and remove the mines they would shoot at us. We had to get them stopped. Once we were sure … and if the mines were on top of the ground and we had time we would put a rope on them, each mine, and back off about 50 yards and pull the mine so to [discover] whether or not it had a booby trap connected with it. And in more than 90 percent of the cases it did not. Now if we were under enemy fire we didn't take time to do that, we'd just go out there and take it out and take the chance on it exploding and we never had one explode on

British infantry double forward near Ulzen. A Bren gunner is closest to the camera, while further up the column are a PIAT-armed soldier and riflemen. (Author's Collection)

us. So that's how we would remove anti-tank mines. Or if they were underground and we didn't know where they were, we'd have a mine detector sweeping – electronic – that could send down signals and bounce back and you could tell if there's metal down there.

Such indeed was the theory, but there were also new classes of German mine, particularly anti-personnel types introduced since 1939, that used very little metal in their construction, and were therefore very difficult to locate until it was too late. Such tricky devices included the 43-type *Glas* mine, and the wooden *Schü* mine. While many Allied soldiers tended to assume that this was something to do with 'shoes', and the very real danger of losing a foot, the name was actually a contraction of the German for 'defensive' or 'protection'.

Much slowed, but undaunted, the American armies ground their way into the 'West Position' as the autumn progressed. General William Simpson's Ninth went in to the north of Aachen, the First under General Courtney Hodges to the south. From Trier down towards the Swiss border Patton's Third and General Alexander Patch's Seventh had first to fight their way through Alsace and Lorraine before they could reach the Moselle or the old German frontier. Patton endured particularly

A British infantryman advances with the PIAT. Approved in August 1942 and weighing 32lb the PIAT was cumbersome to load and not as effective as the new generation of German rocket anti-tank arms. Nevertheless it did score successes and also proved useful against fortifications. (Author's Collection)

heavy losses attempting to batter his way into Metz, in heavy rain, concluding in private that it would be better if the Germans kept the place. Clearly the enemy were masters of defence, as Captain William Dupuy then with 357th Infantry, and post-war battle analyst, remarked, 'They took pieces of terrain and knitted them together into positions from which they were able to fire in all directions... They used cover and concealment and they used imagination... A handful of Germans could hold up a regiment if they sited their weapons properly.'[8]

Nevertheless Aachen, the first German city, fell following encirclement and street fighting in mid October. There were also odd moments of levity when GIs entered the Reich, as Arnold Whittaker of the 10th Infantry related:

He [a fellow GI] found a four gallon bottle with wicker handles on it – of Cognac – and we were on the back of this Sherman tank and every time that we stopped the tank for a 'mother nature call', the word got out the guys at 3rd Squad, and K Company, had some Cognac. So they all run up there with their canteen cup. Well some of the tankers decided to have some, and I think God said, 'These guys been through enough, let's give them a few laughs'... [But] you couldn't take a chance of getting too much and falling off the back of tank with another 32-ton Sherman following you. You know what a 32-ton tank does to a body? Just flattens it all. So we didn't overdo it. But we're all laughing and everything like that and what happens when ahead along the side of the road was a German car, a civilian car ... it had run out of gas. So one of the head tank guys said, 'Let's give it the Sherman test and see what 32 tons will do to the running board on the left side of the car?'... Well he did that and of course that 32 tons did a good job of it and then the next tanker said to himself, 'That cotton picker, I'm not gonna let him over do it – I'll go a little higher.' So as a result after about the tenth Sherman that Volkswagen was flatter than a pancake. And of course, the more we went, the more we laughed, we thought that was great ... it seemed like anyway every ten miles there would be another abandoned car and we would give that the Sherman test and flatten them out.

Fighting in and around the Siegfried Line would ultimately continue well into 1945, particularly in the south where the 'Colmar Pocket' had first to be overcome. In the centre, at Utweiler, just inside the German border, the 3rd Infantry Division suffered a minor disaster while forcing a breach.

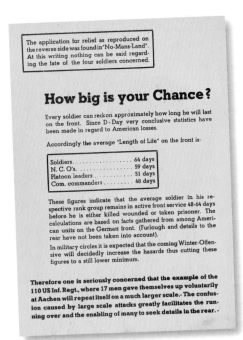

The application for relief as reproduced on the reverse side was found in "No-Mans-Land". At this writing nothing can be said regarding the fate of the four soldiers concerned.

How big is your Chance?

Every soldier can reckon approximately how long he will last on the front. Since D-Day very conclusive statistics have been made in regard to American losses.

Accordingly the average "Length of Life" on the front is:

Soldiers	64 days
N. C. O's	59 days
Platoon leaders	51 days
Com. commanders	48 days

These figures indicate that the average soldier in his respective rank group remains in active front service 48-64 days before he is either killed wounded or taken prisoner. The calculations are based on facts gathered from among American units on the German front. (Furlough and details to the rear have not been taken into account).

In military circles it is expected that the coming Winter-Offensive will decidedly increase the hazards thus cutting these figures to a still lower minimum.

Therefore one is seriously concerned that the example of the 110 US Inf. Regt., where 17 men gave themselves up voluntarily at Aachen will repeat itself on a much larger scale.- The confusion caused by large scale attacks greatly facilitates the running over and the enabling of many to seek details in the rear.-

Attacking on 15 March, the 2nd Battalion of the 7th Infantry and supporting units were quickly counter-attacked by the enemy. Five American tanks were knocked out as they drove over mines, and the infantry were held up by 'thickly sown' *Schü* mines. As Lieutenant Ananich, one of the survivors reported, 'The Krauts rolled six of their tanks on to the high ground north of the town. They had us caught, and caught bad. We only had the weapons infantrymen carry. One of the German tanks worked its way down into the town and the others followed and started knocking down buildings with direct fire. Some of our men were buried alive in those buildings.'[9] As Lieutenant Russ Cloer recalled the problem was that in attacking through minefields and against pillboxes infantry and engineers needed to go first. When tanks appeared the exposed infantry were at their mercy. As a result, the 2nd Battalion of the 7th was cut off and suffered major casualties. Seymour Rosen was amongst the confusion: 'We lost our tank support, the tanks wouldn't come in – the engineers wouldn't go to clear the minefield – our battalion commander hid in a pond'. But gradually, mile by mile, the German resistance was forced to retreat.

The battle of the Scheldt

Although the fighting at Arnhem and on the borders of Germany are regarded as primarily British and American affairs, in late 1944 the Canadians would make their main contribution at the mouth of the Scheldt river. As a prelude, the dykes of the island of Walcheren were breached by the RAF on 3 October allowing the sea to rush in. Successive raids on enemy positions dropped 8,000 tons of bombs before the ground attack. By the end of the month Montgomery described the island as resembling 'a saucer full of water'. But despite the Allied air superiority it would still be a hard fought battle. The reason for the five-week action continuing until 8 November 1944 was simple; for in order to make use of the port of Antwerp the Allies had to control the river.

The task was clear, but in the waterlogged terrain of northern Belgium and Netherlands achieving it was no easy matter. As Bill Davis of the 1st Black Watch of Canada put it, 'That was the dirtiest job we had during the whole war – the taking of the Scheldt. The weather was rotten, cold, snow, rain and no place to get warm or dry.'

In the first phase the 2nd Canadian Division attacked north from Antwerp; fighting booby traps, mines and the weather as well as the Germans. Arguably the worst day was 13 October, so called 'Black Friday' on which the 1st Battalion, the Black Watch, took decimating casualties. According to the unit's war diary the assault began in fine weather just after 06.00am with the Black Watch passing through the Royal Regiment to cut off the Walcheren causeway. However, before 07.00am they were under heavy machine-gun fire, soon joined by air-bursting mortar shells and snipers. Though the Canadians were well supported by artillery the enemy were difficult to locate and casualties grew. By 09.00am two of the companies were back at their start line. That afternoon the Black Watch attacked again, this time supported by flamethrower carriers whose work had a 'considerable effect on the enemy' but still many of the officers were killed or seriously wounded.

Bill Davis got a worm's eye view of the whole affair:

I was getting rather frustrated because we were just getting pelted with machine guns just like you wouldn't believe… The next thing I knew I woke up: the tanks were gone and most of my guys were gone. I got up to look around and my closest buddy knocked me down, said, 'You know you're going to get killed if you keep doing that!' Anyway, somehow or other we worked our way across that deep field to the dyke at the end. But we spent the rest of the day throwing grenades back and forth, the Germans on one side and us on the other side, and they were just murder. The wounded were laying out in the field hollering and yelling.

There were only 19 of us left out of a company of over a hundred, and as we were moving out I came across our company commander, Major Popham, who was laying there – [he] had been shot through the head earlier in the day. So I went to take his map case and his papers and everything so the Jerries wouldn't get it, and it scared the hell out of me… [He] said, 'You are not going to leave me Scoop?' – that was my nickname. I didn't know what to say at first because the back of his scalp was laying open. So I put a field dressing on him, 'Major, I can't carry you, but we'll go as far as we can.' So we did, hanging on

OPPOSITE
Psychological warfare – a German leaflet aimed at reducing the morale of the American troops. This piece of propaganda claims that the American soldier was unlikely to remain in action much more than a couple of months. This was an exaggeration, but it was true that many American divisions had eventual turnovers of personnel greater than their original strength. (Author's Collection)

to each other. Got him back to where there was some Jeeps taking out the wounded, and that was the last I seen [of] him…

Artefacts now held at the Deutsches Historisches Museum. Shown top is the *Panzerschreck* or 'tank terror', with one of its rocket projectiles. The Panzerschreck was introduced on the Eastern Front in 1943. At up to about 160m it was a very effective anti-tank weapon, capable of penetrating about 160mm of armour. At the bottom is the *Panzerfaust klein* also nicknamed *Gretchen*. This was the first of the main production models of the one shot 'tank fist', introduced in 1943. Range was very limited with an optimum of about 30m, but the hollow charge projectile could cope with 140mm armour. Both range and penetration were improved in later models. (Author's Collection)

Heavy fighting continued for the next few days as the Calgary Highlanders took up where the Black Watch left off. Soon the British Second Army joined the battle attacking westwards, and in Operation *Switchback* the Breskens Pocket, a heavily fortified area of German resistance on the southern shore of the Scheldt estuary, was reduced and the Leopold Canal finally crossed – again with the aid of Wasp flame carriers. A third phase, Operation *Vitality* opened on 24 October with the British 52nd Division crossing the west Scheldt, and getting behind the enemy positions. Finally, in the bizarrely named Operation *Infatuate*, the Walcheren causeway and island were attacked. At the point of the amphibious assault on 1 November were Nos 41, 47 and 48 British Royal Marine Commandos using 'Buffalo' carriers and armour. One of them was a disbelieving Jim Kelly of 41 RM Commando, who quickly realized that Montgomery's crockery analogy was correct – but now of course there was only the 'rim' of the water-filled saucer left to fight on. The Germans, naturally enough, had protected it with a minefield of anti-personnel 'S' mines, including the infamous 'Bouncing Betty':

'A' Troop, which I belonged to weren't the leading troop at that time. The men on the left flank, they were caught in a minefield – four men went down. I went across and into the minefield and poked my way across to the first fellow, and a mine popped out of the ground, in between the middle of his back and my chest. I had four seconds… But it didn't go off, and I thought, 'Well I'm going to get killed here', so I just took them out and went back in

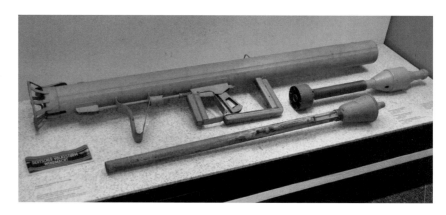

Nicknamed the *Ofenrohr*, or 'stove pipe', the Panzerschreck was a German 8.8cm anti-tank rocket launcher inspired by the American bazooka. Shown here is the second generation type incorporating a shield with a small window to protect the user from the exhaust of the rocket as it left the barrel. Considerably lighter than other conventional anti-tank guns the weapon remained in use to the end of the war. It could not be fired within a confined space due to the considerable back blast. (Author's Collection)

again in my own footsteps, and just probed until the next man... Until I brought the four men out.

Eventually the Commandos managed to fight their way onto the enemy position, discovering that the Germans had survived both air and artillery by dint of their concrete emplacements. Even now some were not ready to emerge. As Kelly remembered:

Once we got on top of them they just locked the doors and stayed there ... we banged on the doors and shouted at them to come out... We ended up for the most part of the time, just lying right on top of them for a night, freezing cold. And the next morning they would come out with all their gear packed, and the little haversacks and what not, and they'd come out and surrender ... and battery by battery we got right the way around the island.

Jim himself did not, however, get all the way round. Some German defenders were still resisting and opened up with mortars and artillery before being overwhelmed. Kelly blamed himself for what happened next – his section were not dispersed enough, and had been walking in the open. He collected shrapnel wounds that put him in hospital for a couple of months, thus becoming one of 8,000 killed, wounded or missing in the week-long fight for Walcheren.

THE ARDENNES
16 DECEMBER 1944 – 16 JANUARY 1945

> " The Ardennes was the most beautiful area, with very narrow roads and dense forest... There were big piles of snow in the valley where they were dug in, and there was a hand sticking out here and a rifle there. They had lost about 25 men, still laying there, dead. "
>
> Arnold Whittaker, US 10th Infantry

The winter of 1944 was cold – and snowy. For many Bing Crosby's Academy Award winning hit *White Christmas*, first heard publicly on NBC during the festive season of 1941, now took on an ironic edge. For, perhaps surprisingly, an American Army that was relatively well paid and fed, and armed with modern semi-automatic rifles and quality artillery, was not so well prepared when it came to combating the effects of Mother Nature. Seymour Rosen was not the only one to complain, 'When I left the States I had a pair of long underwear on, wool pants, olive drab wool shirt, sweater, field jacket, a wool cap and helmet. That was it. We never got warm clothing; most of the line companies never got warm clothing. The rear echelon guys got most of it. You could see them walking around in their fancy coats and fur-lined jackets and stuff: but we were just cold.' Bill Ryan agreed, 'We weren't properly equipped ... all we had was that damned heavy overcoat – [when it] got wet – it weighed a ton'. George McGuire was a little further back, lucky enough to be better dressed, but still, '95 percent of the time you were cold. You couldn't build a fire because of the smoke, and so you just had to endure the cold... They issued some special boots, and we had heavy coats and gloves – but even then, we were still cold.' Some bizarre

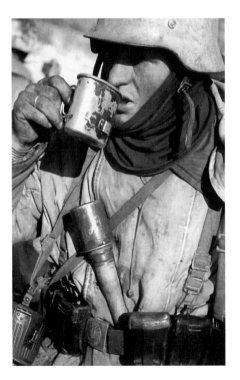

experiments were conducted in attempts to keep warm. Well behind the lines US Army nurse Ellen Levitsky and her comrades from the 164th General Hospital were 'chilly' in their tent, so Levitsky collected 'scraps' for the pot-bellied stove, then, having trouble lighting it, added gin. Two tents were incinerated. The colonel was less than amused – a third and 'you stay outside' was the concluding remark of his interview.

Frank Camm recalled drifts of snow so deep that sometimes the only way to move objects around was to drag them on improvised sledges, using captured horses to pull doors ripped from houses. Harley Reynolds denied there was anything as pretty as snow flakes – just blown 'pellets' creating misery. Typically Arnold Whittaker of the 10th Infantry, US 5th Division, was living in a hole. Clearly, the infantry were the bottom of the heap:

I could parallel it with street people who are living under viaducts and under cardboard and that way. Well that's the way we lived, I spent most of my time in fox holes. It was welcomed to be able to take a small town and have the option of being in a barn which is wonderful over your head ... [but] digging a fox hole was your home away from home. The irony of the whole thing? It was typically an ideal size and depth for a casket. It was 6ft long, 3ft wide and 4ft deep and a casket would fit in it. During the Battle of the Bulge it was cold ... the ground was so hard that it would take four to five hours to dig. We were normally in a combat area where we had to be very careful about noise... Our fear was hitting a stone or hitting anything that would make a loud noise and our fear was in direct relationship to what kind of progress we were making on getting our fox hole to protect us... And then at most times also, this fox hole, if it was in a wooded area it had to have a roof on it ... this is because of tree bursts: mortars, Luftwaffe bombs, 88s – they would hit the trees and explode and then come down like rain, hot hot metal, ragged metal, and hit you. Or, many times guys were injured by splinters from trees. It would hit them and explode and then come down like arrows. So you had to have a fox hole with a roof on it ... we would take our bayonet, we'd cut off sticks and lay them on top and then we'd throw the dirt on top of that.

By December 1944 there were many who assumed that the end of the war in Europe was a mere formality. In the south Allied forces occupied much of Italy and were encamped beyond Pisa and the River Arno. In the East the Red Army had reached Warsaw, while in the West Allied forces were inside Germany, and shipping was now reaching along the Scheldt to Antwerp, a town that an increasingly desperate enemy was subjecting to attack by V-2 rockets. Metz too had fallen to the Americans after several weeks of bitter fighting. Eisenhower's staff calculated that the German Army was being consumed at a rate of roughly 20 divisions every month. In the air the Allies were all but masters of the skies, only intermittently troubled by the rump of the Luftwaffe. The question seemed to be not whether the war could be won, but exactly when. Although it was true that the optimists who had predicted an end of hostilities by Christmas now appeared wrong, it seemed likely that this was inaccurate only by weeks.

For the time being American eyes focused on the Hürtgen forest, a thickly wooded area south of Eschweiler and south-west of Düren,

PREVIOUS SPREAD
This reconstruction shows the damage caused by Allied incendiary bombs. (Jeremy Llewellyn-Jones)

OPPOSITE
German infantryman in winter dress. The padded jacket was reversible, with white snow camouflage on one side only, which proved to be highly practical, but not every soldier received one. Tucked into the belt is a *Stielhandgranate* or stick grenade. This man carries two supplies of ammunition: five-round rifle chargers in the leather belt equipment and a drum magazine for the MG 34. (Author's Collection)

As early as September 1944, Hitler began laying the groundwork for his major offensive into the Ardennes, despite facing crippling losses. The decision was made to hold firm on all fronts until the fresh assault could be launched, believing that decisive offensive action would cause the collapse of the Allied coalition and prove that Germany could not be conquered. The key, as shown in this map, was to break out of the Ardennes and seize the vital port of Antwerp.

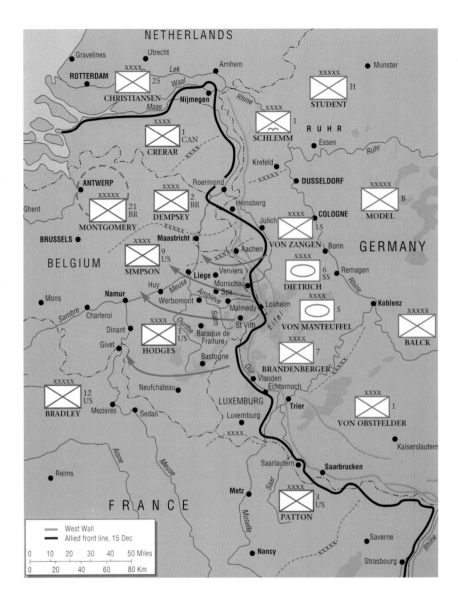

first attempted as early as September 1944. Claimed as the longest single battle the American Army has ever fought, it was famously described by war correspondent Ernest Hemingway, as 'Passchendaele with tree bursts'. As battle continued more forces were fed in, opening General Hodges – the commanding officer – to the accusation that he committed the folly of reinforcing failure. Certainly, a crucial point about the Hürtgen was that it did not favour an attacker, particularly one whose métier was movement, air power or artillery, as for much of the time visibility was poor, and going anywhere slow. Indeed, it was possible to get alarmingly close to the enemy as was realized by Frank Camm, 'We had several of our infantry platoons attack and some of our soldiers got caught behind German lines … while it was dark they had to try to get out and started across a German trench when they ran into German soldiers. And the Germans would say something to them, and they just grunted back and kept on going.'

Early on the 9th and 28th Infantry Divisions bore the brunt. Next came the 1st, 4th, 8th and 104th Divisions – with engineers blasting paths for tanks. Mines remained an ever-present hazard. As Sergeant Mack Morris of the 4th Division remembered:

Private First Class Harvey A. Clark of the Ninth Army compares the Panzerschreck left, with the American bazooka. The Allied weapon was lighter, but had less penetrative power, and at a little over 3lbs its rocket was about half the weight of the German projectile. (Author's Collection)

> Hürtgen had its roads and firebreaks. The firebreaks were only wide enough to allow two jeeps to pass, and they were mined and interdicted by machine-gun fire. In one break there was a teller mine [a common German anti-tank mine] every eight paces for three miles. In another there were more than 500 mines in the narrow break. One stretch of road held 300 teller mines, each one with a pull device in addition to the regular detonator… Sometimes [the enemy] felled 200 trees across a road, cutting them down so they interlocked as they fell. Then he mined and booby-trapped them. Finally he registered his artillery on them, and his mortars.[1]

Often the only hope of getting by was the old-fashioned way, probing and poking at the ground with a bayonet and hoping you hit mines gently, at an angle – and not too hard on a detonator.

So it was that although enemy troop movements westward were detected, as well as mention of Antwerp in intelligence reports, a major offensive seemed quite implausible. The notion was counterintuitive: the Germans ought not to have had the strength to push back the Allies – so for them to attack was only to risk ending the war that much sooner. Eisenhower later admitted that his *laissez faire* attitude to the Ardennes sector was a calculated risk, allowing parts of his line to become stretched, so others could be reinforced to advance:

In order to maintain the two attacks that we then considered important we had to concentrate available forces in the vicinity of the Roer dams on the north and bordering the Saar in the south. This weakened the static, or protective force in the Ardennes region. For a period we had only three divisions on a front of some 75 miles between Trier and Monschau and were never able to place more than four in that region. While my own staff kept in closest touch with this situation, I personally conferred with Bradley about it at various times. Our conclusion was that in the Ardennes region we were running a definite risk but we believed it to be a mistaken policy to suspend our attacks all along the front merely to make ourselves safe until all reinforcements arriving from the United States could bring us up to peak strength.[2]

Yet resolution for the offensive did not rest with any measured professional soldier – but with Hitler. The Führer was at heart a gambler, a chancer who had on many occasions profited from the turn of fate: and the times that fortune had smiled upon him were counted as proof of personal destiny. The rise to power, the failure of the Western powers to intervene early, the failures of bomb plots and a dozen other happy accidents reinforced this dangerous mindset. Now, moreover, the German General Staff had been purged of voices of caution, and as Jodl expressed it, 'in a desperate situation the only possible hope lies in a desperate decision'.[3] Germany was faced with the option to deploy its remaining strength to bolster existing fronts, which could only have served as a delaying tactic, or to concentrate for an attack. A major success might enable disproportionate numbers of the enemy to be eliminated, territory regained, and a shortening of a front achieved. It was the obvious impossibility of decisive efforts on the vast canvas of the Eastern Front, against overwhelming odds, that made Hitler focus on the West.

As Jodl's aide Major Herbert Büchs reported of a meeting on 25 September 1944:

> Hitler firmly believed that we had to try to get out of being endlessly defensive, endlessly on the retreat, and grasp the initiative ourselves on at least one front by going over to the attack, which besides destroying enemy forces would also boost the morale of forces and people. He put the minimum number of divisions necessary at between 20 and 30, about a third of them armoured, and saw them as coming from the new *Volksgrenadier* divisions which were being formed and from the exhausted Panzer divisions in the west after they had been rehabilitated, by about the end of November.[4]

A quick breakthrough required a weak part of the line, maintenance of surprise and timing to coincide with weather unfavourable to Allied air power. From this initial idea were devised the plans submitted in early October offering five options – all of them effectively forms of pincer attack around a key geographical region. Operation *Holland*, a single hook from the Venlo area towards Antwerp, leaving Allied forces trapped in a northern pocket; Operation *Lüttich-Aachen*, encircling American forces in the vicinity of Aachen; Operation *Luxembourg*; further south Operation *Lothringen* (the German translation of the French Lorraine); and Operation *Elsass* (Alsace). From these Hitler selected elements of both *Holland* and *Lüttich-Aachen*, resulting in the final scheme for *Wacht Am Rhein*, a 'grand solution' in which the Panzers would strike from the Eifel to the Meuse seizing Charleroi, Namur and Liege, en route for the goal of Antwerp. A much smaller hook would encircle Aachen.

By this audacious onslaught American and British forces would be sundered, supply lines terminally disrupted. The British, cut off in Holland, might be forced to retreat or be strangled, the Americans shattered and outflanked. The full implications of success were difficult

OPPOSITE

Machine gunners firing during the street battle for Aachen, October 1944. The US 26th Infantry regiment was ordered to take the first German city by attacking east to west across Aachen, two battalions abreast. Colonel Derrill Daniel adopted a combined arms approach following mortar and artillery fire with his rifle companies, closely supported by armour, anti-tank guns, bazookas and, as seen here, two machine-gun teams. This version of the old Browning designed .30 calibre machine gun was belt fed, air cooled and capable of a cyclic rate of about 500 rounds per minute. Notice the litter of spent cartridges and battle damage to nearby masonry. (Author's Collection)

Flamethrower Vehicles: the Crocodile' and the 'Wasp'

The history of flame weapons goes back as far as the 'Greek Fire' of classical antiquity, but the modern flamethrower dates from its introduction to the battlefield by the Germans during World War I. By 1944 infantry and vehicle-mounted flamethrowers were in use by all major combatants. The main types of British flamethrower now included the man-portable 'Lifebouy', the Churchill 'Crocodile' tank and the 'Wasp' carrier.

13ZV71

The Churchill Crocodile. Tough but slow and under-armed the Churchill tank was unable to penetrate the frontal armour of the latest enemy tanks. Nevertheless it was useful for close support of infantry, as a basis for specialist engineer vehicles and in its original concept as a platform for attack through fortified zones. In the flamethrowing 'Crocodile', fuel and compressed air were carried in cylinders in a trailer, while the flame projector replaced the hull machine gun. In this view we see the angular counter-weight shrouding the forward end of the flame gun cradle within the ring shaped housing. (Author's Collection)

A re-enactment of the work of the flamethrower against a building in a Dutch street. Such weapons did not just burn the enemy, but caused suffocating smoke, and could even burn up the oxygen of confined spaces. Thickened fuels stuck to their targets and stayed alight longer. Skilled operators learned tricks such as 'bouncing' squirts off walls, and also flooding strong points, then igniting the pools of liquid to create major conflagrations. (Jeremy Llewellyn-Jones)

A demonstration of the 'Wasp' flamethrower carrier, which had a range of about 80–100 yards. Orders for Wasps were placed as early as 1942, and by 1944 there were several different models. As of June 1944 all production was switched to the Canadian or '2C' type in which there was just one fuel container, mounted to the outside and rear of the carrier, allowing an extra crewman to be carried in the vehicle. (Author's Collection)

to gauge, but could certainly set the Western Allies back many months, cause horrendous losses, and bring Germany undreamed of breathing space in which to regroup and strike again, west or east. The loss of Antwerp alone could have caused the Allies serious problems, since without it they would have remained dependent largely on supplies run from France by road – the so called 'Red Ball Express' that used more fuel than it could deliver.

The Houffalize Panther. Found overturned by a bridge on the road to La Roche in the shallows of the River Ourthe, this tank of the 116th *Windhund* Panzer Division is one of the best preserved in the Ardennes, displayed only a few hundred yards from where it was lost. (Author's Collection)

Opening moves

The blow fell on 16 December with the Germans achieving near total surprise. Where possible convoys advanced at night while the American forces were softened up by a 90-minute barrage from 1,600 guns. In the vanguard went the men of Operation *Grief*; small groups disguised in American uniforms, led by Obersturmbahnführer Otto Skorzeny. From the air came a small night-time parachute drop, Operation *Stösser*, under Oberst Frederich von der Heydte. Three armies were committed to the attack. In the north, General Sepp Dietrich's Sixth Panzer Army was devoted to a drive from Monchau to

A 9th Infantry squad shelter in a ditch on 13 December. The extreme weather conditions exacted a hard toll on the men on the frontline. (NARA)

Antwerp. In the centre was General Hasso von Manteuffel's Fifth Panzer Army, which it was hoped might eventually reach all the way to Brussels. The smaller Seventh Army, under General Erich Brandenburger, protected the southern flank. In the path of the Panzers, defending the front from Ecternach to Monschau, stood a handful of American divisions, three of them battered from previous action – and in theory enjoying respite from combat. In the north, the 2nd and 99th Infantry attempted to thwart *Kampfgruppe* Peiper, the most substantial of the four battle groups of the 1st SS Panzerkorps which acted as the mobile striking arm of the 6th Panzer Army, then advancing towards the Elsenborn Ridge. In the centre was Major-General Norman de Cota's 28th, originally raised from the Pennsylvania National Guard. It was nicknamed the 'Keystone' Division, but now more commonly dubbed the 'Bloody bucket' – due to the shape and colour of its divisional patch. Supported by small Combat Commands drawn from the 9th and 10th US Armored, the 28th Infantry Division did what little they could to defend Bastogne, later described as an 'Alamo in the Ardennes', but it was obvious that if key points were to be held reinforcements were needed fast. Once it was realized how big the enemy offensive was almost a quarter of a million men were earmarked to come to the defence. In the forefront were the 82nd and 101st Airborne.

Holding Bastogne

The 101st Airborne had moved swiftly forward from Reims. The first of the division had arrived late on 18 December. Eugene Madison and many others were driven up on flat bed trucks early the next morning, in dense fog – just as it got 'colder and colder'. As Captain Frank Gregg of the 501st Parachute Infantry Regiment recalled:

> A runner came down to where I was in one of the barracks there and he says, 'The Colonel wants to see you right away'... I knew something was serious. And he says, 'We are moving as soon as we can load the trucks, which are coming in now, and going to a town called Bastogne, because we've got to get there before the Germans do.' We drove all night... Refugees were coming into Bastogne from the way I was going, and I knew what that meant: the Germans weren't very far behind. We went on out to the little village of Bizôry, which is about a mile from Bastogne, and there come the Germans from over the hill... And I deployed my men on both sides of the road, and we fired at one another for the rest of the afternoon.

Men of the 506th Parachute Infantry leave Bastogne for Foy to reinforce the 101st Airborne perimeter, 19 December 1944. (NARA)

The 101st formed a perimeter that Edward Shames now likens to 'the spokes of a wagon wheel', with Bastogne as a 'hub' ringed by the enemy. Yet there was no sure idea where the Germans were coming from. Ominously men reported hearing the 'clinkety clink' or 'squeak, squeak, squeak' of armoured treads – but often nothing could be seen. Others, staring too long at tree stumps through mist, became convinced that they moved. As Carl Beck remembered:

I says [*sic*], man, I don't need this stuff … nobody knew what the situation was. If they did, they wasn't gonna tell… We got hit with German infantry. Company Commander called me up and [said] a machine-gun position had been knocked out in the haystack. He said, 'Beck, get your machine gun and get up there', and fire this, what we call, a final protective line, an 'FPL'… The idea of an FPL is to get interlocking machine-gun fire and let the infantry walk through it… And I was right beside this tank destroyer. It was in turret defilade where he could swing that 76 around … it was pretty stiff fighting. And there was some farmer-type wire up there, I went through that wire … shot that A6 machine gun. I brought it up and I set it down. And just as I set it down, a bullet went bouncing off the bipod. And I'd have been here with a soprano voice if it hadn't been for that! So I set up, fired the final protective line, ran the Krauts off – and as they were leaving they pitched up a mortar or a grenade. You know, I saw it go off at the end of the machine-gun barrel, but it kept on firing. My assistant gunner, by this time, was a kid named Duffy. And those little grenade fragments and frozen earth got all in my face and head… You feel yourself and you're bleeding like a stuck hog, you know. So things had quietened down by this time, so I said, 'OK, I'll go back'. I went back to the Aid Station. He [Duffy] wrapped up my head. And as I was laying there on a stretcher, here came the gunner out of that M18 tank destroyer. He'd been firing a 50-calibre out of the turret. And he had a bullet up in his nose. And I said, 'What the hell happened to you?' He says, 'Well, I saw that round coming and I ducked, but I didn't duck in time.' And what happened? That bullet that hit the ring mount and ricocheted down, hit him in the nose.

For Ed Shames it was patrol actions that were the most stressful:

One evening … Stein [said] lets go a patrol – a listening patrol… We went out not too far from our command station. We picked out a tree overlooking a little town called Foy. While we were listening and waiting we didn't hear too much [but] all of a sudden – out of clear blue sky apparently – a mortar shell had a tree burst on this tree we were under. Course, it frightened the hell out of us. Stein said to me, 'Are you hit?' And I said to him no, I don't think so… He said he didn't feel he was hit but … [but] I felt this blood on his leg: and sure as hell he was hit, and it was gushing … piece of shrapnel had severed an artery in his leg. And it was so cold that the blood was very slow oozing out of it. Saved his life.

The German *Sturmpanzer IV*, nicknamed *Brummbär* (the 'grouser', or 'grizzly bear'), was a conversion of the standard Panzer IV medium tank to enable it to carry a 150mm howitzer for close assault in street fighting, or against fortifications. Used at Kursk in 1943, the *Sturmpanzer IV* was also deployed in Italy before seeing action in Normandy with Sturmpanzer-Abteilung 217. This unit escaped from France before participating in the Battle of the Bulge and its eventual capture in the Ruhr Pocket. Though effective enough only 300 examples of this weapon were produced. Four examples survive, in Russia, America, France and Germany. (Author's Collection)

For the Americans, unlike the Germans and Soviets, death and snow were as yet rather unfamiliar bedfellows. The surreal quality of the aftermath of combat struck more than one of the veterans. As Frank Gregg recalled, 'I looked out the next morning and the Germans were hanging over the barbed wire fence – you know, trying to get through. And those guys next to me did a good job of stopping them. There must have been 25 hanging over those barbed wire fences the next morning.' As to bodies, it appeared to Ed Shames that, for the time being, 'There was no need to do anything with them because they froze up like a block of ice. Hard as granite. And if they came up to us we dropped them out right in front of our foxholes. We sure as hell wasn't going to move them, so we used them as a table. Hell … something to sit down on, they were warmer than the damned snow.' Carl Beck was equally hardened to those that could no longer feel, 'You know to see the enemy dead was just something you just disregard. It's like maybe seeing a dead animal or something.' But not all the bodies were German. Arnold Whittaker would later find 4th Division men where they fell, 'When we got there, they were dug into the woods into a large hill, covered with snow. From a distance it looked like the results of beaver mounds… And when you got closer, there would be a hand sticking out here, an M1 there. We were concerned that with all the snow we were getting that the Quartermaster wouldn't find them until spring: so we took their M1s and put the bayonet on it and stuck it in the ground.' It was, as Frank Gregg put it – 'brutal'.

A Kingtiger (Tiger II) passing prisoners of the US 99th Infantry Division near the village of Merlscheid. Production of the second generation 'Royal' Tiger commenced in mid 1944, and the new tank featured 180mm armour and an improved 88mm gun. Perhaps mercifully, total production would be barely 500 machines. (NARA)

Yet the sacrifice of the airborne troops and those who went before was not in vain. As Manteuffel himself explained the Germans were now in a quandary as to whether to put all their efforts into capturing Bastogne, 'or go back to the original plan for the 26th Volksgrenadier Division to capture this place while deploying the Panzer Divisions for a further advance west'.[5] In the event the enemy split their force, and was slowed, but this was little or no comfort to those trapped within Bastogne. After a few days of fighting supplies were running low, and only when there was a gap in the weather could air drops be made. Shames watched the sky anxiously for aircraft, 'because it was weapons and ammunition which we needed desperately, we were just about out. And food… I had nothing, burlap on my feet, a pair of gloves I'd taken off a German soldier, that had no fingers, and no hat [except] my helmet.' Finally on 23 December the weather did clear, and provisions began to arrive. Shames was disgusted to discover that the first thing to get through to him was a small package containing, of all things, a fountain pen – 'just what I needed'. Then one of the men pointed out to him that it was gold, and engraved with his name – by the girl who was later to become his wife. Moreover, it was not only a pen that the fine weather brought. Waves of Allied aircraft could now come over, both to attack the enemy, and to finally begin the large-scale drops of food and ammunition.

The Allied counter-offensive

From the north British forces moved to block the Bulge, from the south Patton's tanks now advanced on Bastogne. Neither proceeded as fast as they would have liked due to the extreme weather and the continued threat of mines. As Arnold Whittaker put it:

> During the Bulge, the biggest problem we had was weather. And weather was causing casualties equal to the casualties caused by the Germans. So Patton was totally frustrated … the field hospitals were filled with GIs with frozen feet. And when you get 'trench foot' they just amputated it. Your feet turned black, and then gangrene, and you get big blisters – and it's a fooler because your feet go through a period where they're warm, they feel tingly, they feel good and you ignore the one rule they had on dress. And the one rule they had on dress is the fact that they wanted you to carry an extra pair or two of socks around you neck and change your shoes, change your socks, as often as possible. And some, some guys didn't adhere to the rules and were kind of cavalier about it. As a result, their feet caught up with them and they had their toes, or their whole feet amputated.

Many expedients were tried to counter the threat of mines, as Frank Camm remembered:

The 501st Parachute Infantry march on Mageret. The men in the foreground are bazooka teams, one of the few weapons with which paratroopers could confront armour. (NARA)

A bunker busting *Sturmtiger* captured at Drolshagen, Germany, in April 1945. This remarkable weapon was described as an 'assault mortar'. Based on the chassis of the Tiger I it mounted a 38cm mortar and an MG 34 machine gun. It is thought that the total production of these monsters was just 18 pieces, of which a handful fought in the Ardennes. (Author's Collection)

When you hit a mine in the right place it'll explode, and during the Battle of the Bulge I conducted an experiment with some our men by taking different weapons, a rifle, a 30-calibre machine gun, a 50-calibre machine gun, a 37mm gun and a 105 [howitzer] and had them fire at the mines to see which was the most effective way to remove the mines, and we found the least amount of ammunition we had to need in terms of weight was the 30-calibre machine gun. So whenever we saw them we, we tried to shoot 'em out if they were out in the open, or else at night when the enemy couldn't see us, then we didn't mind going in there and try to pull them out ourselves.

It has been said that had Allied forces moved quicker they could have trapped much of the enemy force that attacked in 'the Bulge'. Nevertheless, the US 4th Armored reached Bastogne on 26 December, and the route to Antwerp was also firmly slammed shut. With a paratrooper's pride General Anthony McAuliffe took umbrage at the suggestion that the 101st had been 'rescued' and, indeed, the resilience of the American defenders had been truly remarkable. In a bitter postscript to the Ardennes campaign the enemy attacked again with Operation *Nordwind* on New Year's Day, but by now it was futile – and after just a few days they were forced to desist. Operation *Bodenplatte*, launched by the Luftwaffe at the same time, also failed because while both sides lost heavily in aircraft the Germans were now unable to replace the deficiency. With better weather Allied dominance in the air remained undisturbed. Malcolm Andrade, a Canadian Spitfire pilot who served with both the 91st and 127th Squadrons of the RAF, was just one of the flyers who made it possible. He was still young, and had grown up wanting to fly:

> If you ever saw a Spitfire in the sky as a boy, you never forgot the sound of the engine. The Merlin has a distinctive sound – thrilling at high speed – and depending on the mark, like the Mark IX which I flew, there's a whistle that accompanies the sound of the engine winding up… You're totally in love with this airplane because its gorgeous to look at. The elliptical wings, everything fits together: so we had a saying 'if she looks good she flies good'. And that's the Spitfire. It looks good, it's beautiful, it's too nice to be a war machine. You look at a Hawker Hurricane, it looks like a war machine, it's rugged, it's heavy – looks powerful. The Spitfire is too graceful to be a killer… When you are young you just run and hop onto the wing, there's a door, and your mechanic's already got that down. So you get in there and sit in your seat, your parachute's on your rear end so your seat is curved to fit your parachute. Then you strap in, have a look at the harness where the central clip is and everything plugs into that. If you want to release that you hit the belt and – ching! Quick release, that's the whole idea – or some belts, turn it, and that releases the catch. Once you're strapped in you go through your drill. Hand ready on the throttle. If the mechanic has your engine running you don't have to start up. Normally they warm-up the engine for you… If not then you have to do your wobble pump and get the gas into the carburettor, and then you press your starter button and your magneto. Once that starts the engine will crank over and then usually fire up within the third turn of the prop.

Andrade was barely 19-years-old on the field at Grimbergen in the winter of 1944, moving to Woensdrecht airbase in the Netherlands early in the new year. His Squadron Leader had looked over the new replacements wondering what this 'kid' was able to do, and Andrade had a mighty fear that he would not measure up:

> You're confident in your skills to fly, but you're scared to fly in combat in case you let someone down, you don't keep formation, get lost, something like that… There's many ways you can get picked off either by ground fire, or just plain run out of gas and crash. Those are worst-case scenarios. Usually you're flying in a formation of four, which is a flight, and you follow

your leader, and you're the junior boy so you are a wingman to someone who is more experienced than you are. Your job is to follow that man. So if you get broken up in combat, stay with that man, you're supposed to look after him. If there's someone on his tail you're supposed to get on the tail of the fighter attacking him.

Most missions were in a ground-attack role in direct support of the army, information and map references being relayed from units along the chain to the squadron. Andrade described his first mission thus:

Once that information is up to date we get the scramble… Normally the attack would start at around 8,000ft – we're flying in echelon… The flight leader then would roll over and dive, and we would follow and dive – line up your port cannon, start getting the target into your gun sight. It would [have been] decided at what height we drop our bombs. So you fuse your bombs for the amount of time that you need to get away from the bomb blast. So if you're going down fairly high up and breaking off, let's say one to two thousand feet, well you've got plenty of time to get away at that height. But if you're going lower and closer in you need a lengthy time, so you give it the maximum number of seconds you need to get away from your own blast. So you arm your bombs. Normally a 250lb bomb under each wing – on very rare occasions a 500lb underneath… So you go down on your target, centred through your gun sight. The minute before you break off they're shooting at

A fallen German soldier at Neffe, Belgium, January 1945. The village of Neffe, on the eastern perimeter of the Bastogne defence, was attacked repeatedly shortly before Christmas 1944. But in early January the American armoured divisions broke out here. (Author's Collection)

McAuliffe Square, Bastogne, showing the memorial to American general Anthony C. McAuliffe (1898–1975) alongside an M4A3 Sherman tank. McAuliffe parachuted into Normandy on D-Day with the 101st Airborne as its artillery commander, and later landed in the Netherlands by glider during *Market Garden*, but is best known for commanding the division during the defence of Bastogne. On being called upon to surrender on 22 December McAuliffe replied to the German commander General Lüttwitz with the celebrated one word response, 'Nuts'. He related this anecdote to his troops by way of relief from the otherwise chilling news that they were beset by possibly seven enemy divisions. (Author's Collection)

you. The 88 – a marvellous gun – starts firing when you are coming in at around 10,000[ft]. As you come down lower you start getting 40mm, 30mm, 20mm cannon shells flying up at you, and then the bullets start, right as you get lower… Traces of light like fireworks – and the first time you see it in front of your eyes, you duck. And it's stupid when you think about it. So that's what I did and, of course, you tend to lose your target area, and you hustle back to your gun sight now because you are diving down furiously one after another and we're all being fired at. So you bomb your target and hopefully you hit… We get back to base, a fairly easy run, nobody got hurt. And I was all nerves when I got out of the aircraft, felt sick, and threw up… And that was my first experience of combat: I was the 'new boy'.

Different types of mark required variations to tactical technique. Dug in tanks or artillery positions for, example, offered very small targets. Often the only way to stand a chance of hitting these was to 'go lower than you'd like to'. Machine guns were fired first, and the sight of the rounds striking the ground could allow the pilot to 'walk onto' the target while husbanding cannon ammunition. The amount of damage caused in such an attack, if any, was often difficult to gauge, especially from bombs, as several aircraft might be attacking in rapid succession. However as far as Andrade was concerned, it was, '… a standing rule once you've dropped your bombs – don't come back with any bullets in your guns or cannon shells. Seek out targets of opportunity behind enemy lines.

An SS-Unterscharführer and his team pause their *Schwimmwagen* ('swimming' or amphibious car) on the road to Malmedy, the scene of a massacre of Allied prisoners-of-war during the Battle of the Bulge. (NARA)

That could be a train, troop transports, marching troops, anything in enemy uniform. So when we were free to attack we'd dive on them and let them have it. So we came back with our guns empty.'

If the enemy was in a column then textbook method was to hit the front first, halting and blocking it, then attack the rear. This left everyone inbetween vulnerable as the only way to escape was to the sides across fields; not easy with wheeled vehicles, and often impeded by deep roadside ditches. In such an attack Andrade got his first introduction:

… into really seeing that you were killing people. When you start firing at the wagons you see little 'matchsticks' flying out. Suddenly you realize – as you approach rapidly – that these are men. You know cannon shells and bullets are hitting them and throwing them out with the impact and exploding amongst them. And you don't feel pity for that's what you are there for, and you want to let them have it because you don't want them getting through to attack our armies. So you give it to them with everything you've got, and there's no remorse, believe you me. You don't want them to get away. I was wingman to my leader – he saw a motorcyclist speed out – I don't know what he was thinking, panicked I guess. He was doing about 70 miles per hour, we were doing 250: there's no contest. We just blew him apart, just eliminated this guy then turned back onto the main targets and continued attacking until we ran out of shells and bullets. We felt very good about that one when we got back to base.

Unusually this was one scene that Andrade did actually get to see at close hand. Two days later the Allied ground forces overran the area and some of the pilots visited the road. 'We saw burnt bodies and wreckage everywhere… It was just pretty sickening in a way, but satisfying to see that we had done a good job in eliminating this bunch as much as possible. So we felt good about that: but you don't forget the smell. That's something you don't forget… Infantrymen might laugh at us because they see this every day on the battlefield.'

By February 1945 the frontline was back about the place it had been before the offensive. That month a Belgian friend offered Eileen Younghusband, a Women's Auxiliary Air Force officer and aircraft plotter, a lift through the Ardennes:

> … little realizing what we were going to see. And as we went through the snow was melting – and we could see the bodies of German troops, American troops and some British troops. And of course the shattered tanks that never got away. And then we went on to Bastogne which had been one of the hotspots … and that was very unnerving. That to me was one of the most horrific days… First time I'd ever seen a dead body. It was a shock when we saw them as we drove past on the wooded roads; and in the end there were so many of them I ceased looking.

Exactly how many was indeed a moot point. For while most observers agree that the Bulge was the bloodiest battle fought by the American Army – with about 19,000 dead – the total including wounded and missing of all nationalities is variously estimated at somewhere in the region of 200,000.

Important as it was, the Ardennes was now just one battlefront of several. In Operation *Veritable*, begun on 8 February 1945, the Canadians under Lieutenant General Henry Crear started the drive to the northern Rhine, through the Reichswald. With them were three British Divisions; the 15th Scottish, 53rd Welsh and 51st Highland. Tom Renouf was with the 51st:

> Shortly before 10:00 hours, it was our turn to charge across the mine-strewn field. Just like Tommies in the trenches 30 years earlier our mouths dried and our hearts pounded as we waited to go over the top. Then Sergeant Major Stewart started pushing us through the hedge… I started sprinting across the field taking fire from the Germans on the other side and dashed towards the

cover of the forest. A few yards out, as bullets whizzed past, I spotted one of our lads lying face down in a shell hole. I jumped in to see if he was all right and turned him over, only to find he had a small red hole in his temple… That macabre discovery put a spring in my step and I ran on for all I was worth. But when I dived into the relative safety of the forest, I found there was not as much cover as I had hoped. There were no branches on the trees because the shelling, mortaring and shrapnel had stripped them bare.

Eventually, through street fighting supported by RAF bombing, the small towns of both Goch and Cleve in North Rhine-Westphalia would be taken as the Allied armies pushed on towards the German heartland. Yet it was neither the British, nor the Canadians, who were first across the Rhine. How it came to be the Americans was a mixture of both luck and judgement.

REMAGEN

Amazingly the need to connect the heart of Germany with Western Europe, across the historic Rhine, has been a major concern in wars for two millennia. Julius Caesar spanned the river with a wooden bridge at Neuwied, near Koblenz, and another at Andernach. The bridge fought over at Remagen in early 1945, like Caesar's bridges, was both born of war, and destroyed in war. By 1916 extra capacity was required to support the Kaiser's armies fighting on the Western Front, and so the firm of Grün and Bilfinger were contracted and the building of a new bridge began. By working round the clock viaducts were erected over existing highways and a tunnel was dug into the solid rock of the Erpeler Ley. Over 'Father Rhine' itself rose three grandiose symmetrical arches and a carriageway 1,069ft in length. Rail tracks allowed trains to pass in both

Detail of the 116th Panzer Division Houffalize Panther. (Author's Collection)

directions at the same time, while a pair of narrower foot paths allowed troops to march across. At either end of the bridge a pair of dark brown stone pseudo-medieval towers, complete with gun emplacements and winding stairways, granted the bridge a resemblance to the old castles of the Rhine valley.

In 1918 the bridge was opened and dedicated in the name of Erich Ludendorff, Senior Quartermaster General of the Imperial Army. Paradoxically the Armistice was signed not very long afterwards, and that December American troops crossed the bridge to begin their occupation. Later the French took over, and by another quirk of fate, examined the structure closely enough to discover the existence of two large emergency demolition chambers in each of the main stone supporting piers. Workmen laboriously filled these voids with cement. Another war on, and in the late summer of 1944 the bridge was targeted by American bombers: it was hit on 19 October, and claimed destroyed, but it proved possible to put it back into commission in 15 days. On 29 December another raid got lucky, and again the bridge was put out of use and the town damaged. The process was repeated again twice in January, and again the bridge was badly damaged, but by industry and luck was back in action by mid February.

Although Luftwaffe anti-aircraft guns were also devoted to its protection the permanent garrison of the bridge remained laughably small: a tiny company of just 36 invalids recuperating from wounds, and a company of engineers. Their most potent weapons were a motley selection of machine guns, some of them captured several years earlier from the French and British. Perhaps worse, explosives to blow the bridge were lacking. The whole fell under command of a veteran of World War I, Captain Willi Bratge. Hitler himself inadvertently made the situation even less certain when he reacted to the premature destruction of the Mühlheim bridge at Cologne with instructions that demolition charges on major bridges should only be armed at the last moment, and that detonation could only take place following an order in writing from the responsible officer. While the battered bridge still functioned after a fashion the stress and confusion of early 1945 did not lead to the implementation of a fool-proof defence plan, and the crossing was passed from the jurisdiction of one command to another. Indeed, only hours before the arrival of the Americans, the bridge was put under the orders of General Otto Hitzfeld's LXVII Corps. In the middle of the night, and with directions to counter-attack in another area, Hitzfeld had other pressing matters on his mind. The best he could manage was to dispatch to the bridge a capable deputy in the form of Major Hans Scheller, with instructions to firm up and alert the defenders, and to destroy the bridge in case of necessity. By the time he arrived a little after 11.00am on 7 March, the bridge was crowded with retreating German vehicles, but at least some demolition charges had also appeared: not the 600kg that the engineers deemed necessary, but 300kg of an inferior industrial type. Less than half an hour later, and before Scheller had been able to make a full appreciation of the situation, intelligence was received that American forces were attacking the nearby hill. Villagers had raised the white flag, and the enemy were making rapid progress.

Just a few hours earlier the Americans had had no great expectation of being able to cross the river, still less of taking a major bridge in tact. The Combat Command of the US 9th Armored now approaching the bridge was led by Lieutenant Colonel Engeman: its point was a detachment of tanks and half tracks from the 14th Tank Battalion and 27th Armored Infantry. Near Fritzdorf the Americans pushed their way through a roadblock, and continued to advance. On the threshold of Remagen the columns of retreating German transport were perceived as tempting targets for artillery, but none was registered as the risk of hitting friendly troops, now hard on the heels of the enemy, was seen as too great to open fire immediately. So it was that the leading Americans pursued into the town, being engaged by a machine gun that was quickly overcome by supporting armour. A few minutes later the lead platoon was covering routes to the bridge, cutting off those Germans still on the west bank. By 2.00pm most of Remagen was secured, and fire was brought against the bridge itself.

Not long after came news that another part of the 9th Armored had reached and secured a bridge across the River Ahr at Sinzig. So far the 27th Armored Infantry held back on the expectation that the Remagen bridge would be blown imminently: but oddly nothing happened. Under orders from General William Hoge, commander of the 9th Armoured Division, Engeman was now goaded into action. Smoke rounds were fired to cover the attack, but suddenly there was a massive detonation – the bridge rose, then dropped back, further maimed, yet still unbroken. In the confusion of the last hour Major Scheller had delayed demolishing the bridge to allow more troops across, although his engineers did manage to blow an anti-tank ditch

OPPOSITE
A V-2 launches from Test Stand VII at Peenemünde. The 14 ton A-4 type rocket was the precursor of many long range military missiles and carried a 1-ton payload. Also used in attacks against Paris and London, the V-2 played a part in the battle for Remagen, and was used to bombard Antwerp. (NARA)

OVERLEAF
The battles for Europe throughout the last year of the war caused vast amounts of damage to civilians, homes and businesses, as can be seen here in this reconstruction. (Jeremy Llewellyn-Jones)

An American 155mm self propelled gun comes into action in support of the infantry at Echternach, February 1945. The M12 'GMC', or 'Gun Motor Carriage' was based on the old M3 tank chassis, and also used parts from the M4 Sherman. Having powerful armament and mobility it was something of an ace in the pack in terms of infantry support and on occasion was brought close, or even right into, built up areas to bust buildings and fortifications. (Author's Collection)

to create an obstacle. Finally at 3.20pm, realizing just how close the Americans were, he had given the destruction order. But it was too late: the wires to the charges were severed, probably by shell fire, and an NCO had to crawl forward to light an emergency fuse. The resultant explosion, while powerful enough to move the bridge, was not enough to topple it. Under covering fire from heavy weapons, US armored infantrymen, led by Second Lieutenant Karl H. Timmermann, now worked their way onto the crossing. Not without cost defenders around the bridge were overcome, and most of the remainder pushed back into the railway tunnel under the Erpeler Ley. Remaining charges were located and cut, and the towers searched and cleared. The main resistance now came from the Luftwaffe's light anti-aircraft guns on the top of what would soon be christened 'Flak Hill'.

Gradually three companies of the 27th were pushed across to the east of the Rhine and began to work their way around Erpeler Ley. Major Scheller escaped from the tunnel, but many, including Captain Willi Bratge were left trapped, unable to fight their way forward, or run the gauntlet of fire that now blocked their exit. At about 5.30pm they bowed to the inevitable, and, together with some civilians, emerged under a white flag. The toe-hold across the Rhine was quickly reported up the chain of command as far as an unbelieving Eisenhower, 'That was one of my happy moments of the war... We were across the Rhine, on a permanent bridge; the traditional defensive barrier to the heart of Germany was pierced. The final defeat of the enemy, which we had long

calculated would be accomplished in the spring and summer campaigning of 1945, was suddenly now, in our minds, just around the corner'.[6] Despite local counter-attacks more American troops from other units were rushed to secure the vital point.

One of those to cross was Bill Ryan, 'All I remember is debris everywhere, and there were still Germans laying there – shot and killed. The engineers were at the far end, "Hey you dumb Yanks, you'd best double time it, the bridge is going up any minute!" So we

Men of the US 90th Infantry Division advancing into Wiltz, Luxembourg, pass a body lying in the road, January 1945. The fallen officer is Lieutenant Colonel George B. Randolph, commander of the 712th Tank Battalion, knocked down by a shell splinter. High ranking officers were not immune during the long road to victory. (Author's Collection)

double-timed the whole bridge. It was amazing that it was the last remaining bridge standing, and its just lucky the explosives didn't all go off, or we'd have gone down.' It was not, however, all plain sailing the other side as Bill soon discovered:

> I was point man going through a small German town; I was at 'port arms' with my rifle, I came around a corner and there was a German right in front of me, and he lowered his rifle with his bayonet – as if he were going to fight with the bayonet. So he lunged at me and I backed up, and as I backed up he hit me with a butt stroke. Luckily I was moving back when he hit me. It broke two of my front teeth, but it didn't break my jaw or nothing and I got far back enough and I lowered my rifle and pulled the trigger. I'll never forget the look on that guy's face, because I hit him square in the chest… He was only three or four – maybe five – feet away. That's the closest I've ever seen a guy that I've killed.

The loss of the Remagen Bridge was a mortal blow. As Goebbels confided in his diary on 9 March:

> It is quite devastating that the Americans should have succeeded in capturing the Rhine bridge at Remagen intact and forming a bridgehead on the right bank of the Rhine. Large scale countermeasures are now being initiated since

FROM LEFT TO RIGHT

Following the bridge capture, the First Army rapidly pushed troops over the bridge to create a bridgehead on the eastern bank of the river. Here, a column of M4 medium tanks is seen moving to the eastern bank. (NARA)

An American soldier looks down on the Ludendorff Bridge. (NARA)

everyone is naturally clear on the threat which a bridgehead on the right bank poses for us. During the night Ju 88s were in action and partially destroyed the bridge, but it is not yet known whether this has made it unserviceable. On the enemy side of course people are overjoyed at the news. They act as if they already held the whole right bank of the Rhine. In fact it is a raving scandal that the Remagen bridge was not blown in good time.[7]

The following day his train of thought was darker still, '... people in the USA and Britain are literally intoxicated with victory. Above all, people think that because the Remagen bridge has been captured the war will end quickly. In London it is stated, moreover, that the bridge fell into enemy hands as a result of treachery.'[8] On 12 March the Propaganda Minister was still brooding about the morale implications of this first breach of the Rhine, 'At midday I have a telephone call from Gauleiter Simon, who tells me of his anxiety over this bridgehead. People cannot understand how it came about that the Remagen bridge was not blown at the proper time...'[9] Frank Camm saw evidence of a rapid change of heart of German civilians in the Rhineland first hand. Those who had been saying *Heil Hitler!* only days earlier now threw their pictures of the dictator, 'down on the floor and we'd walk all over them. And frankly, I didn't like the way they changed attitude so quickly.'

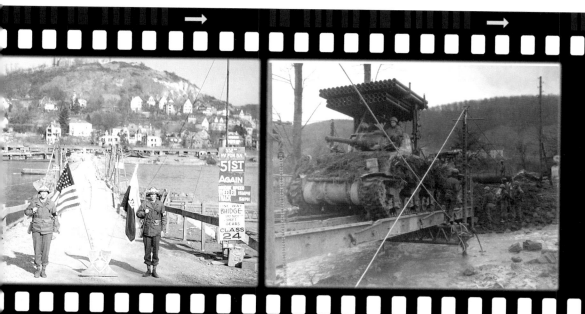

Securing the bridgehead

Not content with one large but damaged crossing, American forces now threw two pontoon bridges across the Rhine, north and south of the Ludendorff bridge. Begun on 10 March these were complete well within two days. By the end of the week 25,000 men were across the river. Yet the enemy had not quite finished with the bridge either. On 11 March German Navy divers were ordered to the Rhine with instructions to enter the river upstream, and float down to the bridge to destroy it with charges. Leutnant Schreiber and six men were duly dispatched by air to Frankfurt, and from there to the Rhine, planning to start about ten miles away from Remagen and drift downstream with the current to the target. However the initial attempt was foiled by blocked roads and the expanding bridgehead.

What Schreiber and his team could not yet have realized was that on 12 March, and despite frantic efforts by two different engineer battalions, the Americans had decided to shut the Ludendorff bridge to traffic. On 16 March during attempts to repair a truss a heavy crane had got stuck on one of the weakest points. In the meantime the crossing had become a target for V-2 rockets – this being the only time that they would be aimed at German soil. About 11 rockets were fired at the bridge from an area north-west of Bellendorn in the Netherlands. Some of these powerful missiles, that shot up through the atmosphere to descend almost vertically,

While the capture of the bridge made headlines, it was the rapid construction of additional crossings such as this pontoon bridge that made the bridgehead viable in the longer term. (Getty)

The remarkable Sherman 'Calliope' which mounted no fewer than 60 rocket tubes atop a Sherman M4. (Author's Collection)

landed in the river itself, and another hit near to the Apollinaris Church, but the closest came down only 300 yards from the bridge. Here the massive explosion created an enormous crater, killed three soldiers and several farm animals, and may well have further shaken the already dangerous bridge. The last of the V-2 rockets struck on 17 March. Nor were these the only munitions aimed at the Ludendorff bridge. Artillery barrages and bombing continued for some time after the Germans were pushed back from the immediate bridgehead. The Americans had replied with batteries of artillery, both to the air attacks, and to the enemy guns, adding to the shaking of the ground.

On 17 March at just after three in the afternoon, and while engineers were still at work on the bridge, a sound like a rifle shot was heard from the structure. Very likely a large rivet had sheared and now a large hanger dangled from the bridge. This was quickly followed by another and the deck of the bridge began to move. Finally as engineers began to run, and with a roar of moving steel and masonry, the Ludendorff bridge collapsed into the Rhine. Of the soldiers working there 29 died immediately, many of whose bodies were never recovered, and a further three later died of their injuries. More than 60 others were hurt but recovered subsequently. According to the commanding officer of one of the engineer units it was not possible to assign any single cause to the end of the bridge at Remagen, but in his opinion continuous vibration from a multitude of sources – added to the many explosions and damage, and the sheer weight of the repair equipment on one portion – had finally overcome its ability to remain standing.

Remarkably, even as the bridge came down, there were still German troops bent on its destruction. Schreiber's team heard news of the demise of the Ludendorff bridge as they were about to enter the water on the evening of 17 March. Nevertheless the mission was not aborted, merely retargeted onto the pontoons that were now obviously supplying the bridgehead on the east bank. They dressed in their diving suits, donned breathing apparatus, and set off with packages of plastic explosive attached to small empty oil drums to give them buoyancy. It would, however, have been far better to have abandoned the effort for the river was by now illuminated, and troops along the banks started to take shots at the figures in the water. The presence of searchlights mounted on tanks came as a complete surprise, and eventually the exhausted divers were pulled from the river and taken prisoner.

No fewer than 13 soldiers were decorated with the Distinguished Service Cross (DSC) for their parts in the seizure of the Remagen bridge. Three more were granted for actions on the fire side, while silver stars rained down on over a hundred more. By a strange coincidence, Second Lieutenant Timmermann, the first officer across, had been born in Germany. The citation to his DSC read:

> For extraordinary heroism in action against the enemy on 7 March, in Germany. Upon reaching the Ludendorff railroad bridge across the Rhine river, Second Lieutenant Timmermann, aware that the bridge had been prepared for demolition, and in the face of heavy machine gun, small arms, and direct 20 mm gun fire, began a hazardous trip across the span. Although artillery shells and two explosions rocked the bridge, he continued his advance. Upon reaching the bridge towers on the far side he cleared them of snipers and demolition crews. Still braving the intense machine gun and shell fire, he reached the eastern side of the river where he eliminated hostile snipers and gun crews from along the river bank and on the face of the bluff overlooking the river. By his outstanding heroism and unflinching valour, Second Lieutenant Timmermann contributed materially to the establishment of the first bridgehead across the Rhine river.

As the Allies celebrated with medals and upbeat reports about the 'miracle of Remagen' the enemy cast about for scape-goats for this 'running sore'. An already out of favour von Rundstedt was finally removed from his post as Commander in the West, and replaced by Field Marshal Albert Kesselring. For those further down the chain of command hasty ad hoc courts martial were organized under Major General Rudolf Hübner: five, including Scheller, were executed.

THE RHINE AND BERLIN

17 JANUARY – 30 APRIL 1945

> " There'll be a hot time in the town of Berlin,
> When the Yanks go marching in,
> I wanna be there boy and spread some joy
> When they take old Berlin. "
>
> Words and music by Joe Bushkin and John de Vries[1]

INTO GERMANY

According to the words of the popular song it was going to be the 'Brooklyn boys' who went into Berlin 'to take the joint apart and tear it down'. Yet, from the failure of the Ardennes offensive to the fall of the German capital, there were still three months of fighting ahead. Who would actually win the race to Berlin depended on several factors: whether the Allies stuck to prior agreements regarding zones, who could finally overcome the defence lines of the Rhine and Oder, and most importantly what the enemy chose to defend. With the Americans already having a toe-hold across the Rhine to the south, Montgomery prepared an amphibious crossing to the north: co-ordinated with airborne landings by the 6th British and 17th US Airborne, and a massive artillery bombardment. As Patrick Delaforce recalled, 'Our job was to plaster all the targets that might hold the remains of the German armies that had been thrown over the river. We fired our guns non-stop for about ten hours, and that was the biggest consecutive bombardment that I'd ever been in… And on the far side we could see the airborne division going over: they dropped within about three-quarters of a mile of the river. You could see them clearly, dropping from about 1,000ft…'

One of those now falling to earth in Operation *Varsity* was Canadian Jan de Vries:

> I remember going out, jumping: I was near the end of the stick. The whole sky was full. And that was quite a thrill to see all the 'chutes but … you didn't know what was happening because you were looking at the ground more than anything else… And I heard the bullets going by. I looked up and saw the 'chute full of holes – 'Jesus get me down!'… The breeze caught me, lifted my 'chute over the trees and I came through the branches with the prescribed feet and knees together. Broke a few branches on the way down and came to a jolt about 7ft off the ground. That was it, I hung there… And then two guys came along and one of them lifted the other one up, and then the weight of the three of us pulled my canopy clear… The three of us were on the ground, so I was a happy boy again.

The 1st Commando Brigade were in the vanguard of the British amphibious attack, and entered Wesel following fierce fighting.

PREVIOUS SPREAD
This reconstruction shows the effect of an RAF bombing raid over Berlin as the Allies closed in on the heart of the Reich. (Jeremy Llewellyn-Jones)

Meanwhile Eisenhower observed the proceedings of the US Ninth Army:

The assault, on the night of March 23/24, was preceeded by a violent artillery bombardment. On the front of the two American divisions 2,000 guns of all types participated. General Simpson and I found a vantage point in a church tower from which to witness the gunfire. Because the guns were distributed on the flat plains on the western bank of the Rhine every flash could be seen. The din was incessant. Meanwhile infantry assault troops were marching up to the water's edge to get into the boats. We joined some of them and found the troops remarkably eager to finish the job. There is no substitute for a succession of great victories in building morale... With the arrival of daylight I went to a convenient hill from which to witness the arrival of the airborne units, which were scheduled to begin their drop at ten o'clock. The airborne troops were carried to the assault in a total of 1,572 planes and 1,326 gliders; 889 fighter planes escorted them during the flight, and 2,153 other fighters provided cover over the target area and established a defensive screen to eastward.[2]

In other operations the Americans also started crossings aimed at pushing into central and southern Germany. With them was Arnold Whittaker:

It's an 800ft wide river. About 10ft deep, travelling about two or three miles an hour and we were eight men in flat bottom row boats controlled by the engineers. In other words, when you got the boat over there, somebody's got to bring it back... Another thing – we didn't have in basic training, we didn't take co-ordinated rowing lessons. So the engineers would [take] their bayonets or whatever, and pound the sound to get us co-ordinated... It wasn't until one of those shells hit the bottom of the river and came up and gushed on us, and got us all wet, that we finally got with it and said, 'Let's get across!' You had 70lbs of gear, so if the boat flipped over and you weren't hit by artillery you just drowned... As soon as we got across, our squad leader got hit with an 88. And then, on the other side, was a large orchard in bloom ... they had irrigated it from the Rhine and they had little canals, and as a result they had little dykes and every time we went over these dykes, there was a sniper picking us off. I remember going over, and I could hear it. And don't tell nobody that you can't hear a sniper's bullet because you can hear it go by your ear – because it's moving pretty fast. That's when Dick

FROM LEFT TO RIGHT
A British artillery bombardment in support of the Rhine crossing. The main 'medium' guns of the Royal Artillery were the 4.5 and 5.5in guns. The latter had a range of about ten miles with an 80lb high explosive round, slightly less with a 100lb round. Approximately 2.5 million 5.5in shells were fired between D-Day and the end of the war in Europe. (IWM BU2143)

Weiss, my buddy got hit and Goldie got hit in the throat. Just in my squad, we lost three men…'

It hit Whittaker harder than he expected:

We had an unspoken word that you don't get too close to your foxhole buddies because you don't know how long you're going to have them, and I got close to Goldie… Dick Weiss, they got him in the left arm, and I said, 'Where's Goldie?', and he said, 'Goldie isn't coming…' Then we [advanced with] walking fire and I started crying… I was a 19-year-old – dirty old – infantry replacement, walking and firing his M1, and crying. I wasn't doing a very good job of firing my M1. I was just doing it mechanically, and I shouldn't have got so emotionally tied.

Beyond the Rhine enemy resistance was often stiff, but there were also opportunities for bypassing and encirclement, and as Patrick Delaforce observed the Rhine crossing was 'a colossal leap forward psychologically'. In arguably the biggest success of the war to date the British to the north and the Americans to the south now managed to close around the Ruhr, the armaments factory of the Third Reich. The juncture of the US Ninth Army and the British 21st Army Group on 1 April created a massive

pocket trapping over 400,000 enemy service personnel. Gradually those within lost the will to fight. Walter Model committed suicide, and German Army Group B ceased to exist. Now there were new scenes for the young soldiers to witness, not all of them pleasant: ruined cities, and veritable armies of victims, refugees, and displaced persons. Near Hameln one of the thousands encountered by the 2nd US Armored was young Polish forced labourer Mathew Sikorski:

We were working in a textile factory. One of the buildings consisted of bunk beds for women and children. After some lessons my mother was manufacturing blankets, and I was changing empty bobbins... On 4 April we were ready to go to work and we tried to open the door to the factory building and it was locked. No Germans in sight anywhere... We decided it would be safer to leave the town and walked a long while in the afternoon, to the outskirts of Hameln. We decided to spend the night in the forest. At dawn I heard some very strange sounds on the roads – and I never heard sounds like that before. There was some kind of heavy vehicle, maybe not even one, but several. And there was some squealing sounds, so maybe these are tanks. So I left my mother behind and climbed the hill and carefully put my head over the top to see what was happening... To my great joy I saw that these were not German tanks, but they were American, with the

American troops use a naval LCVP during the Rhine operations: smoke was used extensively to disguise crossings. (IWM KY59430)

Men of the Cheshire regiment on the Rhine near Wesel following the successful assault crossing. (IWM BU2336)

A column of British vehicles proceed into Germany, spring 1945. (Author's Collection)

beautiful star on the side, moving slowly. I was so elated … but the turret of the first tank was moving slowly back and forth. The GIs were looking for something to shoot at. So I slid back down and presented the situation to the women there… The tallest and oldest of the group said go and bring me a stick, as long and straight as you possibly can. So I ran into the woods and came out with a stick. She was fumbling for something in her bag and I was curious what it was… She started to unfurl this piece of fabric and put it on the end of the stick. Then I realized that this was her underwear, and supposed to be our surrender flag. They could see women and children with the surrender flag, and so the first tank stopped.

By 15 April, the British 11th Armoured Division was near Celle. Initially Patrick Delaforce had no idea what happening, 'We were halted and the medical people came round and, rather rudely, squirted white DDT down all our uniforms – down our trousers, shirts, head, and we said, "What the hell's going on?"… They said, "There's a typhus area up in front"… We didn't know anything about concentration camps – never heard of them… There appeared to be rags all over the place [but] they weren't rags – they were dead bodies, or dying bodies. The smell was appalling.'

The place was Bergen Belsen, and the number of the sick and starving was approximately 55,000. Under a truce British medical personnel entered the camp. A couple of days later Richard Dimbleby reported on the scene:

I picked my way over corpse after corpse in the gloom until I heard one voice raised above the gentle undulating moaning. I found a girl, she was a living skeleton, impossible to gauge her age for she had practically no hair left, and her face was only a yellow parchment sheet with two holes for eyes. She was stretching out her stick of an arm and gasping something, it was 'English, English, medicine, medicine', and she was trying to cry but she hadn't enough strength. And beyond her down the passage and in the hut there were convulsive movements of dying people too weak to raise themselves from the floor. In the shade of some trees lay a great collection of bodies. I walked about them trying to count, there were perhaps 150 of them flung down on each other all naked, all so thin that their yellow skin glistened like stretched rubber on their bones. Some of the poor starved creatures whose bodies were there looked so utterly unreal and inhuman that I could have imagined that they had never lived at all. They were like polished skeletons, the skeletons that medical students like to play practical jokes with. At one end of the pile a cluster of men and women were gathered round a fire; they were using rags and old shoes taken from the bodies to keep it alight, and they were heating soup over it. And close by was an enclosure where 500 children between the ages of five and twelve had been kept. They were not so hungry as the rest, for the women had sacrificed themselves to keep them alive.[3]

Less than a month after the Rhine crossing the American Army was well into Bavaria. By curious paradox the 3rd 'Marne' Infantry Division took Nuremberg, cradle of Nazism, on 20 April, Hitler's birthday. On arrival the Americans found the city's anti-aircraft guns levelled against them, and the town walls, although medieval, were a significant obstacle to the infantry. As the 'Blue and White Devils' divisional history reported:

Veteran campaigners never experienced more accurate enemy sniper fire. Luftwaffe troops, crack SS Panzergrenadiers and Volksturmers held on for three days, finally retiring behind the old city's 20 foot thick wall. A 155mm howitzer, hauled into position 500 yards from the wall, could do no more than nick the outer plaster. The job was one for the doughs again. Scaling the walls, rushing the two gates and probing their way through the pitch black narrow passageways infantrymen reached the inner city, then raced for Hitler Platz and the Royal Castle in the northwest corner of the old town.

Seymour Rosen was with Lieutenant Colonel Jack Duncan's 2nd Battalion of the 7th Infantry:

In Nuremberg we were pinned down by this machine gunner up in a high building: there was a four-way intersection, and he had that pretty much covered. And as we started ahead he killed one guy and wounded two other guys. The first guy was wounded bad enough … he had chest wounds, and was coughing up blood, bleeding at the mouth, and his eyes were kind of glazed over. We knew he wasn't going to last and he kind of 'expired'. The second guy almost lost his ankle, and the third guy got stitched in the shoulder. And we decided to go around the corner to see if we could knock the gunner out… We tried to use the bazooka: we went across the street and I loaded the bazooka and tapped the guy on the head and got out of the room, and he fired and hit the building but he didn't hit the guy. And [the

LEFT
British troops examine a captured bicycle, April 1945. Attached to the front forks are a pair of Panzerfausts. Panzerfaust teams were easy to conceal and the later versions of this hollow charge weapon were capable of penetrating 150–200mm of armour – or enough to knock out virtually any Allied tank. (Author's Collection)

RIGHT
Sergeant Greenley of the 22nd Independent Parachute Company, British 6th Airborne, was claimed to be the first paratrooper to drop during the Rhine crossing. Notice the Sten gun tucked into his harness. (Author's Collection)

bazooka man] came out all bloodied from the back blast, and so we didn't do any good in a sense. In the interim we had radioed for a tanker to come up, and the tank came up and just before the intersection he stopped and our company commander jumped on the tank. He said there's a machine gun up there and we can't get through, he's got us pinned down. And the tank refused to go ahead, because he was afraid of anti-tank weapons. Our company commander pulled out his 45 and held it to his head... He finally moved.

On 25 April at Torgau on the River Elbe came one of the most historic of episodes in modern history, for that day patrols of the US 69th Infantry Division met the Red Army's 58th Guards, just 75 miles south of Berlin. Doc Molloy was not the first American soldier to shake hands with a Russian – but he was caught up in the unfamiliar magic of the moment: 'They were building a bridge towards us, we were building a bridge towards them, and during that time we learnt each others language, through sign language and otherwise. And we traded wristwatches, and tried to speak to each other showing pictures of family from home, if we had something like that... To this day I remember how they count, and how they say "good morning".'

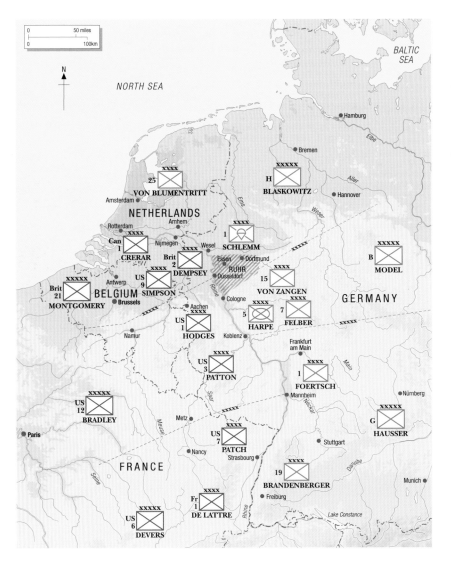

By the spring of 1945 the Allies, including the main British, American and Canadian armies, had successfully reached the Rhine. Crossing this river would be a huge psychological blow to the German defenders. (© Osprey Publishing Ltd.)

BERLIN

Bavaria, the Baltic and the Elbe were outstanding achievements, but in the East matters moved even quicker. On 30 January 1945 the Soviet Fifth Shock Army reached the River Oder. It was frozen hard: by the morning of 3 February the 301st Rifle Division was across the ice. General Vasily Chuikov of the 8th Guards Army had made impressive speed during his advance into Germany, but the last miles now turned into some of the most difficult. The race to the Oder created a massive salient, with enemy forces still very active in both Pomerania to the

The Berlin
defence plan
of March 1945.
The outer
defence line
enclosed eight
zones lettered 'A'
to 'H'. The 'green'
or battle line ran
through the
suburbs close
to the city
boundary, within
which was the
main battle line
following the
tracks of the
S-bahn. At the
heart of the
defence was the
inner line and the
final Citadel.
(Author's
Collection)

north, and Hungary, far to the south. Perhaps tanks could have risked a rush to Berlin but this might have ended in disaster with communications to the motherland threatened from the rear. The Soviet High Command, on Stalin's express instruction, decided to allow other armies to come up. The weather turned to rain, and the Oder thawed. This brief respite allowed German forces a moment of reorganization.

The battle of Seelow Heights

By 9 April the fall of Königsberg in East Prussia cleared the way for Soviet redeployment. Forces of the 2nd Belorussian Front under Marshal Konstantin Rokossovsky now moved south, and the 1st, under Marshal Georgy Zhukov, was able to concentrate against a narrower portion of the enemy front, focusing on the Seelow Heights – the last major defensive line outside Berlin. From the south the First Ukrainian Front also shifted its mass of manoeuvre, the men of Marshal Ivan Konev moving towards the north-west. The awesome bulk of the largest single mass of the Red Army was now poised with 2.5 million troops, over 6,000 tanks, 41,000 guns, 7,500 aircraft and 3,000 Katyuska truck-mounted rocket launchers. On 16 April Zhukov opened his front at Seelow Heights, seeking to force a passage over a ridge beyond the Oder where the main road skirted around the north of the town of Seelow. Though outnumbered German General Gotthard Henrici, commanding the Vistula front, had correctly anticipated the situation, denuding other areas in order to hold significant tactical features. Forward areas were occupied only lightly, with most of the German troops held further back. Battle commenced with a massive bombardment by artillery and Katyushas – answered by a lighter return barrage.

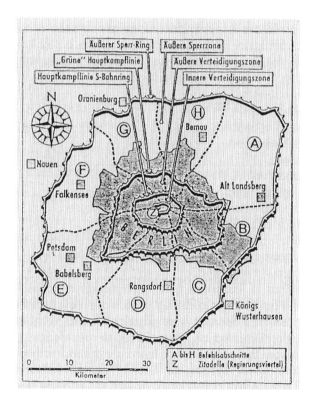

Iacov Krenin was the commander of a four-vehicle rocket battery:

Katyuska is a nickname our soldiers called it. Katyuska was the name of a girl who sang a song about waiting for her fiancé who was fighting in the war… The task was to hit the area, and a miss by 20 or more metres was of no significance… You turned the electrical firing device and it took 25 or 30 seconds for all the rockets to be launched. Not at once, but one after another. First from one side, and then from the other, so they were flying with some distance between. [From far away] you could hear a hissing sound. Then it grew louder and louder. At night the 64 rockets [from the four-piece battery] looks like fireworks… The impact area of a rocket was about 100m by 30. Everything is lit up and on fire. The effect was that a man was either killed or wounded, or started acting like crazy … traumatized. The Germans called Katyuska 'Stalin's Organ' … and were very scared of it: it was a psychological weapon too… Of course it made a noise, but not really music!… Of course, Katyuska could not win the war by itself. So it was used in combination with other artillery, aviation, tanks and infantry. Altogether it was an effective interaction of different kinds of troops.

The Soviet 82mm mortar. Being the standard medium type mortar, no fewer than 98 were allotted to rifle divisions in the latter part of the war. Of a simple tube and bipod design the weapon was capable of firing 3.3kg bombs to a maximum range of just over 1.5 miles. All the crew had to do was aim the tube and drop the projectiles down the barrel. (Author's Collection)

The rocket-battery attack was swift and hard. A complete salvo from a battery of four BM-13 launchers dumped more than 4 tons of munitions on the enemy, and might devastate several acres of ground. Massing batteries created concomitant increases in destruction. Although the Katyuska was slow to reload it was relatively easy to drive the vehicles away to a new location before the enemy had time to react. By the end of the war the Red Army had approximately 500 batteries of three major types, mounted on a variety of vehicles including the American Studebaker, Ford, GMC and Chevrolet trucks as well as Soviet Zis machines. As well as doing damage to the enemy the mobile rocket battery was a morale raiser for those it supported. As infantry officer Jakov Jarchin, a veteran of hand-to-hand combat in Moldavia noted, 'We saw how efficient our Katyuskas were, and we could see the rockets flying in the air. Artillery preparation was very effective at the beginning of an attack.'

Following bombardment Zhukov threw forward both his first attack, and then his tank reserve, taking heavy casualties – at least in part because the river and boggy ground made for difficult going. Russian progress was further hindered by the inability of observers to see what was happening on the high ground. Zhukov's uncharacteristic tactical errors were expensive in time and men – but not terminal. After two days Konev's forces had begun to unhinge the German positions from the south, by the third day Soviet forces were making their way around the Seelow Heights to the north. With the defence in tatters and no reserve, the road to Berlin was now forced open.

The Allied air offensive

Another factor in Soviet success was air power: Stalin himself was reported as saying that the Stormovik ground-attack aircraft was 'as essential to the Red Army as oxygen or bread'. This particular aircraft began life as a not very effective 'light bomber' but extensive modification such as the addition of a rear gunner and a variety of new armaments, including rockets – plus mass production – had turned it into a highly effective killing machine. According to aircraft technician Leonid Sheinker the Stormovik was no miracle weapon, but reliable, and if flown low enough, a good platform to hit enemy concentrations. To encourage the right spirit in pilots authorities held up the example of Nikolai Gastello, who, early in the war, had dived his stricken craft into a column of vehicles to devastating effect. This 'fire-ram attack' may have been either deliberate, or an intentional act of heroism, but Sheinker and his comrades were left in no doubt of the sort of thing that might be expected of them. By the end of 1944 the Soviets had sufficient control of the skies that while many Stormovik units were directed onto specific targets in support of ground operations, others were left as roving 'free flights'. These patrols were given freedom to attack targets of opportunity. As Soviet pilot Benjamin Danzig described it, 'when you found some troops moving, we were supposed to

'The Air Defence': a pamphlet outlining various first aid kits, priced from 19 to 87 Reichsmarks, that the German householder or civil defence organization could purchase for protection of home or business. Nevertheless, however well organized there was a limit to what chloroform, tablets and bandages could achieve in the face of high explosive and incendiaries. (Author's Collection)

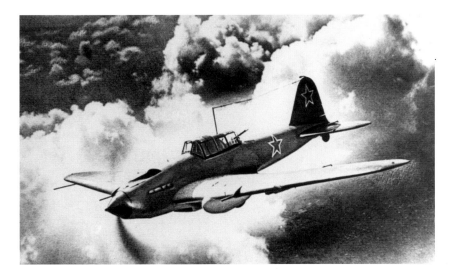

The Russian Stormovik ground-attack aircraft was an essential Soviet weapon for the final part of the war, attacking troop movements on the ground as the Allies closed in on Berlin. (Cody)

bombard and annihilate them'. Towards the end of the war he was flying two such sorties a day.

Despite successes aircrew attrition remained high as the Berlin area defences were still strong in anti-aircraft weapons. According to Danzig the lower and faster you went, the better. For heavier German weapons aimed at higher altitude marks, and light Flak had little time to respond and swing onto target if ground-attack aircraft swept past at top speed. Despite his tactical flying skill Danzig's luck ran out as the Soviet Army's final advance began. Anti-aircraft fire found his aircraft, successfully taking a chunk out of his leg as well as his Stormovik. He was no stranger to injury, having been wounded before, but this time it was serious. Danzig turned his Stormovik east, looking for a place to put down:

> The shell had hit me. I saw that my boot was full of blood, so had to land as soon as possible. I found a field and landed – but saw that it was full of trenches, part of a Polish position: I tripped on a trench and turned upside down. From there they took me and drove to the hospital. The journey took 5 hours, and later, at another hospital, they discovered gangrene and had to amputate ... they decided to send me home on a train – unconscious.

Four months of hospital treatment were required, but Danzig survived.

Berlin was, of course, being hit from the West as well as the East, and some of the biggest loads were dropped by the RAF – but it was loathed as a target by aircrew. As Leonard Levy explained, when the Wing

A Berlin street is devastated by simulated bombing. The RAF campaign now dubbed the 'battle of Berlin' commenced in November 1943 and continued until March 1944, costing about a thousand aircraft. Nevertheless raids were continued by the British, Americans and Soviets almost until the last, with the USAAF launching a particularly impressive thousand-bomber mission on Hitler's last birthday. (Jeremy Llewellyn-Jones)

Commander pointed at the map and indicated Berlin, 'in one voice 150 voices would say "Oh shit!"... Berlin was the most heavily defended city in all Europe... There's going to be six, seven, hundred aircraft in the air at the same time – night fighters, Flak, searchlights – they had "88" guns that were unbelievable', and when an aircraft spiralled down, and no parachutes were seen, that was seven young men lost. Levy nearly went the same way while returning from a mission pursued by enemy fighters. The 'port outer engine was damaged and ceased to function, two of the three fuel tanks were holed and leaking, the aircraft filled with smoke and fire. We lost our hydraulics, we lost our electronics ... the night fighter on our tail was eventually shaken although 8,000ft of altitude was lost... We [ended] up crash landing at a fighter drome called Coltishall.' Despite the dangers for Allied aircrew, by mid April 1945 Berlin had endured approximately 378 air raids reducing large portions to rubble, killing about 30,000 of its citizens, and rendering perhaps as many as a million homeless. Yet the strength of its construction and broad streets prevented the sort of total conflagration that gutted Hamburg, and while many structures were no longer habitable the vast majority still offered cover in street fighting. The raids had also encouraged the evacuation of part of the population, as well as the building of substantial new shelters capable of housing an estimated

300,000 people, and the improvement of many existing cellars and U-bahn stations. At some points 'Flak' towers had been erected to provide platforms for anti-aircraft batteries. Three of these, at Freidrichshain, Humboldthain and the Zoo were monstrous keeps. The Zoo tower, for example, projected 132ft above the ground, as well as deep into it, and mounted eight 128mm guns on the roof in addition to 37mm and 20mm weapons. At the height of the crisis it sheltered about 15,000 civilians as well as accommodating the garrison and hospital. Clearly, despite Allied air superiority the battle for Berlin would need to be won on the ground – street by street.

The final battles

As early as February it became increasingly apparent that the capital itself could soon be a battleground. General orders for holding the city were issued by General Hellmuth Reymann on 9 March 1945. These instructions were the 'spiritual' guidance of every commander and designed to achieve 'uniformity' of purpose. Their tone was at once determined, desperate and propagandistic. Put simply the defence was to be to the 'last man and the last cartridge'. As far as combat was concerned the battle for Berlin was not to be 'an open battle', but:

OVERLEAF
Soviet bombers over Berlin. These aircraft are either Petlyakov Pe-2s or Tupolev Tu-2s, both of which were light attack aircraft that could carry 3,000kg of bombs. The Soviets rarely undertook strategic bombing, concentrating the efforts of the air force on tactical and operational objectives in support of the ground forces. (Topfoto)

German Machine Guns

Allied servicemen faced a variety of machine guns ranging from older examples based on the designs of Hiram S. Maxim, through captured types from France, Czechoslovakia and Denmark, to the latest German models. The MG 34 was tested in action during the Spanish Civil War and is recognized as the world's first true 'general purpose' machine gun, being capable of both sustained volume fire and tactical battlefield mobility. In the 'heavy role' it fired from a tripod while in the light support role it was used with a small bipod. The MG 42 fired even more rapidly, and was more economical to manufacture. Well used from enfilading fire positions machine guns could be every bit as deadly as in World War I. Sometimes it was possible to hit MG nests with artillery, but all too often it was the job of the infantry to deal with them – perhaps by pinning them with fire from one direction as a soldier crept close enough to throw a grenade.

During the making of the documentary, photography of the MG 42 posed a number of technical issues, not least catching the motion of mechanism and projectiles as they cycled through the gun at rates up to 20 rounds per second. The solutions included high-speed equipment and multiple cameras to capture the action. (Jeremy Llewellyn-Jones)

A German MG 34 machine-gun team fire through a barbed wire obstacle. The *Richtschütze* of the squad fires the gun while his assistant checks the 250-round belt feeding from the steel ammunition box. The gun could also be used with 50 or 75-round drum magazines. It had a cyclic rate of over 800 rounds per minute – or rather faster than most Allied machine weapons. Used wisely from camouflaged positions with alternative firing points and several guns covering a sector, it was capable of stopping unsupported infantry in its tracks. (Author's Collection)

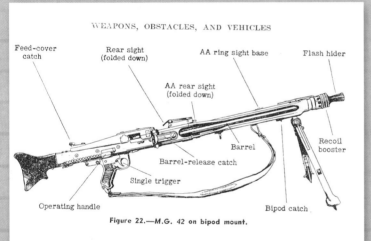

WEAPONS, OBSTACLES, AND VEHICLES

Feed-cover catch

Rear sight (folded down)

AA ring sight base

Flash hider

AA rear sight (folded down)

Barrel

Recoil booster

Barrel-release catch

Single trigger

Operating handle

Bipod catch

Figure 22.—M.G. 42 on bipod mount.

The MG 42 from an American manual illustration. It improved on the earlier MG 34 in several ways, being quicker to make and having an even faster cyclical rate of 1,200 rounds per minute. However, it was similar enough to its predecessor that it took the same belts and 7.92mm rounds and required little additional training for its crews. Best fired in very short bursts, the MG 42 made an ideal squad support weapon, heavy machine gun or vehicle piece. (Author's Collection)

Pre-war photo showing an MG 08 machine-gun team with the 70cm coincidence type range finder, left. The hefty 1908 model heavy machine gun was a water-cooled Maxim, and a veteran of the trenches of World War I with a relatively slow rate of 450 rounds per minute. Nevertheless it soldiered on with reserve and police formations all the way through to 1945, and as a design was only marginally older than the British Vickers. (Author's Collection)

OPPOSITE

A member of the SS *Feldgendarmerie*, or military police. Nicknamed *Kettenhund* or 'chain dogs' due to the gorget of office hung on a chain about the neck, they were a key element in the maintenance of discipline. Already widely feared the draconian 'last ditch' orders issued in the final weeks of the war granted virtually untrammelled authority to take all measures, up to and including death, to keep troops to their posts. (Author's Collection)

chiefly in the form of street and house-to-house fighting. It must be conducted with fanaticism; imagination; with all means of deception, craft, and cunning, with planned and spontaneous raids of all kinds, on, above, and below the ground. What is important here is to exploit mercilessly the advantages of being on our own soil and the presumed fear of most Russians faced with an unfamiliar sea of houses. Precise knowledge of place, the utilization of the underground railway and sewer system, of existing communications, the excellent potential of houses for combat and concealment, the fortress like extension of blocks of houses – particularly reinforced concrete houses – into bases of operation render the defenders invincible to any foe…

The enemy was not to be allowed a minute's peace, but made to 'burn and bleed to death' in the tight network of pockets of resistance. Every feature, house, shell hole or hedge, was to be defended 'to the last'. Every house or base of operations was to be recaptured by counter-attack, and 'shock troops' penetrating behind the enemy by means of subterranean passages emerging in order to 'surprise and destroy him from behind'. Success depended less on 'perfect grasp of the techniques of military science' but sheer willpower, every fighter being 'inspired and permeated by the fanatical will to want to fight', in a battle that 'may decide the outcome of the war'. Such words were intended to rouse defiance in the breasts of the outnumbered: but to many it appeared nothing more than a matter of kill or be killed. The presence of Hitler himself was also a factor. By staying in Berlin he granted himself the 'moral right' to 'take action against weakness'. He could not 'keep threatening others if I myself run away from the Reich capital in the crucial hour'.[4] In the event discipline was maintained by more than just idle threats. Hitler's 'order of the day' warned that there were enemies within as well as without:

Whoever fails in his duty now behaves as a traitor to our people. Any regiment or division that abandons its position will be acting so disgracefully that it will be shamed before the women and children braving the terror of the bombing in our cities. Above all be on your guard against those few treacherous officers and soldiers, who, in order to preserve their pitiful lives, fight against us in Russian pay, perhaps even wearing German uniform. Anyone ordering you to retreat, unless personally known to you, will be immediately arrested and, if necessary, shot on the spot, no matter what rank he may hold.

While German methods of instilling determination into the resistance were draconian and murderous, Soviet proceedings were hardly less brutal. For according to Stalin's orders, 'all agents, saboteurs and terrorists must be captured, [likewise] all those who have served in German police units, as public prosecutors, leaders of fascist organizations, editors of newspapers and magazines, members of the so-called "Russian Liberation Army" as well as other suspicious elements'. Such apprehension often spelled death. Not least amongst the 'suspicious elements' to be held were members of the Red Army who had been captured by the enemy and lived to tell the tale. To the Communist leadership it was considered incomprehensible that a Soviet soldier should allow himself to be captured, and some Russians prisoners-of-war had indeed acted as 'Hiwis' or 'voluntary helpers' to the enemy. Yet 'voluntary' was a relative term, as Nazi captivity in this war of annihilation was itself a likely death sentence.

On entering German territory Soviet troops were informed that they were going to 'tread the ground that gave birth to the fascist monsters who devastated our cities and homes, slaughtered our sons and daughters, our brothers and sisters, our wives and mothers'.[5] As the Russian journalist Ilya Ehrenburg explained in a hard-hitting morale raising piece:

> Not only divisions and armies are advancing on Berlin. All the trenches, graves and ravines filled with corpses of the innocents are advancing on Berlin, all the cabbages of Maidanek and all the trees of Vitebsk on which the Germans hanged so many unhappy people. The boots and shoes and the babies' slippers of those murdered and gassed at Maidanek are marching on Berlin. The dead are knocking on the doors of Joachimsthaler Strasse, of the Kaiserallee, of Unter den Linden and all the other cursed streets of that cursed city…[6]

Jakov Jarchin recalled that the Russian soldier now felt that he was, '… equal to the Germans … we had a long period of advancing behind us, we were supported by Katyuskas and the morale was quite high'.

Goebbels' propaganda had it that Germans would be murdered indiscriminately and rape and pillage could be taken for granted. Although very moderate compared to the Soviets, the Western Allies were not entirely guiltless. GI Seymour Rosen came across 'some pretty bad dudes in our army', and remembered at least some cases of rape, and a 'Kentucky guy who took delight at shooting at civilians' until the authorities 'got him out of there'. Yet such serious matters were the exception rather than the rule in the West, and as Rosen himself observed maltreatment of prisoners was counter-productive in the long run. Certainly, 'You did not want to let the German Army know that you were mistreating prisoners, because [then] they had nothing to lose. If they knew they were going to be mistreated or killed, they would just stay and fight longer. It didn't make any sense...' Even so thousands of civilians died in air raids, and enthusiastic 'souvenir hunting' was widespread. Although, as acknowledged by Rosen, the frontline soldier had to be careful as German watches, personal trinkets and weapons might be taken as an indicator by the enemy that you had been personally responsible for killing the original owner. So it was that, 'if you were in danger of being captured, you discarded any enemy souvenirs you had'.

Compared to what was about to happen in the East much of this was trivial – and most Germans knew it. For the Russians had now crossed a thousand miles of territory once held by the enemy. In it they had been angry witnesses to mass evidence of killings, starvation, burnings and wanton destruction. Huge numbers of refugees began to trek west. As one Russian officer recalled, 'The hate ran so deep we wanted to end the war, and annihilate that force that wanted to kill us.'[7] Many were prepared for similar revenge; almost all were ready for a taste of the apparent luxuries of the West, so long denied to them by the Spartan and brutal existence of an 'Ivan' in the Red Army. Even in Poland there were clear signs of what to expect. Peter Kemp was a British observer of the arrival of the Red Army in a Polish town, where the soldiers:

behaved with calculated brutality and contempt. They broke up furniture for firewood, they pilfered every article of value and marked or spoilt what they did not care to take away; they urinated and defecated in every room … the hall, the stairs and passages were heaped and spattered with piles of excrement, the walls and floors were splashed with liquor, spittle and vomit – the whole building stank like an untended latrine. It is a pity that those communists who declared that they would welcome the Red Army as liberators never saw that particular army at its work of liberation.[8]

When American engineer officer Frank Camm encountered the rank and file Russian soldiery he concluded that they were, 'ordinary guys … not very many were very intelligent: they're much more like farmhands than anything else, and I noticed that they couldn't take care of their equipment'. Perhaps this was more of a comment on the education of the masses under Stalin's rule, rather than the quality of the individual. Surprisingly some of 'Ivan's' own officers came to much the same conclusions. As Jakov Jarchin put it, 'In my opinion it's a lack of upbringing, lack of ethics in some soldiers, and it's also a feeling that he can do anything he wants' that was to blame for some of the excesses witnessed in the final months and weeks of the war.

In October 1944 the Red Army had made its first incursions into East Prussia, seizing Nemmersdorf and other German settlements. A local counter-attack by Hossbach's Fourth Army wrested the area back again just a few days later. Women and children had been slaughtered; perhaps even more remarkably the dead included known critics of the Nazis and French prisoners-of-war who had been working on the land. This terrible incident, widely reported in the most colourful and prurient manner, was a gift to Nazi rabble rousers intent on influencing their countrymen to do, or most likely die, in the face of the Red 'hordes'. Ulf Ollech was one young gunner on the route into town:

I was only 17, but suddenly I had to shoot at human beings in order to preserve my own life. We were trained with artillery, and were stationed on one of Berlin's arterial roads, the Prezlauer Allee, it was called. Work began at 0700 hours – practice with artillery and training, training. Then we were transferred to the north-east, to the eastern edge of Bernau. We set up positions on the road, but were then transferred at night to a place called Malchow, where we had a free field of fire on the road closer to Berlin, near

OPPOSITE
Dr Joseph Paul Goebbels (1897–1945) was born at Rheydt in the Rhineland, and died by his own hand, along with his family, in the Berlin bunker. Joining the Nazi party in 1922 he was soon identified as a gifted speaker and vitriolic propagandist. As Minister for Public Enlightenment and Propaganda his key wartime role was to uphold home morale, but he also became Defence Commissioner for Berlin, playing a part in the final campaign as a right-hand man to Hitler. (Author's Collection)

OPPOSITE

A Soviet late model T-34 tank in the Imperial War Museum collections mounting the 85mm gun introduced in 1943. The vehicle in the background is the Jagdpanther a tank destroyer version of the Panzer V, Panther, mounting the potent 88mm L/71 anti-tank gun. The Jagdpanther was fast, boasted 80mm of frontal armour against the 45mm of the T-34, and came into production in January 1944. It has been described, not unfairly, as 'Germany's most effective tank destroyer of the war'. (Author's Collection)

the Weissensee… The *Volkssturm* troops were in the trenches in front of us. Behind us were residential areas with trees and houses and gardens, so that we were well camouflaged; and we expected, quite rightly, that the Red Army would come along this road straight past us. We had to be patient… We spent the night there, half awake, half asleep, and the next morning, when the sun rose, we heard they were slowly advancing along this road. Because it was an asphalt road, the Russians could see exactly whether or not someone had been laying mines there. But it was free of mines, and so they advanced.

Four T-34s, two Shermans and an assault gun came along. The road had a small bend and before the first tank had reached this bend we started firing. We had a gun which had a velocity of 1,200m per second, the only gun in the world from which the shell left the barrel at such speed. This meant that the discharge and impact, especially at a distance of 200, perhaps 300 metres, was so short you thought the discharge and impact were the same sound. The tanks were all destroyed and the Red Army infantry at the rear of the tanks dispersed.

The wrecked tanks glowed red throughout the night and the ammunition inside them exploded. We spent the night there, and the next morning the weather was dry, we discovered that the infantry units, in the shape of the *Volkssturm*, had gone, vanished. They were supposed to be in front of us and we had seen them the day before, but now they were nowhere to be seen. That, of course, scared the wits out of us…[9]

It is often said that in the last days of the war Hitler was totally out of touch with reality moving now non-existent armies around on the Berlin bunker maps. While this familiar image has more than a grain of truth there were certainly moments of awful clarity. Detailed reports of military conferences, ostensibly recorded word for word by official stenographers, continued to be made until as late as 27 April 1945, revealing flashes of dreadful realization. In fragments of the surviving situation report of 2 March Hitler exclaims to Jodl that the 'divisions' on the upper Rhine are merely 'unit symbols', 'junk' that the commander on the spot will have to use to create 'something' while orders given by SS General Heinz Reinefarth could not be followed through because the troops simply were not there. In another part of the same document it suddenly dawns on the Führer that the Russians possess, on one modest sector, greater armoured strength than the entire German force in the whole of Italy. Interestingly, one thing that seemed to make sense of the vain hopes of the defenders was a growing awareness in the bunker that the Allies were moving to prearranged 'demarcation lines'. These could be exploited as they might either hamper enemy movements, or even cause friction between East and West if any forces could be induced to cross them.

But any significant change of fortune depended upon intervention of German forces from outside. On 21 April SS General Felix Steiner, commanding 'Army Detachment Steiner', was ordered to attack Zhukov's forces encircling Berlin from the north. Steiner refused, instead requesting permission for his forces to fall back to avoid annihilation. As a result, General Walter Wenck's Twelfth Army, currently facing westward, was ordered to disengage from the Americans and

drive east, linking up with the Ninth Army of General Theodor Busse, so striking at the Soviet stranglehold from the west and south. At the same time XLI Panzer Corps under General Rudolf Holste would attack from the north. Wenck sent the encouraging message to Berlin that he understood the significance of his task and was gathering together the remnants of various formations for this final effort. He was 'proceeding with all forces against ordered objectives'. Yet Wenck's formations were already completely drained by previous exertions, and his movements were stymied by their own entanglement with American forces.

Nevertheless, Wenck at least succeeded in performing the about face required to bring his army into action with the Russians, and while Busse and Holste made little progress Wenck drove his men almost as far as Potsdam before being halted by superior Soviet forces. In explaining why he had continued to fight Wenck later stated that the battle was no longer about the Reich, nor even about Berlin, but about allowing as

Der Panzerbär –
'The Tank Bear',
issue of 27 April
1945, for 'reading
and passing on'.
This 'battle paper
for the defenders
of greater Berlin'
was intended as
a morale raising
news sheet. Its
symbol was the
bear of Berlin,
carrying a spade
and Panzerfaust,
the key arms of
those who dug
and manned the
anti-tank
defences. The last
edition came out
on 29 April
detailing the final
'heroic struggle'.
(Author's
Collection)

many people, military or civilian, to make their way to the West. In this he was partially successful, and some of Busse's men did indeed manage to escape to join with Twelfth Army, though the majority were captured or killed during their final stand in the Halbe Pocket when the German Ninth Army was entirely encircled by Marshal Konev's forces. What was left now retreated westward. Realistically even if other formations had broken through to Berlin, this would only have delayed the inevitable. For, as troops were sucked in to the defence of Berlin from surrounding areas, the Reich itself would shrink, and, within days or at most weeks, there would be nothing left. Nonetheless, as late as 29 April messages were still being sent from the bunker enquiring what points Twelfth Army and other possible relief forces had reached.

Hitler maintained the fanciful illusion that only by remaining in Berlin, and by continuing some sort of resistance against the Russians, could the Western Allies still be convinced, long past the eleventh hour, to turn their guns upon the Communists. While this was extremely unlikely it would also have been an exaggeration to suggest that the relations of the Western Allies with 'Uncle Joe' were entirely open and trusting. For, as late as just a few days before the opening of Operation *Berlin*, Stalin informed the West that his main target was in fact Dresden. Within the Chancellery, and isolated from accurate information, the Führer was in danger of becoming an irrelevance after years of behaving as demigod: but there appeared little point in leaving. As he put it to Krebs and Goebbels on 25 April, 'as an inglorious refugee from Berlin, I would have no authority in either northern or southern Germany, and in Berchtesgaden even less'. A few moments later Hitler broke off in the midst of another subject to observe that, '... if we were to leave the world stage so disgracefully, then we would have lived in vain. It's completely unimportant if we continue to live for a while or not. Better to end the battle honourably than to go on living in shame and dishonour for a few more months or years.'[10] The die was cast.

The final defence of Berlin

The hopelessness of the German situation was obvious to most. As General of Artillery Helmuth Weidling, who was appointed to the unenviable task of leading the defence of the Reich capital, recorded:

> The 24th of April had already convinced me that it was impossible to defend Berlin, and that it was also senseless from a military standpoint, since the German High Command did not have sufficient forces. In addition, the commander did not have a single regular unit at his disposal in Berlin at the time, with the exception of the *Grossdeutschland* regiment and an SS Brigade that was guarding the Reich Chancellery. The entire defence was handed over to the Peoples' Reserve (*Volkssturm*), the police, the fire-brigade and various troops of the rear area service and various administrative departments.
>
> The city was divided into eight outer and one inner defence sector. Communication among the various sectors was poor... Berlin had food and munitions reserves for thirty days. Since the store houses were on the outskirts of the city, however, supplying food and munitions became increasingly difficult the more the ring of Russians tightened around the defenders. On the last two days we had neither food, nor munitions. I think that the Volkssturm, the Police detachments, the fire-brigade and the anti-aircraft units consisted of about 90,000 men, not counting the troops of the rear area services. There were also the Volkssturm of the second mobilisation as the various firms were closed in the course of the battle. The LVI Tank

Volkssturm marching through Berlin following a speech from Goebbels. This photo, disseminated through 'a neutral nation', found its way to American press agencies on 31 December 1944. Though older than most regular troops, every man is equipped with Panzerfaust anti-tank weapon, greatcoat, air defence helmet and Swastika arm band. Some also have pistols. The parade, and appearance of the picture, helped give an impression of a well armed, well disciplined, force. (Author's Collection)

OPPOSITE

Soviet infantry armed with the iconic PPsh 7.62 submachine gun seen here in a battle for a village. With its distinctive 71-round drum magazine it was the main close combat arm of the Red Army. About five million were manufactured during the war. Many were captured by the enemy who found it simple and robust, giving excellent fire power at close quarters. Some were therefore converted to fire 9mm ammunition. (Author's Collection)

Corps reached Berlin, that is, retreated to Berlin, with 13,000 to 15,000 men. It is impossible to give an exact figure of the number of people who defended Berlin, since I did not receive figures on the troop strength of the individual units under my command.[11]

The *Volkssturm* (literally 'Storm of the People' or 'People's Army'), who provided a significant part of the close defence of the city, were of greatly varying quality. Effectively a 'people's militia', the formation was a last ditch levy for home defence, and in theory could include every able-bodied German male between 16 and 60 not already under arms. With fit men from their late teens to late 30s already largely swept up by the regular forces the emphasis was inevitably on the older, and on the young. Not technically part of the German Army, but a scion of the Party, the Volkssturm was originally decreed into existence, by Hitler, on 25 September 1944, but formally announced on the propitious date of 18 October, anniversary of the victorious 1813 battle of Leipzig. The vision of the Volkssturm was impressive indeed, calling for a total of six million men throughout the Reich. These were to be organized in over 1,000 battalions, in a series of enlistments; the first being for service in 'frontline' battalions; the second in factory and local battalions for area defence; the third of youths in the 16 to 19 bracket, as well as volunteers as young as 15; and the fourth for guard duty, but including enthusiasts of over 60 who still wished to serve. The best of the crop, the battalions of the first enlistment, were supposed to be 649-men strong, organized in three companies, each company having three five-man anti-tank squads as part of its establishment. In the event about 700 battalions actually saw service, and those of the third and fourth levies received few arms other than those they could procure for themselves. Volkssturm training, focusing essentially on weapons handling, was a basic 48-hour programme, often fitted around the continuation of work, such as that on fortification construction.

Goebbels in his capacity as both 'Reich Defence Commissioner for the Reich Defence District of Berlin', and Gauleiter, attended the swearing in ceremony of the Wilhelmplatz First Battalion on 12 November – a unit actually including employees of his own Propaganda Ministry. He described them enthusiastically as 'modern troops, with the spirit of 1813, but the weapons of 1944'. This was partially true in that the Volkssturm did receive issues of new Panzerfaust and Panzerschreck anti-tank weapons and grenades, plus rifles, some of them obsolete – but which unit got what, and how much, appears to have been something of a lottery. The vexed question of uniforms was never really solved for although the Volkssturm had a ranking system of pips worn on the collar, not everyone had a suitable costume to put them on. The fortunate got German Army greatcoats and caps, others wore brown Party uniforms, a few captured uniform with new badges – but some received nothing more than an arm band. Not everyone had head protection, but many wore the *Luftschutz* helmets of the civilian air defence organization. One provincial newspaper offered constructive advice:

> Uniformity of clothing in the *Volkssturm* is, in itself, of no importance: but camouflage is. To wear bright, or very light coloured clothing is inadvisable. It has therefore been decided that light coloured clothing, such as the party uniform, shall be dyed the new *einsatzbraun* [service brown]. The dyeing of civilian suits, however, will only be carried out if the original colour is unsuitable for field service and provided that the suit, after being dyed, can still be worn by its owner for his lawful, civilian occasions.

Some Volkssturm would fight bravely, virtually to the last man, knocking out tanks at pointblank range: others failed totally through lack of weapons or training, and some did not make it into battle at all. At least one Berlin Volkssturm battalion, receiving no uniform or ammunition for their limited number of old Danish rifles, were able to procrastinate long enough to remain uncommitted.

The physical lines of the Berlin defence were formed by a series of concentric positions. The outer rested on a chain of natural obstacles between the Dahme and Alte Oder rivers, stretching for about 50 miles, and there were obstacle belts blocking major road junctions north and south of the city. Another zone of defence, the 'green line', was formed on the city boundary, supported where possible, by fall back positions. Within this the next layer of the onion was the main inner defence ring, or *Hauptkampflinie*, based on the S-bahn, or suburban rail circuit. Finally came what was optimistically dubbed the *Zitadelle*, or citadel, resting on the strength of what was effectively an island formed by the River Spree, the Landwehr canal and 'bastions' east and west around Alexanderplatz and Am Knie. To create a sufficient labour force for the improvement of the physical defences the only army engineer battalion available was supplemented by two of the Volkssturm and a mass of semi-skilled personnel drawn from the Reichs Labour Service (RAD); Organization Todt; civilians; prisoners-of-war; and outright slave labour. By such means 70,000 were gathered for the works. In the absence of enough fuel and motor vehicles loads of materials were moved mainly by rail, or horse and cart.

The outer rings, being of great length, could only be improved with basic field defences consisting of at least one fire-trench line, and, over a significant span, an anti-tank ditch. Bridges were blown, or prepared for demolition. Yet, what should be destroyed and when was a matter for argument. Hitler's orders called for crossings to be obliterated indiscriminately, but at the same time some bridges were useful to the defence, and others carried gas, electrical and water supplies as well as carriageways. Speer's account is that he argued for bridges to be preserved, with an eye to the post-war situation, while generals Henrici and Reymann conspired to keep some for tactical reasons. According to one post-war calculation only 127 of Berlin's 483 bridges were therefore cut at this stage. The S-bahn was a significant obstacle to attackers in that the multiple rail lines formed fields of fire, and in many places cuttings or embankments provided ditches or ready-made ramparts. Artillery was the main defensive weapon, with many of the anti-aircraft guns, that had hitherto pointed skyward, being dug in against tanks alongside existing anti-tank weapons. In the city centre masonry and more limited fields of fire were turned to advantage with barricades blocking streets, machine-gun positions on roofs and in cellars and holes broken between buildings allowing defenders to move unseen from one place to another. Blocks were created in some U-bahn tunnels, and others were prepared for demolition or flooding. Weidling's communications problems were exacerbated by the fact that many of the recently raised militia had no radios, and therefore had to rely on the civilian telephone network – and runners who might fall victim to a sniper's bullet or bombardment at any moment. Like an orange, viewed from above, the eight main segments of the city were lettered clockwise 'A' to 'H'. Each had its own commander, but the citadel was entrusted to SS

Brigadeführer Wilhelm Mohnke whose final reserve was a 1,200 man detachment of the *Liebstandarte Adolf Hitler.*

The Red Army assault

Soviet strategy, as assessed by General Krebs, was essentially tripartite. The first objective would be to encircle in general; the second to divide the larger isolated area into parts; and the third to mount specific thrusts to fragment the city centre into ever smaller and manageable parts. The final assaults were likely to be made against Potsdamer Platz, Alexanderplatz and the Charlottenburg railway station. Tank rider Lieutenant Evgeni Bessonov encountered the enemy on a reinforced railway line position as the Soviet forces enveloped Berlin from the south:

A Soviet Katyuska battery at work. First used in action in 1941 this truck-mounted rocket launching system was developed by the Leningrad Gas Dynamics Laboratory and was used in significant numbers during the final campaigns of the war. (Getty Images)

> At dawn on 22 April we approached a high railway embankment and were stopped by intensive fire. We could quickly have destroyed the German delaying force and moved on forward, but the problem was that the passage under the railway bridge was filled with sand and fortified with big logs, connected with metal girders. We did not manage to destroy that barricade... We rode on tanks for some time and all of a sudden came under fire from trenches on the right-hand side of the road. The tanks stopped, I ordered, 'Dismount! Fire!' and the whole company ran towards those trenches firing non-stop from our submachine guns. Right in front of me was a Fritz in a trench. I tried to cut him down with my German submachine gun, but apparently during the skirmish at the embankment some sand had got into

the bolt. I jerked the bolt, pulled the trigger, but it did not fire. The German did not think long, grabbed his rifle and aimed it at me… Right at that time a submachine gun burst sounded in the air and the German dropped dead at the bottom of the trench. It turned out that it was Drozd who cut him down with a Soviet PPsh submachine gun, which never jammed in battle. Why the hell did I carry that German submachine gun? We jumped across the trenches, some Germans fled, while the rest were killed. Andrey took away my submachine gun, took out the magazine and threw the submachine gun away.[12]

By the last days Soviet and German soldiers were so closely locked in street battles that air power ceased to have much meaning, for aircraft were as likely to strike friend as foe. Instead it became a short-range infantryman's war. As Soviet infantry officer Jakov Jarchin explained:

I can give you an idea. For example when we attacked an individual building, before entering, we used guns and mortars, to shell the building so that the soldiers would have easier access. Then, under support of our mortars, we attempted to surround the building, and cause the Germans to surrender. Then we threw grenades into the building. If that didn't work we had to go in – despite the danger, advancing step by step, and sometimes fighting hand-to-hand with the Germans… In my unit we had rifles, submachine guns and spades. That's all… Berlin was all in ruins, all because of massive American and British [air] bombardment. The population was in basements; no water and no electricity; lacking food. Equally some men were completely ruined…

OPPOSITE
With the Western Allies reaching the Elbe river the Soviet Armies began their encirclement of Berlin and the final destruction of the German armed forces (here depicted in blue). Marshal Zhukov began his main attack on 16 April 1945. Just nine days later the encirclement of the capital was complete. (© Osprey Publishing Ltd.)

Early in the afternoon of 30 April Red Army Sergeant Kantaria reached the second floor of the Reichstag and succeeded in waving the Red banner. Although German troops were still on the floor above him the distance to the *Fürherbunker* in the Chancellery garden in Wilhelmstrasse could now be measured in just hundreds of metres. Soon afterwards Eva Braun took poison and Hitler put his pistol into his mouth and pulled the trigger. By that evening the Red flag had finally reached the top of the Reichstag.

An important witness of the final fall of Berlin was Vasily Grossman, special correspondent for the Russian Army's *Red Star* newspaper. Grossman was an experienced journalist, and had witnessed both Stalingrad and the aftermath of the liberation of the concentration camp at Treblinka. Yet even he was almost dumbfounded by this 'monstrous

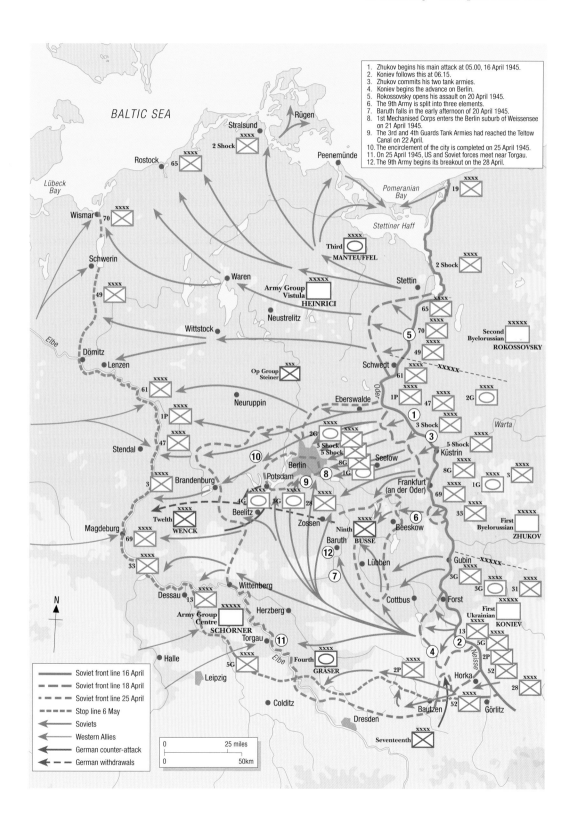

BALTIC SEA

Pomeranian
Bay

1. Zhukov begins his main attack at 05.00, 16 April 1945.
2. Koniev follows this at 06.15.
3. Zhukov commits his two tank armies.
4. Koniev begins the advance on Berlin.
5. Rokossovsky opens his assault on 20 April 1945.
6. The 9th Army is split into three elements.
7. Baruth falls in the early afternoon of 20 April.
8. 1st Mechanised Corps enters the Berlin suburb of Weissensee on 21 April 1945.
9. The 3rd and 4th Guards Tank Armies had reached the Teltow Canal on 22 April.
10. The encirclement of the city is completed on 25 April 1945.
11. On 25 April 1945, US and Soviet forces meet near Torgau.
12. The 9th Army begins its breakout on the 28 April.

Rügen

Stralsund
2 Shock

Rostock 65

Peenemünde

Lübeck
Bay

Wismar 70

Stettiner Haff

19

Third
MANTEUFFEL

2 Shock

Schwerin

Waren

49

Army Group
Vistula
HEINRICI

Stettin

65

Wittstock

Neustrelitz

Schwedt

70

49

Second
Byelorussian
ROKOSSOVSKY

Elbe

Dömitz

Lenzen

Op Group
Steiner

Schwedt

61

Oder

61

1P

47

2G

Warta

Neuruppin

Eberswalde

1

Stendal

1P

47

3 Shock

3

Küstrin

5 Shock

2G

3 Shock
5 Shock

8G

1G

Seelow

8G

1G

3

Berlin

Potsdam

9

8

10

Brandenburg

3

Frankfurt
(an der Oder)

69

33

First
Byelorussian
ZHUKOV

4G

3G

28

Beelitz

Zossen

6

Beeskow

Twelfth
WENCK

Magdeburg

69

Ninth
BUSSE

Baruth

12

Gubin

3G

3G

31

33

Lübben

7

Cottbus

Forst

First
Ukrainian
KONIEV

Wittenberg

Dessau 13

Herzberg

Army Group
Centre
SCHÖRNER

Torgau

11

13

5G

2P

N

Halle

5G

Elbe

Fourth
GRÄSER

Leipzig

2P

Horka

Bautzen

52

Görlitz

28

Colditz

Dresden

Seventeenth

Soviet front line 16 April
Soviet front line 18 April
Soviet front line 25 April
Stop line 6 May
Soviets
Western Allies
German counter-attack
German withdrawals

0   25 miles
0   50km

concentration of impressions', wreathed in fire and smoke, where he saw:

> Enormous crowds of prisoners. Their faces are full of drama. In many faces there's sadness, not only personal suffering, but also the suffering of a citizen. This overcast, cold and rainy day is undoubtedly the day of Germany's ruin. In smoke, among the ruins, in flames, amid hundreds of corpses in the streets. Corpses squashed by tanks, squeezed out like tubes. Almost all of them are clutching grenades and sub-machine guns in their hands. They have been killed fighting. Most of the dead men are dressed in brown shirts. They were party activists who defended the approaches to the Reichstag and Reichschancellery. Prisoners – policemen, officials, old men and next to them schoolboys, almost children...[13]

The Red flag being raised over the Reichstag by sergeants M. A. Yegorov and M. V. Kantaria. This was a reconstruction soon after the actual event for the lens of photographer Yevgeny Khaldei. (Topfoto)

Other sights he observed that day ranged from the homely to the terrible: a little child crushed into the mud by tank or shell; infantry making a bonfire in the Reichstag to heat their mess tins; celebrations, looting and laughing; dead animals and hungry lions in the Tiergarten; curious soldiery and Hitler's furniture together with his appropriately crushed globe. As Leonid Sheinker recalled, 'we were happy and sad at the same time ... [we] were euphoric, we hugged and kissed each other'.

Grossman also hinted at other occurrences when he described a meeting with a young Frenchman arguing that the Soviet Army's treatment of women in the city was going to damage its fine 'fighting reputation'. Indeed, one of the most remarkable things about the violation of Berlin was its scope and variety. One Danish journalist who witnessed it described it as less to do with sex than a 'destructive, hateful, and wholesale act of vengeance'.[14] At one end of the scale were children and old women gang raped to death: at the other some Russian officers, endowed with a strangely old world gentility, who made more or less willing German women semi-official mistresses, so preserving them from the worst defilement. Rape was certainly very widespread, and although a round figure of 100,000 Berlin women attacked is often quoted the true figure may never be known: some victims went unreported, some suffered more than once. Much was down to guesswork. A significant number of people – men as well as women – committed suicide, either before or after facing the rough hand, or summary justice and pillage, of the victors. As General Weidling himself described it, 'the moment had come to settle the bill for the sins of the past years'.[15]

For the victor the spoils

Property was target of both unofficial robbery and strategically directed official looting. The Russian *Frontoviki* took anything and everything and often spoiled what they could not take – even the humble private being allowed to send back East a 5kg parcel every month. Yet there were many more significant removals. The Allies had long since agreed that Germany would pay reparations for her war of aggression, and this was quickly expressed in appropriation of plants and 'deindustrialization'. The Soviets installed General Nikolai Bersarin as 'City Commandant General' as early as 27 April assuming total 'administrative and political authority' – even before Hitler was dead. A campaign of seizing machinery began prior to the arrival of the Western Allies in July, focusing effort on the western part of the city. The works of Siemens, AEG, Osram and various chemical plants were all targeted. The Schering laboratories were visited by a 300-man Russian team before the end of May who removed scales, pumps, motors, microscopes and anything vaguely transportable. This was in no way unusual. Over half of western Berlin's industrial capacity quickly vanished, a larger proportion than that destroyed in the aerial onslaught and street fighting. Men and women alike were conscripted for labour, though at least this was usually accompanied by organized feeding. The arrival of the British and Americans did not spell the end of the process, but merely the onset of a new phase, and seizures of property continued in the West until 1949, and in the East to as late as 1953. While living under the Soviets meant simply exchanging one totalitarian regime for another, life in the western part of the city would be no idyll either. Physical shortage and hardship were accompanied by military administration, 'denazification' enquiries including the American '*fragebogen*' questionnaires, the closure of businesses run by active Nazis, and initially at least, injunctions against troops 'fraternising' with the conquered. After 12 years as Hitler's capital, Berlin was now both a conquered and a divided city.

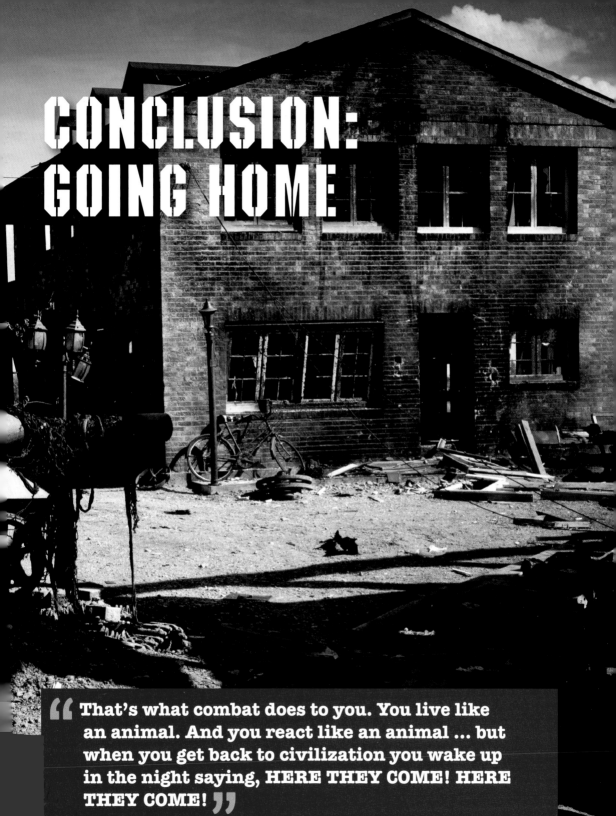

CONCLUSION: GOING HOME

"That's what combat does to you. You live like an animal. And you react like an animal ... but when you get back to civilization you wake up in the night saying, HERE THEY COME! HERE THEY COME!"

Carl Beck, US 501st Parachute Infantry

**PREVIOUS
SPREAD**
This recreation
shows just one
small part of the
destruction of
Berlin, using a
Berlin street
as a source
of inspiration.
(Jeremy
Llewellyn-Jones)

OPPOSITE
Erected in 1791
as the royal
entrance gate
to Berlin, the
triumphal arch
had already been
a victim of war in
1806 when the
sculpture of the
winged goddess
of victory was
taken away by
Napoleon.
During the final
struggle of 1945
hospital trains
were parked in
the S-bahn
nearby and the
long straight road
in front of the
gate served as
emergency
runway for light
aircraft. Tanks and
guns were dug in
to support the
defence.
Eventually strong
Soviet forces
converged
towards this
point from
multiple
directions.
(Author's
Collection)

Just as every German appeared to be claiming they had never been a Nazi, everybody else was staking symbolic claim to having been the first to capture the Eagle's Nest above Berchtesgaden, Hitler's mountain retreat just inside Germany, on the Austro-Bavarian border. Folklore suggested the honour was claimed by the US 101st Airborne. French troops were certainly also nearby. Neither actually took the Eagle's Nest, and the glory – if such it is – belongs to some anonymous 'dogface' scout of the 3rd Infantry Division, whose regimental history records that the 1st and 3rd Battalions of the 7th Infantry, 'raced to capture Berchtesgaden. There they raised the American flag at Hitler's Eagle's Nest.' Official US Army photographs dated 4 May 1945, now in the National Archives, confirm this version of history – showing somebody in American uniform hauling down the swastika. Snow is still on the ground from the previous night while in photographs taken by other units it has already melted. The first group onto the mountain was a detachment commanded by Lieutenant Sherman Pratt. According to one report the flag was taken to the German-born American regimental commander, Colonel John Heintges, who ordered it cut into pieces and distributed to his officers. Veterans of Iwo Jima might disagree, but in many respects the taking down of this particular flag was more important than the putting up of any number of your own. Actually the 3rd Division had not raced from the beaches of Normandy at all as is the common misconception – having been landed in the south of France. So much for popular myths. Veterans are certainly aware of problems in interpretation of the past – both for historians, and for eyewitnesses. As Canadian John Thompson put it with a laugh, 'We exaggerate. The stories get better as you get older too you know, because there's fewer people to call you a bloody liar!'

Ultimately, however, history does come down to just one thing: interaction of people with each other, ideas, places and objects. The last year of World War II in Europe was a tragic example on a vast canvas – a titanic clash of ideology, in which democracies aligned at least temporarily with Communism to crush Fascism. Personalities in the towering forms of Stalin, Churchill, Roosevelt and Hitler bestrode the stage in every way as forcefully as kings and emperors of old. The persecution of the Jews added not only further hideous depth to suffering, but an almost medieval – millenarian even – dimension to a war that gobbled millions of lives into its maw. Nazi iconography had cast 'the

movement' in the guise of ancient Rome and Sparta, complete with eagles, monumental architecture, all the trappings of slavery and the annihilation of those who stood in its path. 'Total war' had been awakened both for and against totalitarianism, and ultimately Berlin, the heart of the 'Third Empire', the new Rome on the Spree, had been sacked every bit as comprehensively as had the classical city of the empire on the Tiber. New technologies of destruction were harnessed and tested against human flesh and bone every day. Nevertheless as Eisenhower observed of this new 'crusade' in Europe, 'the important people in this war were the ordinary soldiers under the Western Allied banners. They had to be, because in democracies the compunction to put them on the battlefield had to be used so lightly: they had to be motivated by persuasion, duty, and comradeship, even the vision of a better, fairer, world'.[1]

Oftentimes we are given an impression of history as a seamless narrative: not only through the eyes of the victors, but those of the mighty. Yet raw history is made up of fragmentary impressions, sometimes even of collections of events that scarcely make sense to the participants. War in particular tends to have causes, beginning, middle, end – and results – only in retrospect. As Eisenhower stated, or perhaps quoted, in a moment of reflection, 'Interest in battles of the past, for soldier and civilian alike, often centres on points that were either of no great moment at the time of their happening, or did not impress the actors as being so'.[2] If talking to veterans demonstrates anything about World War II it is that it was

OPPOSITE

A Soviet T-34 mounting the 76mm gun atop the memorial in the Tiergarten, overlooking the Strasse des 17 Juni. Literally hundreds of T-34s were used in the assault on Berlin, as despite the recent introduction of new 'Joseph Stalin' tanks this older model remained the most numerous in Soviet armoured formations. It is traditionally maintained that the two tanks on the Sowjetisches Ehrenmal were the first to enter the capital. Remarkably the monument was designed and erected in time for unveiling on 11 November 1945. (Author's Collection)

not one big war – but many tiny ones. It doubtless comprised large areas of boredom and suffering and hardship, with islands of respite and comradeship: but perhaps most characteristically it was a series of small battles and almost individual combats. Much of the time the battlefield appeared empty, and on the ground horizons were often more limited than we might imagine. Those who genuinely remembered their part recalled the fragments and their comrades, not the big picture.

Why this was so for the combat soldier is perhaps best articulated by Charles Scott-Brown, a 'Canloan' ('Canadian Loan') officer to the Gordon Highlanders:

> From an infanteer's point of view you have got to look at it that the highest rank that actually physically leads men in action is a corporal. He has a section of ten men. The lieutenant platoon commander is looking after three sections, and he will guide them, and help them. Do you have a bigger perspective than the men? No. I could see 150 yards, and 100 yards left and right, and that's what I knew about. And all these people, including our veterans, that talk about great things, and what they saw, and everything like that – you still only know about 150 yards… Everything else is hearsay. Same as you. You don't know what the end of the picture is going to look like, but you know what you have taken, and what you have heard, and what you can see. And the military is exactly the same.

The fundamental truth that no ordinary soldier, indeed no ordinary officer, could see the wider vista of the war was also echoed by many veterans. As Soviet pilot Benjamin Danzig expressed it, 'I couldn't see it from on high. I don't want to lie to you or imagine. All I know is just the task that they gave me – go there and bomb, and that's it… Even my colonel did not know the whole picture. Only the most senior officers knew the whole picture.' British infantryman Jim Tuckwell said almost exactly the same, 'As an ordinary private soldier you just did what you were told. You didn't know what you were doing half the time.' For Ken Sturdy it was simple, 'when fighting there isn't a big picture, you're almost blinkered. You are in a bubble.'

Why individuals fought varied, but the idea that many did so for their comrades, or simply to get back home quicker, remains persuasive. As Malcolm Andrade put it, 'The only thing you're really scared of is letting the squadron down, letting your mates down. My biggest fear at the

start was would I measure up. These guys are experienced. I'm expected to fit in and contribute. And you make up your mind this is what you are going to do'. Another Canadian, Chan Katzman, told a similar story:

> We were scareder than hell! There was nobody that wasn't and if they ever told you they weren't they're full of shit. Everybody was scared. You didn't know. We were never in a situation like that. As much as we practised in Scotland and on the Isle of Wight, we knew that nothing much was going to happen to us. But this was the real thing … you know when they say you die for King and country? Well, most of us looked after each other, the guy next to you. They didn't give a hoot about what I just mentioned. You gave a hoot about the guy next to you because if you saved his life he'll save your life. My life depended on the next guy. The King and the country were fine but they weren't there to help us. We had to do it ourselves.[3]

Carl Beck agreed, 'Fear becomes part of your life … you deal with it. There's this thing inside you that's saying, you've got to go. You're not gonna let your friends down. OK? It's just hard to explain.'

Some of those with the clearest motivation to fight were the Russians, and amongst them were sometimes to be found what might be described as higher, or at least more idealistic, notions. As Iacov Krenin put it, 'I was not very high in rank, but I felt patriotic. I felt like I was defending my motherland, and punished the thieves who tried to enslave our country. Later we came to know horrible things about Auschwitz…' For Krenin duty was not merely to one's country, but global, 'Victory over Germany. It was the most important event of the twentieth century. Can you imagine what would have happened to mankind if Hitler had won over the Soviet Union? Then only the UK and America would have remained… So the Soviet Union was concerned not only with its own survival, its life and freedom, but for the life of all the world.' Ken Angell puts such ideas much more simply, he fought because, 'it was the right thing to do'. Benjamin Danzig might well agree, 'I don't like those who think they are heroes – it's just a job; just a hard bloody job, and there is no time to think whether or not you are a hero'.

It is also worth noting that the happy 'band of brothers' oversimplifies the relationships of fighting men. As Jim Tuckwell explained, 'We were 30 blokes in a hut – we were a family. Some you didn't like, some you did.' Others were conscious that to love anybody too much could be a serious mistake. Malcolm Andrade was just one of several veterans to indicate this:

> Funny thing… The older guys of the squadron, who'd been flying for a while and doing this stuff as routine for over a year – they weren't very friendly. I thought they were kind of 'stand-offish' – superior. A fellow who had been in there about two or three months ahead of me, after a few beers, said, 'Look, no, no, they just don't want to get to know you too well because you get to know people too well, and when you lose them it affects [you] – you feel it. So you don't want to get close to anyone.'

Carl Beck rationalized the same phenomena in a slightly different way, 'Replacements just went away. They just didn't stay with you.' Certainly, Arnold Whittaker was painfully aware of his initial infantry replacement status – 'that's about as low as you can get'.

Officers were, to a greater or lesser extent, part of a different club. Officialdom recognized and encouraged this by not returning the newly promoted officer to the same unit from which he had come as a ranker. Nevertheless, most junior officers, and all of the conscientious ones, worried about their men. As Charles Scott-Brown put it, 'They are your responsibility: if anything happens to them it behoves you to sit down and write a letter and tell the next of kin what happened'. He had to perform this painful duty twice, and six more times on behalf of his wounded, 'and it's probably the hardest thing you do in your life: tell somebody else how you killed their son or husband … and I was 20-years-old on D-Day plus one'. Exactly what you should say to break the news to the bereaved was open to some degree of compassionate, if creative, interpretation. Scott-Brown's missives had a basic outline. 'I would say I regret to inform you that your son was killed on such and such a day, and such a time. I thought you might be interested in knowing exactly how your son lost his life. To the best of my ability to remember, this is what happened … [in the description the casualty] always had "a white hat on". Did I lie? Well I crossed my fingers a little bit.'

Death did become very much one of the team. Feared certainly, yet many adopted strategies to get along with him. For the many who did not simply crack up or run away, faith or fatalism were just two of the most obvious attitudes. Arnold Whittaker soon became one of the genuinely faithful, 'Having a strong faith is important. I've always said there's no such thing as atheist in a fox hole… I believe that God got me through.' Clayton Byrd simply accepted the 'Grace of God' – about which one could give no further explanation. Nelson Horan was one of the more fatalistic school, 'Well, of course, everything just goes through your mind, you don't know what's going to happen, and, of course, it's noisy, dead people all over the beach and equipment spread out all over the beach and ships being sunk from artillery fire… But you just had to do what you had to do.' Ken Angell was probably swung towards fatalism by the experience of Normandy, 'There's nothing more: I'm going to get it or I won't. I think you protect yourself with those thoughts.'

Designed by Paul Wallot and built in 1894 the Reichstag was extensively renovated by Sir Norman Foster after reunification. (Author's Collection)

Excitement and fear may have been the common currency of combat, but for many, much of the time, it was a case of 'hurry up and wait'. For some like Frank Rosier it was actually inactivity that was the work of the devil, as when you are 19, 'the last thing you want to be is laying in a wet field for a couple of days – and nothing happens. Sheer boredom is the worst thing, because if you get bored, you might want to do something dangerous.' Love and death were often the opposite sides of the

'Best wishes from Berlin', 1933 to 1945–46: an artist's postcard impression of the physical change wrought to the Reichstag, home of the German parliament, from beginning to end of the Nazi era. Despite remaining empty following the Enabling Act of 1933, the building was seen as a prize of huge symbolic importance to the Russians. It was finally taken on 30 April 1945. (Author's Collection)

coin, and perhaps some of the female veterans were more aware of this than most. As the Levitsky sisters remembered some key attributes of humanity simply could not be extinguished by war:

Dorothy Levitsky: 'I'll tell you one thing – they were 18-year-old men. They were men but they were 18-years-old.'

Ellen Levitsky: 'These kid's were terrific… And they loved nurses.'

Battle fatigue, stress, shell shock – call it what you will – could catch up with anyone. Experts thought that essentially every man had his own reserves, larger or smaller, but sooner or later they ran out. This was part of the significance of leave, however infrequent; the rotation of divisions, and for aircrew, the concept of the 'tour' of 25 or 30 missions. By such small mercies a man was given something to aim for, an idea in his mind that death or disablement were not the inevitable end of his service. Nevertheless Malcolm Andrade noticed what he called 'the twitch' in fellow pilots. It could start as a 'tickle of the eye', or perhaps an involuntary movement of the mouth, that others began to watch. The squadron leader in particular had a weather eye for such symptoms, because the sufferer might become dangerous to himself or his comrades. One palliative was to declare the man 'tour-expired – tour ex'ed' for some reason – and send him 'back to blighty' for leave. Family and relaxation might be calming enough to get the nerves back for another period of service. For aircrew in particular there was stark juxtaposition between the extreme stress of air combat, and a brisk return to a base behind the lines where there was some semblance of everyday normality. This might include not only a bed and clean clothes, but proper food and an officers' mess. It was odd nonetheless, as Andrade explained, 'You go back – there's an empty place beside you. You talk about it – but you don't carry on with it for the simple reason it's not good for morale.'

Although combat fatigue was recognized, post-traumatic stress had not yet been studied as a specific phenomenon. Nevertheless many veterans exhibited what we might now regard as classic symptoms.

As Morton Waitzman explained, 'I never talked about the war, about the camps that we saw … never talked about any of the experiences I had from D-Day on to the Elbe river. It was something which brought on the nightmares and difficulties that I had for so many years afterwards. For 50 years I didn't talk about it.' Tom Renouf also had problems with sleep, 'I frequently woke up in a cold sweat as horrific episodes from the war flooded into my mind'. Another veteran, George Dangerfield, was more optimistic that most humans had an inbuilt ability to forget the bad and remember the good. Nonetheless, war could still 'make a mess of you'. Trauma could take odd forms, depression and anxiety being common enough, but some could get acclimatized to virtually anything. As Benjamin Danzig observed, 'anyone who was in the war was traumatized', but still he could not sleep when the guns stopped, 'this is how society gets used to the noise of war'. For Alex Adair it was not so much society as youth that was adaptable, 'We were young and impressionable, 19, 20, 21 … and you just did as you were told… To some extent you became immune… It's not terrifying when you are pumped up.'

Arguably combat experience in World War II helped create a generation gap as big as that existing after World War I. As Seymour Rosen analyzed it:

> It's very difficult in terms of explaining it to people. My grandchildren are from 26 to 32 and over the years they've said to me, 'Grandpa, why have you never talked about the war?' And I try to say to them it's very difficult to explain to you how a guy in the infantry lives. You're constantly out of doors, not enough sleep – sleep was a luxury you never had. Got cold food, and an opportunity to heat up a C-ration once in a while. How do you explain living in the rain and the mud and the snow? If you haven't experienced it, it doesn't mean anything to you: it's just a number of words that say, 'it must have been rough'. It was a sub-human life essentially. Always understaffed, always undermanned, guys getting killed and wounded. A constant turnover of people and you're living in a very narrow environment: you didn't have any idea what was going on 20 yards away from you, or even behind you. You just focused on the front and surviving.

Across the ideological divide Benjamin Danzig had a similar perspective, 'What can I tell you, in summary? War is a dirty, bloody job. There is no

A swastika armband: one of American paratrooper veteran Carl Beck's war souvenirs. (Courtesy of Carl Beck)

romanticism in war. I know that young guys want to be pilots: what I can tell them is that war is a dirty, hard, bloody job. One day you have lunch with a guy, the next he's dead. If somebody tells you they're not afraid of anything, don't believe them. They are lying, or they are crazy. I can [you] tell that a normal person always has some fear...'

Just how long blood lust and will to combat should, or could, last was a moot point. Official surveys of GIs suggested that even when they set out to war there was rather less overt desire to kill a German than to kill a Japanese, and presented with a starving population, and the demise of Nazism, genuine and personal hatred does seem to have been difficult to sustain in the long term. Indeed, there were some who took a genuinely optimistic view. As Peter White, a junior officer with the King's Own Scottish Borderers, mused at the end of the war:

I often found myself thinking of what it must be like for these ordinary German families and I realized I had a deep sympathy for the situation, keeping in mind what it would have felt like if the boot had been on the other foot. I was therefore more than pleased on reflection to realize how outstandingly well, on the whole, the average Jock behaved as an ambassador for his country, rather than a conqueror, once the fighting had stopped ... and if he stayed clear of the fatal 'wee droppie'. He had a tremendous sense of humour, a wealth of kindness, especially to young children and old people which was very pleasant to see and he never seemed to retain the anger or hate generated in the heat of a conflict. I was rather interested to notice as time went on that on learning the Jocks were from 'Schottland' the news appeared to act as a magic lubricant in our relationship with the inhabitants, with its usual crop of queries about 'doodlesacks' and kilts.[4]

Attitudes to the enemy certainly varied. British Royal Engineers Sergeant Wally Harris was apt to think the best of any human being, but not to let this get in the way of the job, 'I just felt they was the enemy, but they're like me. A family man: probably got photos in their pocket, as like I had, of my wife. But at the time you can't consider that, can you?... If I hadn't killed them, they'd have killed me.' Frank Rosier took a similarly pragmatic stance, 'I don't hate Germans – they are just somebody I had to fight'.

Jim Tuckwell assumed that everybody had his duty: it was just different, 'I didn't feel any hatred: they were doing what we were doing, fighting for their country. We didn't know about all these other atrocities which were going on.' As Len Mann put it, 'I don't believe in killing anyone, but you don't have any choice... I mean if you don't want to cut yourself don't get a job as a butcher.' Jim Holder-Vale was careful not to

An idealized view of the young Soviet soldier complete with rolled greatcoat, bayonet and red star with hammer and sickle. From a painting in the Latvian military museum, Riga. (Author's Collection)

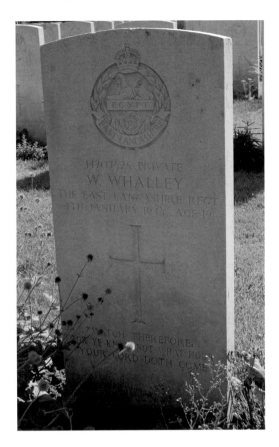

feel sorry for the enemy, as, 'if you started feeling sorry for them you might feel sorry about shooting them'. US airborne officer John Marr drew a more subtle distinction: he didn't hate the Germans, but hated 'what they were doing'. There are, however, as many different opinions as veterans, and attitudes have changed with time. In 1963 the D-Day Victoria Cross winner Stanley Hollis famously snubbed a former German officer by very publicly refusing to attend a showing of the film *The Longest Day* at which the former enemy would be present. Interviewed by his local paper Hollis was reported as saying, 'I killed 102 German soldiers in the last war. Although I am not proud of it, I find it impossible to treat a man as an enemy one minute and then shake his hand. I saw the results of too many of their atrocities ever to trust, or like, the Germans again.' He may not have forgiven the enemy, but also, as his daughter expressed it, 'he never really forgave himself'. According to his commanding officer, he was 'absolutely personally dedicated to winning the war – one of the few men I ever met who felt like that'.[5]

Remarkably not everyone has totally negative feelings about the war in retrospect. There were even moments of joy when one was glad to still be alive. For Arnold Whittaker one such was 25 December 1944, 'it was the most beautiful Christmas morning that I had ever experienced in my life, and every Christmas for the last 67 years I remember that Christmas morning. The sun was out and it was beautiful, clear, crisp…' Bruce Melanson looked back on the war as 'an adventure', but also extremely hard. All in all he felt lucky to have got through – and lived to tell the tale. Hal Baumgarten's near death experience at Omaha taught him to value every moment, 'because you never knew when your time is going to be up'. Many of the veterans, and probably not coincidentally some of those who have lived the longest, have philosophical, even relaxed stances, regarding the hand that they were dealt. As Charles Scott-Brown reflected, 'Changed my attitude to life? No. Did I hate or anything like that? No. Was I worried about it? No. Was I proud of it? No. I did my job, I didn't do any more than anybody else.' However, 'I didn't like writing letters to next of kin because it meant I had screwed up'. For Clayton Byrd, the pain of going away was almost balanced by the sheer joy of coming back, 'It was wonderful. And in World War II, to the people, returning, no matter what you had done, you were considered to be a hero – which is so drastically different than some of the other wars that we have been in since that time. So that was a good feeling.' So it was that almost everybody wanted to go 'home' – if they still had one to go to. As sisters Ellen and Dorothy Levitsky put it they were, 'tired of living in these foreign joints'.

While many felt enervated by the war, physically, spiritually or emotionally, in a circuitous way some actually felt improved by the experience – however traumatic at the time. Seymour Rosen described himself before the war as, 'an 18-year-old kid from New York City' who never went hunting or camping, inexperienced, and not particularly well educated. Afterwards he got the opportunity to go to college, and have 'a sense of values and a sense of responsibility' that he did not have before. Interestingly he felt that being Jewish may have made him 'a little more determined' – but that teenagers with his background really did not have 'the luxury of philosophical thinking' at the time. He was 'trying to survive the war… I wanted to get my ass out of there and try to live'. Army nurse Ellen Levitsky put the case more positively, her memory of 1945 having been warmed by the passing decades, 'I went in at 23 and came out at 25.

OPPOSITE
The grave of Private William Whalley, 1st Battalion, East Lancashire Regiment, of Sutton Oak, St. Helens, who died on 4 January 1945, aged just 19. Hotton in Belgium, where Private Whalley is buried, marks the western limit of the German advance through the Ardennes. This soldier is just one of 666 Commonwealth servicemen interred at Hotton War Cemetery. While combat losses were much lower than in World War I the British Army still suffered 126,734 killed or died of wounds. Many of these were infantrymen killed in Europe after the invasion of 6 June 1944. (Author's Collection)

Detail of the memorial in the Schwartzenburg-platz, Vienna, commemorating the 17,000 Soviet soldiers who died in the course of the fighting for Vienna. The edifice was clearly put up with propaganda in mind: nonetheless it should not be forgotten that upwards of 20 million citizens of the Soviet Union paid with their lives during World War II. (Author's Collection)

I was more mature, ready to settle down, but there was so much more in me… I was married for 49 years, never did ever speak anything of this to my husband. My big regret is that I didn't stay in the army.' Patrick Delaforce saw the war for what it was only when it ended, 'You are on a high, of fairly controlled excitement. And my God it was exciting. And then suddenly it stopped. They'd all quit. And all you saw around you was wounded Germans, defeated Germans, sad Germans… It was a great anti-climax… It was like a drug. Because that's what war is – a drug.'

But as a final comment, did the last great war really bring out the best in people? In the words of veteran Jim Tuckwell – 'I think they realized they were on this earth to do what was right'.

ENDNOTES

Introduction: The Great Crusade

1. Eisenhower, the Eisenhower Centre
2. Montgomery, *Normandy to the Baltic*
3. S. Darlow, *D-Day Bombers: The Veterans Story*
4. Eisenhower, *Crusade in Europe*
5. All interviewees are listed in the appendices
6. Jan de Vries, the Memory Project Archives, the Historica-Dominion Institute
7. Eisenhower, *Crusade in Europe*
8. C. Partridge, *Hitler's Atlantic Wall*
9. Jack Swaab, *Field of Fire: Diary of a Gunnery Officer*

Chapter 1: D-Day

1. W. G. Ramsey (ed.), *D-Day Then and Now*
2. Robert Barr, BBC War Report
3. Jan de Vries, the Memory Project Archives, the Historica-Dominion Institute
4. Joseph Gautreau, the Memory Project Archives, the Historica-Dominion Institute
5. W. G. Ramsey (ed.), *D-Day Then and Now*
6. D. Burgett, *Currahee! A Screaming Eagle in Normandy*
7. M. Windrow (ed.), *The Soldier's Story: D-Day*
8. W. G. Ramsey (ed.), *D-Day Then and Now*
9. S. Darlow, *D-Day Bombers: The Veterans Story*
10. BBC War Report
11. M. Windrow (ed.), *The Soldier's Story: D-Day*
12. J. Thompson, *Victory in Europe*
13. Roy Armstrong, the Memory Project Archives, the Historica-Dominion Institute
14. Chan Katzman, the Memory Project Archives, the Historica-Dominion Institute
15. Ibid.
16. Tom Settee, the Memory Project Archives, the Historica-Dominion Institute
17. Bill Halcro, the Memory Project Archives, the Historica-Dominion Institute
18. Ken Duffield, the Memory Project Archives, the Historica-Dominion Institute
19. Orval Wakefield, M. Windrow (ed.), *The Soldier's Story: D-Day*
20. Richard Harris, P. Warner, The D-Day Landings

Chapter 2: Normandy

1. Frank Gillard, BBC War Report
2. S. A. Hart, *Sherman Firefly Vs Tiger*
3. S. Hills, *By Tank Into Normandy*
4. 'Ultra' was the designation given to enemy signals intelligence obtained through the code-breaking efforts of the British government Code and Cypher School at Bletchley Park.
5. South Lancashire Regiment, Regimental History

Chapter 3: Breakout

1. Montgomery, *Normandy to the Baltic*
2. M. Reynolds, *Sons of the Reich: II Panzer Corps*
3. Don Marsh, account of the breakout from St. Lô, available at:
   www.3ad.com/history/wwll/memoirs.pages/marsh.pages/st.lo.breakout
4. A. Featherston, *Saving the Breakout*
5. S. P. Hirshon, *General Patton*
6. Montgomery, *Normandy to the Baltic*
7. C. Shore, *With British Snipers to the Reich*

8. Ibid.
9. Ibid.
10. Ibid.
11. Ibid.
12. Montgomery, *Normandy to the Baltic*
13. Quoted in C. D'Este, *Decision in Normandy*
14. Ibid.
15. Eisenhower, *Crusade in Europe*

CHAPTER 4: ARNHEM AND THE SIEGFRIED LINE

1. M. Middlebrook, *Arnhem 1944: The Airborne Battle*
2. B. Horrocks, *A Full Life*
3. E. Treacher, statement to the National Army Museum, 1988
4. J. Sims, *Arnhem Spearhead: A Private Soldier's Story*
5. D. G. Van Buggenum, *B Company Arrived*
6. S. Westphal, *The German Army in the West*
7. Eisenhower Centre
8. M. D. Doubler, *Closing with the Enemy*
9. History of the 3rd Infantry Division, available online at: www.lonesentry.com/gi_stories_booklets/3rdinfantry/index

CHAPTER 5: THE ARDENNES

1. J. C. McManus, *The Deadly Brotherhood*
2. Eisenhower, *Crusade in Europe*
3. H. M. Cole, *The Ardennes*
4. J. P. Pallud, *The Battle of the Bulge Then and Now*
5. Ibid.
6. Eisenhower, *Crusade in Europe*
7. H. Trevor-Roper (ed.), *The Goebbels Diaries*
8. Ibid.
9. Ibid.

CHAPTER 6: THE RHINE AND BERLIN

1. 'They'll be a hot time in the town of Berlin', words and music by Joe Bushkin and John de Vries, 1943
2. Eisenhower, *Crusade in Europe*
3. Richard Dimbleby, BBC War Report
4. Hitler, Fuhrer Order 74, 15 April
5. A. Werth, *Russia at War*
6. Ibid.
7. C. Merridale, *Ivan's War*
8. P. Kemp, *No Colours or Crest*
9. R. Carruthers and S. Trew, *Servants of Evil*
10. H. Heiber, *Hitler and his Generals: Military Conferences 1942–45*
11. R. Rürup (ed.), *Berlin 1945*
12. E. Bessonov, *Tank Rider*
13. V. Grossman, *A Writer at War*
14. R. Rürup (ed.), *Berlin 1945*
15. Ibid.

CONCLUSION: GOING HOME

1. Eisenhower, *Crusade in Europe*
2. Ibid.
3. Chan Katzman, the Memory Project Archives, the Historica-Dominion Institute
4. P. White, *With the Jocks*
5. M. Morgan, *D-Day Hero: CSM Stanley Hollis VC*

APPENDIX

We are very grateful to the following veterans who were interviewed in the making of the documentary series and whose recollections are used throughout this volume. Ranks, units and ages are listed at the time of D-Day and they are grouped according to their current country of residence.

UNITED KINGDOM

Private Ken Angell, Oxfordshire and Buckinghamshire Light Infantry (age at D-Day: 20)
Guardsman Richard Alan Appleby, 2nd Battalion, Welsh Guards (age at D-Day: 25)
Corporal Bill Bloys, 2nd Battalion, the Parachute Regiment (age at D-Day: 20)
Lieutenant Edwin Bramall, King's Royal Rifle Corps (age at D-Day: 20)
Lieutenant John Cloudsley-Thompson, 4th County of London Yeomanry (age at D-Day: 23)
Guardsman Ray Cumbley, 2nd Battalion, Welsh Guards (age at D-Day: 24)
Trooper Harold Currie, 4th County of London Yeomanry (age at D-Day: 19)
Sick Berth Attendant George Dangerfield, Royal Navy (age at D-Day: 18)
Trooper Peter Davies, 1st East Riding Yeomanry (age at D-Day: 21)
2nd Lieutenant Patrick Delaforce, Royal Horse Artillery (age at D-Day: 20)
Guardsman Bill Dyer, 2nd Battalion, Welsh Guards (age at D-Day: 21)
Private Bill Edwardes, 1st Battalion Worcestershire Regiment (age at D-Day: 17)
Private Bill Evans, 2nd Battalion, South Wales Borderers (age at D-Day: 23)
Medical Officer John Forfar, 47 Commando, Royal Marines (age at D-Day: 27)
Lieutenant Ian Hammerton, 22nd Royal Dragoon Guards (age at D-Day: 22)
Sergeant Wally Harris, Royal Electrical Mechanical Engineers (age at D-Day: 21)
Brigade Major Tony Hibbert, 1st Parachute Brigade (age at D-Day: 26)
Staff Sergeant Bill Higgs, No. 1 Wing, the Glider Pilot Regiment (age at D-Day: 24)
Gunner Jim Holder-Vale, Fox Troop, 92 LAA, Royal Artillery (age at D-Day: 20)
Marine Vincent Horton, 48 Commando, Royal Marines (age at D-Day: 23)
Marine Jim Kelly, 41 Commando, Royal Marines (age at D-Day: 21)
Private Len Mann, 12th Battalion Devonshire Regiment, 6th Airborne Division (age at D-Day: 19)
Trooper Cecil Newton, 4th/7th Royal Dragoon Guards (age at D-Day: 20)
Private Johnny Peters, 1st Battalion, the Border Regiment (age at D-Day: 21)
Bombardier Frank Quelch, 59th Anti-Tank Regiment (age at D-Day: 23)
Private Tom Renouf, 5th Battalion, the Black Watch (age at D-Day: 19)

From left to right: Tony Hibbert, Brigade Major on the bridge at Arnhem and prisoner-of-war escapee; Jim Kelly who fought with the 41 Royal Marine Commando at Walcheren; and British Arnhem veterans: Bill Bloys of the 2nd Parachute Battalion, left, and Johnny Peters, right, who fought with the glider troops of the Border Regiment. (Impossible Pictures)

Private Ted Roberts, Highland Light Infantry, Glasgow Highlanders (age at D-Day: 19)
Private Frank Rosier, 2nd Battalion Gloucestershire Regiment (age at D-Day: 18)
Able-Seaman Bill Smail, Royal Navy (age at D-Day: 19)
Petty Officer Ken Sturdy, Royal Navy (age at D-Day: 24)
Corporal Ron Titterton, 2nd Derbyshire Yeomanry (age at D-Day: 23)
Private Jim Tuckwell, 1st Battalion Dorsetshire Regiment (age at D-Day: 21)
Section Officer Eileen Younghusband, No. 33 Wing, 2nd Tactical Air Force (age at D-Day: 23)

CANADA

Rifleman Alex Adair, Queen's Own Rifles (age at D-Day: 20)
Platoon Sergeant Ronald 'Andy' Anderson, 3rd Brigade, 6th Airborne Division (age at D-Day: 19)
Pilot Officer M. (Malcolm) L. R. Andrade, No. 127 Squadron, RAF (age at D-Day: 18)
Assault Trooper Al W. Armstrong, 8th Reconnaissance Regiment, 14th Canadian Hussars (age at D-Day: 19)
Private Walter Balfour, Lincoln and Welland Regiment (age at D-Day: 19)
Bill Betteridge, Queen's Own Rifles (age at D-Day 23)
Private Kelmann Cohen, Royal Hamilton Light Infantry (age at D-Day: 19)
Corporal William (Bill) Davis, the Black Watch (age at D-Day: 20)
Private Arthur F. Haley, North Nova Scotia Highlanders (age at D-Day: 28)
Able Naval Seaman Andrew A. Irwin, Canadian Navy (age at D-Day: 19)
Flight Sergeant Leonard Levy, Royal Canadian Air Force (age at D-Day: 23)
Lance Corporal (later Corporal) Stan Matulis, the Black Watch Regiment (age at D-Day: 18)
Bombadier Bruce Melanson, 3rd Light Anti-Aircraft Division, Canadian Artillery (age at D-Day: 19)
Private Bob Ross, Lincoln and Welland Regiment (age at D-Day: 20)
Lieutenant (later Acting Captain) Charles Scot-Brown, 1st Battalion Gordon Highlanders (age at D-Day: 20)
Private (later Corporal) William Standfield, Carrier Platoon (Flamethrower), Royal Regiment of Canada
    (age at D-Day: 18)
Gun Position Officer Assistant Okill Stuart, 14th Field Canadian Regiment, Royal Canadian Artillery
    (age at D-Day: 23)
Pilot Officer John Thompson, No. 254 Squadron, RAF (age at D-Day: 21)
Private Douglas R. Vidler, Stormont, Dundas and Glengarry Highlanders (age at D-Day: 20)
Private Jan de Vries, 1st Canadian Parachute Battalion (age at D-Day: 20)
Corporal Jim Wilkinson, 1st Battalion, the Black Watch (age at D-Day: 21)

From left to right: Walter Balfour of the Canadian Lincoln and Welland Regiment, who fought at the battle of the Falaise Pocket; 'Canadian Loan' infantry officer Charles Scott-Brown pictured with the 'Projector Infantry Anti-Tank'; and Douglas Vidler of the Canadian Dundas and Glengarry Highlanders, a mortar crewman in Normandy. (Impossible Pictures)

UNITED STATES

Private Harold 'Hal' Baumgarten, 1st Battalion, 116th Infantry Regiment, 29th Division (age at D-Day: 19)

Private Carl Beck, 1st Parachute Infantry Regiment, 501st Airborne (age at D-Day: 18)

1st Lieutenant William Blair, 333rd Regiment, 84th Infantry Division (age at D-Day: 20)

Private Clayton Byrd, L Company, 302nd Infantry Regiment (age at D-Day: 18)

Captain Frank A. Camm, 303rd Engineer Company Battalion, 95th Division (age at D-Day: 20)

Platoon Sergeant William Doyle, 175th Infantry Regiment (age at D-Day: 30)

Lieutenant Frank A. Gregg, 501st Parachute Regiment, 101st Airborne Division (age at D-Day: 21)

Platoon Sergeant Nelson Horan, 175th Infantry Regiment (age at D-Day: 22)

Private Leo Liberman, 320th Engineer Battalion, 95th Division (age at D-Day: 19)

2nd (later 1st) Lieutenant Ellan Levitsky-Orkin, 164th General Hospital (age at D-Day: 23)

2nd Lieutenant Dorothy Levitsky-Sinner, 164th General Hospital (age at D-Day: 26)

Private Donald A. McCarthy, 1st Battalion 116th Infantry Regiment, 29th Infantry Division (age at D-Day: 20)

Private George McGuire, 29th Infantry and 84th Infantry Divisions (age at D-Day: 18)

1st Lieutenant John W. Marr, 507th Parachute Infantry Regiment, 82nd Airborne (age at D-Day: 26)

Private Doc Molloy, 82nd Engineer Combat Battalion (age at D-Day: 19)

Private First Class Gil M. Nelson, 3rd Battalion, 290th Regiment, 75th Infantry Division (age at D-Day: 19)

1st Lieutenant Rose Doria Paras, 48th General Hospital, United States Army & Nurses Corps (age at D-Day: 22)

Staff Sergeant Harley Reynolds, 16th Infantry Regiment, 29th Division (age at D-Day: 18)

Private Seymour Rosen, 2nd Battalion, 7th Regiment (age at D-Day: 18)

Private 1st Class William F. Ryan, 16th Infantry Regiment and later 1st Division, 82nd Airborne (age at D-Day: 18)

Operation Sergeant Ed Shames, 3rd Battalion, 506th Regiment, 101st Airborne (age at D-Day: 19)

Mathew Sikorski, Hammelin Labour Camp and Holocaust Survivor (born in 1929 he entered the camp at the age of 15)

Private Morton Waitzman, 115th Infantry Regiment, 29th Division (age at D-Day: 20)

Private (late Platoon Sergeant) Arnold Whittaker, 10th Infantry Regiment, 5th Infantry Division (age at D-Day: 19)

RUSSIA

Captain Benjamin Danzig, 22nd Division of the Reserve of the High Command (age at D-Day: 22)

Senior Lieutenant Jakov Jarchin, 270 Guards Infantry Regiment, 1st Infantry Battalion, 89th Guards Infantry Division (age at D-Day: 21)

Senior Lieutenant Iacov Krenin, 303 Red Banner Guards, Mortar Regiment (age at D-Day 21)

Captain Leonid Sheinker, 59th Guard Regiment

From left to right: American soldier Hal Baumgarten: wounded repeatedly on Omaha Beach but lived to tell the tale; Moreton Waitzman, veteran of the US Army 29th Infantry Division in France and Germany; and Arnold Whittaker, US 10th Infantry, 5th Division, veteran of the Battle of the Bulge. (Impossible Pictures)

FURTHER READING

PRIMARY SOURCES
Altner, H., *Berlin Dance of Death*, Staplehurst, 2002
Bessanov, E., *Tank Rider*, London, 2003
Burgett, D. R., *Beyond the Rhine: A Screaming Eagle in Germany*, New York, 2001
Burgett, D. R., *Currahee! A Screaming Eagle in Normandy*, New York, 2000
Borthwick, A., *Battalion*, Stirling, 1946
Carruthers, R. & S. Trew, *Servants of Evil: New First Hand Accounts of the Second World War from Survivors of Hitler's Armed Forces*, London, 2001
Darlow, S., *D-Day Bombers: The Veterans Story*, London, 2004
Eisenhower, D. D., *Crusade in Europe*, London, 1948
Grossman, V., *A Writer at War*, English edition, London, 2006
Heiber, H. (et al), *Hitler and his Generals: Military Conferences 1942–1945*, English edition, New York, 2003
Hills, S., *By Tank into Normandy*, London, 2002
Horrocks, B., *A Full Life*, London, 1960
Jary, S., *18 Platoon*, Bristol, 1987
Kemp, P., *No Colours or Crest*, London, 1960
Küne, R. T., *Der Westwall*, Munich and Berlin, 1939
de Lee, N., *Voices from the Battle of the Bulge*, Newton Abbot, 2004
Lewis, J. E. (ed.), *D-Day: The Normandy Landings in the Words of those who Took Part*, London, 2001
Liddle, P., *D-Day by Those who were There*, Barnsley, 2004
MacDonald, C. B., *Company Commander*, Washington, 1947
Montgomery, B. L., *Normandy to the Baltic*, London, 1946
Neillands R. & R. Norman, *D-Day 1944: Voices From Normandy*, London, 1993
Renouf, T., *Black Watch*, London, 2011
Rürup, R. (ed.), *Berlin 1945: A Documentation*, Berlin, 1995, 5th revised English edition, 2007
Shore, C., *With British Snipers to the Reich*, new edition, London, 1997
Sims, J., *Arnhem Spearhead: A Private Soldier's Story*, London, 1978
Speer, A., *Inside the Third Reich*, English edition, London, 1970
Steinhoff, J. (et al), *Voices from the Third Reich*, Washington, 1989
Swaab, J., *Field of Fire: Diary of a Gunnery Officer*, Stroud, 2005
Trevor-Roper, H. (ed.), *The Goebbels Diaries*, English edition, London, 1978
Warner, P., *The D-Day Landings*, London, 1944
White, P., *With the Jocks*, Stroud, 2001
Windrow, M., *The Soldier's Story: D-Day*, London, 2001

SECONDARY SOURCES
Ambrose, S. E., *Citizen Soldiers*, New York, 1997
Anon., *Churchill Tank: Vehicle History and Specification*, reprinted HMSO London, 1983
Balkoski, J., *Beyond the Beachhead*, Mechanicsburg, 1989
Balkoski, J., *Utah Beach*, Mechanicsburg, 2005
Barnes, B. S., *The Sign of the Double "T": the 50th Northumbrian Division*, Hull, 1999
Blumenson, M., *Breakout and Pursuit*, Washington, 1961
Bruce, R., *German Automatic Weapons of World War II*, Marlborough, 2000
Van Buggenum, D. G., *B Company Arrived: 2nd Parachute Battalion at Arnhem*, Renkum, 2003
Bull, S., *Encyclopedia of Military Technology and Innovation*, Westport, 2004
Cantwell, J. D., *The Second World War: A Guide to Documents in the Public Records Office*, Second edition, London, 1993
Carrell, P., *Hitler's War on Russia*, three volumes, English translation, London, 1964
Chamberlain, P. & C. Ellis, *British and American Tanks of World War II*, London, 1969
Cole, H. M., *The Ardennes: Battle of the Bulge*, Washington, 1964
Delaforce, P., *The Fighting Wessex Wyverns: From Normandy to Bremerhaven with the 43rd Wessex Division*, Stroud, 1994
Delaforce, P., *Churchill's Desert Rats: From Normandy to Berlin with the 7th Armoured Division*, Stroud, 1994
Delaforce, P., *Monty's Ironsides: From the Normandy Beaches to Bremen with the 3rd Division*, Stroud, 1995

Delaforce, P., *The Polar Bears: Monty's Left Flank From Normandy to the Relief of Holland with the 49th Division, Stroud*, 1995

D'Este, C., *Decision in Normandy*, London, 1983

Doubler, M. D., *Closing with the Enemy: How GIs Fought the War in Europe, 1944–1945*, Kansas, 1994

Ellis, & C Chamberlain, P. *The 88: The Flak / Pak 8.8 cm*, London, 1998

Featherston, A., *Saving the Breakout*, Novato, 1993

Fleischer, W., *Panzerfaust*, Atglen, 1994

Fletcher, D., *Tiger! The Tiger Tank: A British View*, London, 1986

Ford, R., *The Tiger Tank*, Staplehurst, 1998

Forty, G., *United States Tanks of World War II*, Poole, 1983

Fritz, S.G., *Frontsoldaten: The German Soldier in World War II*, Kentucky, 1995

Gander, T., *German Anti-Tank Guns*, New Malden, 1973

Gander, T., *The Bazooka*, London, 1998

Gander, T., *Anti-Tank Weapons*, Marlborough, 2000

Gunter, G., *Last Laurels: the German Defence of Upper Silesia*, English edition, Solihull, 2002

Handrich, H., *Sturmgewehr!*, Ontario, 2004

Harrison, G. A., *Cross Channel Attack*, Washington, 1951

Hart, S. A., *Sherman Firefly vs Tiger*, Oxford, 2007

Hechler, K., *The Bridge at Remagen*, New York, 1957

Hirshson, S. P., *General Patton: A Soldiers Life*, New York, 2002

Jones, I., *Malice Aforethought: A History of Booby Traps*, London, 2004

Kaufmann, J. E., (et al), *Fortress Third Reich*, Cambridge, 2003

Kershaw, R.J., *It Never Snows in September*, Marlborough, 1990

Lefèvre, E., *Panzers in Normandy, Then and Now*, London, 1983

Magenheimer, H. *Hitler's War*, English edn, London, 1998

MacDonald, C. B., *The Last Offensives*, Washington, 1973

McManus, J.C., *The Deadly Brotherhood*, New York, 1998

Merridale, C., *Ivan's War: The Red Army 1939–1945*, London, 2005

Middlebrook, M., *Arnhem 1944: The Airborne Battle*, London, 1994

Monin, L & Gallimore, A., *The Devil's Garden: A History of Landmines*, London, 2002

Morgan, M., *D-Day Hero: CSM Stanley Hollis VC*, Stroud, 2004

Pallud, J. P., *The Battle of the Bulge Then and Now*, London, 1984

Partridge, C., *Hitler's Atlantic Wall*, Castel, 1976

Ramsey, W. G. (ed.), *D-Day Then and Now, London, 1995*

Reynolds, M., *Sons of the Reich: The History of II SS Panzer Corps*, Spellmount, 2002

Rolf, R. & Saal, P., *Fortress Europe*, Shrewsbury, 1986

Ryan, C., *The Last Battle*, London, 1966

Saunders, A., *Hitler's Atlantic Wall*, Stroud, 2001

Saunders, H. S. G., *The Red Beret: The Story of the Parachute Regiment*, London, 1950

Senich, P. R., *The German Assault Rifle*, Boulder, 1987

Schmeelke, K. & M., *Fortress Europe: Hitler's Atlantic Wall Guns*, Atglen, 1993

Schmeelke, K. & M., *German Defensive Batteries and Gun Emplacements*, Atglen, 1995

Skennerton, I., *The British Sniper*, Margate, 1984

Thompson, J., *Victory in Europe*, London, 1994

Werth, A., *Russia at War*, London, 1964

Whiting, C., *The West Wall*, Staplehurst, 1999

Film and Sound

More than 80 interviews were made especially for the series with veterans in North America and Europe during 2010 and 2011, during which more than 150 hours of first hand material was recorded. While only a small part of this could be broadcast, transcripts of the collection have been used in the preparation of this volume. The words of the speakers have been edited as little as practicable for clarity, but significant omissions are indicated by dots in the quotations. In some instances veterans were questioned on the same point more than once, and naturally versions of the answers most suitable for either broadcast or print have been selected accordingly. It is also worth noting that a minority of the veterans also contributed material to the online BBC 'People's History' project, and this has also been consulted. A couple of additional sound interviews were arranged in by the North West Sound Archives in Clitheroe, UK, for which thanks are due to Andrew Schofield. Additionally many contemporary film and sound items have been consulted in archives in Canada, the US and the UK mainly by the programme researchers. The most significant of these resources are the US National Archives and the British Imperial War Museum.

INDEX